Britpop Cinema

From Trainspotting to This Is England

By Matt Glasby

I0893800

intellect Bristol, UK / Chicago, USA

First published in the UK in 2019 by
Intellect, The Mill, Parnall Road, Fishponds, Bristol, BS16 3JG, UK

First published in the USA in 2019 by
Intellect, The University of Chicago Press, 1427 E. 60th Street,
Chicago, IL 60637, USA

Copyright © 2019 Intellect Ltd

All rights reserved. No part of this publication may be reproduced, stored in a retrieval system, or transmitted, in any form or by any means, electronic, mechanical, photocopying, recording, or otherwise, without written permission.

A catalogue record for this book is available from the British Library.

Copy editor: MPS Technologies
Cover designer: Matt Dykzeul
Production manager: Amy Rollason
Typesetting: Contentra Technologies

Print ISBN: 978-1-78320-987-3
ePDF ISBN: 978-1-78938-036-1
ePUB ISBN: 978-1-78938-035-4

This is a peer-reviewed publication.

Britpop Cinema

Author's Note

Britpop Cinema would not have been possible without many hours of interviews with the actors, writers and filmmakers who made 1990s/2000s British cinema so remarkable. The resulting quotes have been edited for clarity, brevity and, in places, legality. I would like to thank everyone involved for sharing their stories, even the unprintable ones.

Contents

Foreword

By Hardeep Phull, music journalist

If you came of age in Britain in the mid-1990s, there is something you need to know: Noel Gallagher envies you.

Our first meeting came at the *NME* Awards in 2003. At the time, I was a writer for the esteemed UK music weekly, and in a room full of celebrities such as Coldplay, Kate Moss and The Clash, Noel was the guest of honour.

Although it is not the done thing for journalists to betray their cool exteriors and unleash their inner fanboys (or girls), I cared too much to pretend I did not care. I had to take him aside and quickly, efficiently, explain to him that the first two Oasis albums were not just the soundtrack to my youth, they made me believe that our little island was the centre of everything, that the doors of opportunity were open to even the most provincial of hopefuls like me, that the world was mine for the taking. Being a wide-eyed teenager, bereft of any cynicism, during the Britpop years was an incredible feeling, and something that I still consider myself fortunate to have experienced.

But back to those awards. As a rookie music journalist, I had learned this much: pop stars enjoy flattery (especially those who deny it). So, I adopted my best faux-Mancunian accent, my best wide-groined walk, and approached Noel with a compliment.

'Alright Noel, I'm Hardeep and I'm a writer for the *NME*. Thanks for coming to the awards. I just wanted to say that one of the reasons I do what I do is because of you.'

It worked. He was engaged, and nodded his approval, which I took as a sign to continue.

'You know, I was 15 years old when *(What's the Story) Morning Glory?* came out.'

His eyes grew large, and before I could even cobble together another sentence, he blurted out the following three words: 'You lucky bastard!'

During Britpop's imperial phase, Noel was essentially the benevolent, beloved ruler. There was no drug, no drink, no sordid whim that he could not indulge in, and no shortage of acolytes willing to offer them. But even with his first-hand experience of the last truly bacchanalian phase of British rock, he was jealous of me because he never experienced what I did; that sensation of invincibility that comes from simultaneously coming of age, becoming interested in music, alcohol and sex, and having the stirring roar of songs like 'Live Forever' and 'Acquiesce' in your ears.

The musical history of the 1990s has been pored over ad nauseum. There have been thousands of articles, documentaries and books, and to this day you cannot swing a vintage *Select* magazine down Camden High Street without hitting a fortysomething musician with a funny story about how they once supported Blur. But Britpop was not just about what you heard, it was also about what you saw, and that is why *Britpop Cinema: From Trainspotting to This Is England* is so long overdue.

It was no accident that the groundswell of British music coincided with the revitalization of British cinema, helping it move away from stuffy heritage films starring Anthony Hopkins and Kenneth Branagh. Britain had a new beat, and it was not just coming from the radio, it was all over the nation's silver screens.

Movies such as *Shallow Grave*, *Trainspotting* and *Human Traffic* gleefully welded contemporary sounds to modern visions, while the likes of *Billy Elliot* and *24 Hour Party People* used their period settings to highlight the forerunners of Britpop such as The Jam, T-Rex and New Order, returning them to our cultural conversations.

In hindsight, Britpop's reverence to the past may feel reactionary, but at the time, anyone eager to learn about the history of British pop culture had countless roadmaps at their disposal, to which these films added vivid colour and detail. Following where they went and rediscovering the treasures of the past only added to the thrill.

Taking pride in British pop culture is something that British people are seldom keen to do. It is easier (and more amusing) to make fun of ourselves. But for all its failings, Britpop gave young, curious Brits a feeling that we were in the ascendancy.

Maybe that is why Noel envies us. During the grinding recession and socially oppressive Conservative rule of the 1980s (when he grew up), harbouring pop-cultural aspirations was unlikely, if not downright dangerous.

'When I was 17 I was a typical northwest scally, going to football matches, smoking dope and collecting my dole,' he told *The Times*' Michael Odell. 'People say to me, "Oh, but you must have been writing songs, getting your foot on the first rung of the ladder." I didn't even notice the ladder was there. The people I hung out with – if you had any ambitions you were seen as a bit of sissy, so I didn't even pick up a guitar' (2011).

Viewed in this light, it is no wonder he thinks those of us who were teenagers in the mid-1990s are 'lucky'. When he was young, being interested in music and film were things you had to hide. During the Britpop era, they felt like a ticket to somewhere. Anywhere. Everywhere.

Hardeep Phull, New York Post, January 2018

Acknowledgements

Britpop Cinema would not have been possible without the help of friends, family and colleagues too numerous to name here, but a few need singling out.

Thanks to Matthew Floyd, Amy Rollason and the team at Intellect.

To Jon Glasby, Sara Hewitt, Susi Holliday, Hannah Knowles, Alison Shaw, Veronique de Sutter, Howard Trent and Andy Tuohy for their support and advice.

To Jeremy Baxter, Claire Bennie, Holly Bruce, Ali Catterall, Rosie Fletcher, Jane Giles, Andrew Harrison, Roz Kidd, Matthew Leyland, Joff Oddie, Cathy Smith and Josh Winning for their expertise.

To Matt Dykzeul and John Hitchcox for their wonderful designs; to Mel Hoyes and the staff at the BFI for their invaluable research; and to Hardeep Phull for his smashing foreword.

Most of all, I'd like to thank Mina Spatha and Flo for looking after me; Imogen Harris for her insight; John Glasby for believing in me; and my wife Vari Innes, whose name should be inked on every page.

Introduction: Don't Look Back in Anger

Introduction: Don't Look Back in Anger

Britpop cinema, definitions and antecedents...

Colin (Eddie O'Connell): After so many dreary years of bombs and blitz and slow rebuilding; no sugar, no jam, nothing sweet anywhere; with the whole English world dressed in grey, it seemed, forever... Suddenly life broke out in warm colours again, so young and beautiful that a lot of people couldn't stand to look at it.
Absolute Beginners (Temple, 1986)

The Britpop movement of the mid-1990s defined a generation. Mine, as it happens. Retro-styled but spiked with the bright, brittle irony of the era, it was cheery but cynical, proudly, sometimes cringingly, parochial and – crucially – popular. It freed the charts from the chokehold of US rock and, in the process, changed the UK's cultural landscape for a brief, sunny spell.

Beginning with uncharacteristic modesty, Britpop's first salvos were the 1992 indie guitar anthems 'Popscene' by Blur, which charted at No.32, and Suede's 'The Drowners', which reached No.49. The movement soon gathered momentum, creeping towards the mainstream the following April with a *Select* magazine cover featuring Suede frontman Brett Anderson, posing in front of a (superimposed) Union Jack with the legend, 'Yanks go home!' Over the next few years, Britpop would reach critical mass, resulting in albums as wonderfully of-the-moment as *Suede* (March 1993), Blur's *Parklife* (April 1994), Oasis's *Definitely Maybe* (August 1994) and Pulp's *Different Class* (October 1995), all of which reached No.1. By the time Oasis released their stratospherically self-satisfied third album *Be Here Now* (August 1997), they had blown the nation's patience on endless string sections and cocaine and the party was as good as over, although it was Pulp's *This Is Hardcore* (March 1998), rattling with comedown panic, that finally pulled the shutters.

But before it became a parody of itself, Britpop was a byword for a period of cultural cross-pollination, the like of which the UK had not experienced since the 1960s. It was New Labour optimism meets New Lad irony. Blur vs. Oasis on the *News at Ten* and Noel Gallagher at No.10 Downing Street. Pulp's Jarvis Cocker showing his mettle at Glastonbury 1995, and his arse at the Brit Awards 1996. It was Euro '96 and the Young British Artists, Cool Britannia and Swinging London Mk II. It was everywhere, and it was ours. Though much has been written about the music, it was also a golden age for UK film – perhaps our very last.

In the mid-1990s, something strange happened to British cinema. People actually started to watch it. Beginning with Danny Boyle, John Hodge and Andrew Macdonald's *Shallow Grave* (Boyle, 1995), going global with the same team's *Trainspotting* (Boyle, 1996), and encompassing hits as diverse as *Lock, Stock and Two Smoking Barrels* (Ritchie, 1998), *Human Traffic* (Kerrigan, 1999), *Billy Elliot* (Daldry, 2000), *Sexy Beast* (Glazer, 2001), *24 Hour Party People* (Winterbottom, 2002), *Shaun of the Dead* (Wright, 2004), *The Football Factory* (Love, 2004) and *This Is England* (Meadows, 2007), a genre I call 'Britpop cinema'[1] sprang up. It pushed boundaries, paid Hollywood little heed and, all too briefly, placed a booming UK film industry at the centre of its own movie universe.

While Britpop music peaked fast and petered out well before the millennium, film (especially British film) takes longer to react, and longer still to change course. After all, you only need a day to record a hit single – Blur's 'Song 2' (1997) was written in an enviable 30 minutes; Oasis's debut, 'Supersonic' (1994), a third of that time[2] – whereas even the most modest of films takes months to reach the screen. This is why *Britpop Cinema*'s timescale runs from *Four Weddings and a Funeral* (Newell, 1994), which kick-started the UK's 1990s cinema boom, to *This Is England*, which provides a fitting swansong for the era.

This is no Britpop history,[3] rather an attempt to view an exciting period of indigenous cinema through a Britpop prism, assessing how far each film adheres to the formula laid down by Boyle and co in *Shallow Grave* and, most of all, *Trainspotting*. *Nil by Mouth* (Oldman, 1997), *Ratcatcher* (Ramsay, 1999) and *The War Zone* (Roth, 1999), for example, are works of bruising beauty, but they are also (bar some shocking stabs of violence), part of the same decades-old kitchen-sink traditions as Mike Leigh and Ken Loach. *The Full Monty* (Cattaneo, 1997), on the other hand, shows no trace of Britpop cinema's formal experimentalism; in fact, for a disco-infused comedy about stripping steelworkers, it is remarkably unadventurous. But its runaway box office success – currently just under $258 million and counting (Box Office Mojo, 2018d) – and spin-doctored optimism offer a fascinating reflection of the times, and it is included here (with *Brassed Off* [Herman, 1996]) as a contrast to *Billy Elliot*, a genuine slice of Britpop cinema. One of the best films of the era, Shane Meadows' desolate revenger's tragedy *Dead Man's Shoes* (2004), does not qualify either; it is too plain-spoken, too brutal, too broken; whereas Meadows' later *This Is England* contains scattered moments of joy that seem to stand outside the downbeat narrative. *Shooting Fish* (Schwartz, 1997), meanwhile, is Britpop cinema to its chirpy core, but – newsflash – it is awful.

Pinning down a functional definition of Britpop cinema, then, proves tricky – it is more a frame of mind than a genre – but most of its exemplars tick some or all of the following boxes. Just as the art-school graduate members of Blur, Suede and Pulp fashioned a visual identity through their bands' styling and album sleeves, Britpop cinema should be, first and foremost, *cinematic*, a holiday from the familiar drabness of 1980s UK film. Often this means being formally adventurous: with ambitious camerawork rather than TV two-shots; postmodern structures that take in flashbacks and fantasy sequences; and a conspiratorial knowingness, whether through voiceovers, direct address, intertitles or winking cameos from the likes of Soho gadabout/sometime actor Keith Allen[4] or football bruiser Vinnie Jones.

Britpop cinema also has music in its DNA, something Danny Boyle's films have always excelled at: just try and imagine *Trainspotting* without the pulse of Iggy Pop's 'Lust for Life' (1977) or Underworld's 'Born Slippy' (1996); *Human Traffic* without its party-starting Pete Tong soundtrack; or *This Is England* without the raucous ska of Toots & The Maytals or Clayhill's heartsick cover of The Smiths' 'Please Please Please Let Me Get What I Want' (2006). Not, you will agree, a pretty thought.

Much like the music of proudly working-class Britpop bands such as Pulp and Oasis, Britpop cinema rejects gritty realism for something more aspirational, while giving voice to the experiences of ordinary people. It allows regional accents, whether from Edinburgh in *Trainspotting* or the Midlands in *This Is England*, to grace the screen, replacing the usual Received Pronunciation – so what if America needs subtitles?[5] As Blur's Damon Albarn told *Empire* magazine, '[*Trainspotting*'s] going to open the floodgates for a lot of really good British films that aren't *Hugh Grant Poncing Up the Hill*' (Morrison 2003: 121).

Just as Britpop bands repackaged the sounds of the 1960s and 1970s, much of Britpop cinema looks, ostensibly, backwards while nodding to modernity. Set in the (recent) past but speaking of the now, *Trainspotting*'s impossible timeline seems to run from Iggy Pop (late 1970s/early 1980s) to Britpop (mid-1990s), even though its characters barely age; *24 Hour Party People* celebrates the 1970s/1980s birth of the post-punk, rave and Madchester music genres, all of which were still relevant at the turn of the millennium; *This Is England*, meanwhile, rages against the Falklands conflict of 1982, with a vehemence that perhaps has more to do with the Iraq War of 2003. Mostly it felt as if Britpop era filmmakers, still furious from the deprivations of the Thatcher years, had discovered a safe space to work through their anger.

While it might seem, on the surface, that not much unites *Shallow Grave*'s Edinburgh yuppies with *Trainspotting*'s Leith junkies; *Human Traffic*'s Cardiff ravers with *The Football Factory*'s London soccer casuals, they are all ramshackle gangs looking to escape, whether through violence, drugs or economic advancement. They are also all, or almost all, white men, often struggling to cope with changing masculine roles in post-industrial society. Clearly, the inclusive spirit of the times did not extend as far as women or people of colour, still to this day painfully underrepresented in the industry.[6]

To distinguish it further from TV, Britpop cinema often requires an 'adult' rating with 'strong scenes of sex or violence' and 'explicit language, which will frequently mean sexual swearwords', as Radio 1 DJ Simon Bates warned VHS viewers.[7] Whether indulging in the former, the latter or – gasp – both, Britpop cinema protagonists are usually anti-heroes, like *Trainspotting*'s Mark Renton (Ewan McGregor), providing forward narrative thrust rather than moral probity, which leads to endings that are either unresolved (see *Lock, Stock and Two Smoking Barrels*) or unrepentant (*The Football Factory*).

However, the most important factor is that Britpop cinema *feels* positive; alive with the possibilities of the times; woozy with the exuberance of territories new. Usually this means being pacey – post-*Trainspotting*, an opening chase sequence was practically essential (see *Lock Stock and Two Smoking Barrels*, *Twin Town* [Allen, 1997] and *Shooting*

Fish) – contemporary, and full of joie-de-vivre or, at least, the largesse of huge piles of money lost, won or stolen (as in *Shallow Grave*, *Trainspotting* and *Sexy Beast*). Should the movement require a slogan, it would simply be: 'choose life'.

If all this makes Britpop cinema sound superficial, well, some of it is, but at least it never collapses under the weight of its own seriousness. Often, in the years leading up to the 1990s boom, watching UK movies felt less like a treat than a punishment. But film's first job is to entertain, to transport, and the best of Britpop cinema offers not a mirror, but a skylight.

When it comes to Britpop cinema, *Trainspotting* is, of course, the poster boy – and what a poster – and most of the films mentioned in this book owe it at least a stylistic debt. But there has always been a rogue, rebellious element in British film. Though often reduced to heritage flicks, such as the works of Merchant Ivory,[8] and kitchen-sink dramas, such as the Angry Young Man cycle of the late 1950s/early 1960s,[9] the industry's outliers have always been more interesting, and are worth exploring in some detail.

One of Danny Boyle's avowed inspirations, not to mention one of the greatest documents of the Swinging Sixties committed to celluloid, *A Hard Day's Night* (Lester, 1964) is, to all intents and purposes, 87 minutes of the Beatles dicking about London, with no respect for geography, narrative logic or the old fogeys they encounter. But even half a century later it is still a joy to behold. As John Lennon, ever the charmer, told *Rolling Stone* magazine in 1970, 'We didn't want to make a fucking shitty pop movie' (Catterall and Wells 2002: 3). In which case, job done.

Commissioned by United Artists (UA) as a loss leader, in order to cash in on the soundtrack album, the film shows the band – surely the ultimate gang? – trying to escape their constraints (in this instance, fame) through music. In the case of the title track and 'Can't Buy Me Love', this means some of the greatest pop songs ever written. The film also gives fine voice to the boys' Scouse wit (Reporter: 'How did you find America?' John Lennon: 'Turned left at Greenland'), although, like *Trainspotting*, UA executives wanted the accents dubbed for the US release. Apparently, this caused Paul McCartney to complain, 'Look, if we can understand a fucking cowboy talking Texan, they can understand us talking Liverpool' (Mersey Beat 2018).

An American émigré who had cut his teeth translating *The Goon Show* to TV, Richard Lester brought a freewheeling sense of the cinematic to these gonzo proceedings. Prefiguring Renton's Princes Street dash by three decades, the iconic opening chase has the boys fleeing crazed fans at Marylebone Station, and features genuine tumbles by George Harrison and Ringo Starr. The 'Can't Buy Me Love' sequence, meanwhile, sees them racing down the fire escape of Hammersmith Odeon to a convenient field, where they attack the camera – and each other – jump from impossible heights (à la Renton) and gleefully break the fourth wall. As Paul's grandfather (Wilfred Brambell) puts it, both the boys and the film would rather be, 'Parading the streets, trailing your coat, bowling along, living!' Or, in other words, choosing life.

The enthusiasm was infectious. The film smashed records upon release, and received Oscar nominations for Alun Owen's screenplay and, oddly, George Martin's adapted score. Lester may have asked for a paternity test when he was labelled the father of MTV (Kashner 2014), but his work did help sire Britpop cinema. As the authors of *Your Face Here: British Cult Movies Since the Sixties*, one of the best books on the subject, put it, 'Cheekily mixing and matching techniques from the great directors of the cinema's past, *A Hard Day's Night* carved out a hip new youth-orientated lifestyle and postmodern template that has become cult movies' stock in trade' (Catterall and Wells 2002: 22). Fast forward 30 years and this could be *Trainspotting*'s manifesto, too.

Just as audacious, in content rather than form, was *Alfie* (Gilbert, 1966), adapted by Bill Naughton from his 1963 play. Here the key figure was Michael Caine's cocky Cockney chauffeur, shagging his way around a just-about-to-start-Swinging London like the stray dog we see in the opening and closing scenes. A clear inspiration on McGregor's portrayal of Renton, Alfie is an amoral chancer who steals (women, rather than money), from his friends, simply because he can. Equally, like Renton, as the irreverent, unapologetic narrator of his own tale, Alfie is extremely hard to judge because his use of direct address makes us complicit in his actions – such as when he turns to the camera to ask the audience, 'I suppose you think you're going to see the bleeding titles now?' 'Nobody in this world has any right to stop you doing what you want to do,' he tells one conquest, a self-serving mantra on a par with Renton's 'choose life' speech.

Standing apart from the Angry Young Man cycle thanks to, among other things, its sense of mischief, colourful cinematography and vibrant Sonny Rollins sax score, *Alfie* displays a touch of the *Carry-On* in its love scenes, such as when our hero entertains a nurse while an onlooker peels a banana. But for the most part, its sexual frankness made it the first film 'suggested for mature audiences' in America, the precursor of the Parental Guidance (PG) certificate. Like Renton, Alfie undergoes a change of heart when faced with the death of an infant. But it is his own child, illegally aborted in an upsetting sequence that caused actors Terence Stamp, who played Alfie on Broadway, and Richard Harris to pass on the role. Music provides something of a salve, with the wistful Burt Bacharach/Hal David theme sung by Cilla Black, asking, 'What's it all about, Alfie?' as our hero walks off over Waterloo Bridge to an uncertain future, like the Britpop cinema protagonists who would come after. If he had seen the Jude Law-starring remake (Shyer, 2004), he might have jumped in.

Based on Anthony Burgess' shocking 1962 novel, written in the sometimes-indecipherable teen slang of 'Nadsat,' *A Clockwork Orange* (Kubrick, 1972) is one of *Trainspotting*'s closest forebears. With Kubrick giving vent to Wagnerian levels of cinematic excess, the slyly satirized fall and rise of juvenile thug Alex DeLarge (Malcolm McDowell, playing another proto-Renton) feels more like a grotesque pantomime than a state-of-the-nation horror show. Amid relics of woebegone post-war brutalism such as London's Thamesmead South Housing Estate, Kubrick shows Alex and his gang of Droogs raping, pillaging and murdering as if they were characters in a demented Looney Tunes cartoon, with impossibly bright pops of colour and hokey back-projection making proceedings seem, as McDowell told *The Face* magazine in 1990, 'like being on drugs' and 'real, but not realistic' (Catterall and Wells 2002: 119).

There is music in its dark heart, too. For a while, Kubrick considered casting the Rolling Stones as Alex and his Droogs, whose look also inspired The Sex Pistols' John Lydon. Beethoven's 'Ninth', meanwhile, sends Alex into raptures. 'Oh bliss! Bliss and heaven!' he coos. 'Oh, it was gorgeousness and gorgeousity made flesh. It was like a bird of rarest-spun heaven metal or like silvery wine flowing in a spaceship, gravity all nonsense now.' Later, Alex/McDowell croons (an unscripted) 'Singin' in the Rain' while sexually assaulting Mrs Alexander (Adrienne Corri). Gene Kelly, the star of *Singin' in the Rain* (Donen and Kelly, 1952) the movie, may not have been impressed, deliberately blanking McDowell at a Hollywood party,[10] but a young Boyle was spellbound, telling writer Amy Raphael:

> *A Clockwork Orange* blew me away; the risk-taking was phenomenal. It was really refreshing. *Trainspotting* was certainly inspired, in part, by [it]. With *Clockwork Orange* and, to a lesser degree, *Trainspotting*, people objected to the notoriety that comes with taking risks. But I would argue that it's partly why people go to the cinema.
>
> (2013: 15)

Ironically, it was only after Kubrick's death in 1999 that the Britpop generation could actually see *A Clockwork Orange* at the cinema, rather than on pirate VHS. Faced with (rumoured) death threats and (real) accusations of irresponsibility, the director requested that the film be withdrawn from distribution in Britain, lending its infamy a further frisson of illicitness of which Alex DeLarge would have approved. Damon Albarn and co certainly did: the video for Blur's 1995 single 'The Universal' saw them styled as Alex and his Droogs.

Another Blur favourite was *Quadrophenia* (Roddam, 1979), a Mod coming-of-age flick based on The Who's 1973 album and featuring most of the main Britpop cinema signifiers. Although The Who themselves only appear on the soundtrack, they are glimpsed on TV (to which dad Michael Elphick remarks: 'What's this rubbish then?'). Musicians Sting and Toyah Wilcox, meanwhile, have small but memorable acting roles, and star Phil Daniels would go on to provide the geezer-ish vocals on Blur's 1994 hit 'Parklife'. Made in the economically depressed 1970s, it looks back to the (relative) innocence of the 1960s, the first time young, working-class men like Jimmy (Daniels) had money to spend on sharp suits, cool scooters and bad speed. The rest, to paraphrase W.C. Fields, they wasted.

Bored of the suburban London drudge, Jimmy and his associates – watch out for Britpop cinema stalwarts Phil Davis as Chalky and Ray Winstone as Kevin – escape to Brighton for weekends of sex (with 1990s pin-up Leslie Ash, no less), drugs and Rocker-bashing. Conventional enough as a drama, as an introduction to the Mod subculture it is alluringly inclusive, inviting viewers to ride alongside Jimmy, Chalky and co while fetishizing, in this past that never dates, their own misspent youths. Bar the swooping helicopter shots at the film's climax showing Jimmy riding along the south coast cliffs, it is not formally adventurous, but the uncertain ending is pure Britpop cinema. As Jimmy rides his scooter off Beachy Head (a notorious suicide spot), the Mod dream shattering on the black rocks beneath, he is left alone, frozen in time, to choose life or, perhaps, death.

Re-released in 1997, '*Quadrophenia* and its iconography fitted the decade like a bespoke three-button suit' (Catterall and Wells 2002: 183), and it continues to win new fans. Says Phil Davis, now, 'It's a film people hold with enormous affection. I'm 63 and I'm still getting calls across the street: "CHALKY!" People love it and it's personal to them in some ways, even kids who weren't born when it was first released… it's a phenomenon really' (2016).

A phenomenon for all the wrong reasons, *Absolute Beginners* is a dayglo musical adapted from Colin MacInne's 1959 cult novel, and, according to *The Guardian*'s Jacques Peretti, 'The unintentional template for all [1990s/2000s] Brit-flicks […] with its strange mix of over-choreographed action, low-rent acting and soaring ambition, it has provided Brit-flicks with their holy trinity' (2000). Peretti was responding to a glut of gangster films such as *Rancid Aluminium* (Thomas, 2000) and *Circus* (Walker, 2000) – most of which were so bad that even some of their cast members criticize them.[11] But *Absolute Beginners* was an acquired taste and, with box office takings of £1.8 million against an £8.4 million budget (Walker 2005: 33, 54), one that few viewers even tried.

Looking back at a stylized, late 1950s London that Guy Ritchie might recognize (except there are women in it), the film plays like a middle-school *Bugsy Malone* (Parker, 1976), particularly in the scenes between gauche young lovers Colin (Eddie O'Connell, from *Sexy Beast*) and Crepe Suzette (Patsy Kensit, the future Mrs Liam Gallagher). Elsewhere, it features spirited musical cameos from David Bowie, whose eponymous title track reached No.2 in the UK charts; The Kinks' Ray Davies, who offers the more modest 'Quiet Life'; and Sade with 'Killer Blow'. These are joined by non-singing performances from James Fox (*Sexy Beast*), Steven Berkoff and Mandy Rice-Davies.[12] As such, it is never boring, even if the famously crotchety *Evening Standard* critic Alexander Walker dubbed it, 'Absolutely all over the place, wasteful in its effects and huge sets, dazzling but confused, with the restlessness of an extended pop video, not the rhythm of a movie musical' (2005: 52). The camerawork, in particular, is often beautiful, especially an audacious opening tracking shot that jazz-hands its way through a bustling, Blitz-torn Soho, and was mentioned in *The Player* (Altman, 1992).

Unfortunately, *Absolute Beginners*' failure almost toppled its production company, Goldcrest Films, and distributor, Palace Pictures. The British film industry, its fingers burned, retreated into a bleak depression for the rest of the decade. Said Boyle:

> In America, lower middle-class parents would give their kids Super-8 cameras and, years later, a Spielberg would turn up; in Britain we just don't have that tradition of talented or expressive people going into film. You join a band instead.
>
> (Raphael 2013: 12)

Indeed, it was only when British music began to flourish in the early 1990s that our film industry took its first stumbling steps back towards the light. But before Britpop cinema arrived, surging with life, music and enthusiasm, salvation came in the most unlikely form.

Notes

1 Debate still rages about the origins of the term 'Britpop', although journalist Andrew Harrison of *Select* magazine makes a very good case. The phrase 'Britpop cinema' was coined by the author in late 2015.

2 'Song 2' was written as a send-up of the soft-loud-soft-loud theatrics of grunge. Producer Stephen Street explained in the *NME*, 'Damon [Albarn] went, "Woo hoo!" [in the chorus] because he had nothing else prepared'. 'Supersonic', meanwhile, was the result of Noel Gallagher challenging himself to write a song as fast as possible. 'I remember being off my nut and going into the back room and setting the goal of writing a song in ten minutes', he said. 'That was "Supersonic"' (Barker 2015). Imagine what he could have achieved in twenty.

3 Readers seeking more illumination on Britpop music should read John Harris's masterly *The Last Party: Britpop, Blair and the Demise of English Rock* (2003) or Luke Haines' miserly *Bad Vibes* (2010).

4 At one stage it seemed like a legal requirement for all British films to feature Keith Allen turning up either naked, dead or with drugs/money, as he does in *Shallow Grave*, *Blue Juice* (Prechezer, 1995), *Trainspotting*, *Twin Town* and *24 Hour Party People*, among others.

5 US distributor Miramax asked for the opening of *Trainspotting* to be redubbed for American audiences. 'It just meant cleaning it up so the pronunciation is clearer,' producer Andrew Macdonald told *The Independent*, 'We didn't want them to reject it from the beginning. After that, they either get it or they don't' (Jenkins 1996).

6 Depressingly few Britpop cinema releases were directed by woman or people of colour – perhaps *Face* (Bird, 1997) comes closest. Notable non-Britpop cinema films of the era include *Young Soul Rebels* (Julien, 1991), *Bhaji on the Beach* (Chadha, 1994), *Priest* (Bird, 1994), *Stella Does Tricks* (Giedroyc, 1996), *Under the Skin* (Adler, 1997) and *Bend It Like Beckham* (Chadha, 2002). The picture doesn't improve much when actors of colour are included. The 2017 BFI *Black Star* survey by Melanie Hoyes found that, between 2006 and 2016, 59 per cent of UK films didn't feature any black actors in named roles (2016).

7 In the mid-1990s, Radio 1 DJ Simon Bates became the inexplicable face of UK censorship when clips of him explaining a film's certification by the British Board of Film Classification (BBFC) were placed on all VHS releases.

8 Founded in 1961 by producer Ismail Merchant and director James Ivory, Merchant Ivory Productions became known for its genteel literary adaptations, such as *A Room with a View* (1985) and *Howards End* (1992).

9 The British New Wave included works such as *Look Back in Anger* (Richardson, 1959), *Saturday Night and Sunday Morning* (Reisz, 1960) and *A Taste of Honey* (Anderson, 1961), which dramatized the experiences of socially mobile working-class men with a previously unthinkable frankness.

10 After Gene Kelly's death, his widow Patricia Ward explained to Malcolm McDowell the real reason Kelly had given him the cold shoulder: 'Gene was not pissed off with you. He was pissed off with Stanley… because he never paid him!' (Brown 2014).

11 *Rancid Aluminium* co-star Nick Moran says, 'I've been in worse films, but it was right down there, an amazing mess of egos and everything. One of the reviews just said: "Rancid shit"' (2016).

12 A some-time model and actress, Mandy Rice-Davies (1944–2014) gained notoriety for her involvement in the Profumo affair that rocked the Conservative government of the early 1960s, and was filmed as *Scandal* (Caton-Jones, 1989).

Chapter 1

Things Can Only Get Better

Starring: *Four Weddings and a Funeral* (Newell, 1994)

Chapter 1: Things Can Only Get Better

The beginning of the boom...

Charles (Hugh Grant): Do you think there really are people who can just go up and say, 'Hi, babe, name's Charles, this is your lucky night...'?
Matthew (John Hannah): Well, if there are, they're not English.
Four Weddings and a Funeral

When screenwriter Colin Welland held aloft his Oscar at the 54th Academy Awards on 29 March 1982, he issued Hollywood with a friendly warning: 'The British are coming!' Cheekily quoting Paul Revere, who helped defeat Team GB during the American Revolution, Welland was actually referring to a more recent, and successful, British campaign. *Chariots of Fire* (Hudson, 1981), a historical drama about UK runners triumphing against the odds at the 1924 Olympics, won three more Oscars that evening, including Best Picture. It was the first UK film to do so since *Oliver!* (Reed, 1968). And when *Gandhi* (Attenborough, 1982) followed suit the next year, it gave credence to Welland's claim. Unfortunately, it proved many years premature.

Throughout the late 1980s, the British film industry had little to boast about, suffering much the same fate as the rat in *Riff-Raff* (Loach, 1991), stamped to death by a succession of half-hearted kicks. It was, in the words of critic Alexander Walker, 'a near-disaster area', with investment dropping from £272 million in 1985 to under £79 million in 1989 (2005: 137–138), an unsympathetic Tory government, and plucky production companies such as Palace Pictures and Goldcrest Films collapsing left, right and centre.[1] Ironically, Goldcrest's *Revolution* (Hudson, 1985), set during the same conflict that made Paul Revere a hero, was one of several costly flops that banished British film to the margins. Our only hopes seemed to come from TV stations such as the BBC and Channel 4, the film production wing of which, started in 1982 and later styled as Film4, impressed with *My Beautiful Laundrette* (Frears, 1985) and *My Left Foot* (Sheridan, 1989). But even these minor successes felt like works of the small, rather than the silver, screen.

'When I started, the film industry was in a terrible state; terrible kitchen-sink movies of no interest to anyone', says producer Michael Kuhn, who ran PolyGram Filmed Entertainment (hereafter PolyGram) from 1991 to 1999, perhaps the chief sponsor of the Britpop cinema boom. 'And it seemed to collapse on itself, so instead of thinking bigger, it thought smaller' (2016).

By the beginning of the 1990s, the country was in a terrible state too. The 1990–91 recession was the longest since the Great Depression of the 1930s, and the bleak winter of Conservative rule had been prolonged a further five years at the 1992 general election. Meanwhile, a *Financial Times* report estimated that American films earned ten times more than UK offerings at the British box office (Walker 2005: 166), with most indigenous efforts proving unspeakable (*Carry On Columbus* [Thomas, 1992]), insufferable (*Peter's Friends* [Branagh, 1992]) or profoundly depressing (*Naked* [Leigh, 1993]). Indeed, the latter, starring David Thewlis as the sociopathic Johnny, prowling London's purgatorial streets spitting existential poison at everyone he meets, suggested a Britain – and, by extension, a British film industry – broken beyond repair.

Even the odd genre film produced, such as the spirited, if silly, sci-fi *Split Second* (Maylam, 1992) and by-the-book cop drama *The Young Americans* (Cannon, 1993) were in thrall to the United States; featuring slumming-it international stars such as Rutger Hauer and Harvey Keitel, and treating London as just another location. 'Not exactly Hollywood is it, sir?' says one British lackey to Keitel's hotshot NYC detective in *The Young Americans*. Director Danny Cannon clearly wished it were: his next film was the studio comic-book adaptation *Judge Dredd* (1995) starring Sylvester Stallone, a film so garishly overblown it made *Split Second* look like *2001: A Space Odyssey* (Kubrick, 1968). Says *Four Weddings and a Funeral* producer Duncan Kenworthy:

> I remember thinking that if the British film industry stopped tomorrow, nobody would notice. The audience wouldn't notice, they'd still go to the cinema on Friday and Saturday and still be seeing the same films. If the British TV industry stopped tomorrow, however, within three days there would be riots in every city in the UK.
>
> (2016)

In due course, Britpop cinema would produce Friday and Saturday night films aplenty, but it was the success of *Four Weddings*, perhaps better thought of as a Sunday night film, that ignited 'the firestorm in UK film production, which continued to burn through the rest of the decade' (Watson 2005: 83).

For a film that grossed $245 million worldwide (Box Office Mojo 2018e), turned lead actor Hugh Grant into a star and reinvigorated the British film industry, *Four Weddings* was hardly the most prepossessing of projects. 'When I commissioned it, no one really rated its chances very highly, because it wasn't commercial', says David Aukin, head of film at Channel 4 from 1990 to 1998, 'I remember I showed it to my colleagues and they said it would play alright on television' (2016).

Formed in 1982, and co-chaired by Tim Bevan and Eric Fellner since 1992, *Four Weddings*' UK production company was Working Title, which had just released a string of disappointments such as *London Kills Me* (Kureshi, 1991) and *The Young Americans*. Writer Richard Curtis, though responsible for *Blackadder* (1983–89, UK: BBC1), one of Britain's best-loved sitcoms, had only *The Tall Guy* (Smith, 1989) on his cinematic CV. Kenworthy, meanwhile, was making his feature debut, and had been more used to working with the Muppets at Jim Henson Productions. Indeed, says Aukin:

> Its prospects were rated so low that our investment, collateralized against the territory where it was least likely to perform, namely the USA, was something like £800,000. That's how little it was thought of. The other financiers thought we were taking the wooden spoon in America. Which all goes to show, as William Goldman says, nobody knows anything.[2]

Inspired by the deluge of weddings he had attended over the years, Curtis split his script into five distinct sequences/services,[3] to which we, the audience, are cordially invited. Combined, they tell the story of bashful London bachelor Charles and his pals, as they search for true love in the marquees of Middle England's recently matched and dispatched. At one such gathering, Charles meets Carrie (Andie MacDowell), a glamorous American, and they start a faltering affair. The real-life inspiration, it turns out, was even more faltering. As Curtis told *The Telegraph*'s David Gritten:

> After a dance at a wedding, for the first time ever, a girl asked me, 'Where are you staying tonight?' I told her and she said, 'That's lucky, I'm staying there, too.' And I said, 'But I told some friends I'd go over to their house.' Instead of doing what any human being would do, I said, 'I'd better go with them.' I remember being so angry, playing Boggle with them at midnight, thinking, 'Oh god, what might have happened in the hotel?'
>
> (2003: n.pag.)

Charles, of course, does go to the hotel and, with Boggle left untouched, begins an on-again/off-again romance distinguished by Carrie's flightiness and his own furious indecision. To Grant's credit he manages to make the character's dithering more charming than exasperating. This is, after all, a man who, out of terminal politeness or social terror, never says what he means or asks for what he wants. Even his eventual declaration of love to Carrie on London's South Bank is a masterpiece of stammered self-sabotage: 'In the words of David Cassidy in fact, er, while he was still with the Partridge Family, er, "I think I love you," and, er, I just wondered by any chance you wouldn't like to…' he begins, before deciding, 'No, no, no of course not'. And all this before she's even spoken.

After years of being, as he put it, 'the Nazi brother' (Lamont 2014),[4] Grant clearly relished the chance to play a romantic lead, but it almost didn't happen. The filmmakers estimate that he was the 70th actor auditioned, and his agent demanded £5,000 more than the £35,000 offered, until Kenworthy explained there was nothing left in the budget. Though it is difficult to imagine anyone else in the role, back then Grant was hardly classic pin-up material – among his hobbies was playing football… for the V&A museum's side. 'We're not the hardest team in the world', he admitted. 'Our left-back is keeper of seventeenth-century sculpture' (Walker 2005: 183).

With the leading man in place, and veteran director Mike Newell (*Dance with a Stranger* [1985], *Enchanted April* [1991]) onboard, a high-profile actress was sought, because, as Kenworthy notes, 'For all the British work it's the American star name that gets us the budget'. Funding delays gave Curtis the chance to further sharpen his script (he claimed to have written nineteen drafts), while Newell and Kenworthy went to LA to audition actresses.

During casting, the producer found himself playing Charles to several prospective Carries, in a scene that could have come straight from Curtis's next rom-com, *Notting Hill* (Michell, 1999). One of the auditionees, the wife of a very famous Hollywood actor, threw herself into the role. Recalls Kenworthy:

> We were sitting in chairs opposite each other, I mean some distance apart, and then when it came to the kissing, she just got up out of the chair and kissed me, and I thought, 'Fuck, what do I do?' Of course, the last thing to do was embarrass her by laughing, so I had to get out of my chair and kiss her back. Mike had his fist stuffed in his mouth trying to stifle this laugh and the camera was shaking. At the end we all laughed and she said that her husband had been away for a long time and she thought when she flew down, 'I wanna kiss someone today!' so she did. But she didn't get the part! She came that close. That nearly swung it.

Eventually, back in London, the filmmakers met with model-turned-actress Andie MacDowell, star of *Green Card* (Weir, 1991) and *Groundhog Day* (Reitman, 1993), who was offered the role for a correspondingly large fee. Not that it mattered. When *Four Weddings* was released in 1994, it was Grant, Curtis and the British film industry that were the biggest beneficiaries. And not necessarily in that order.

While the finished film is about as far from the Britpop cinema that followed as it is from the cutting edge, if you squint your eyes, there are similarities. *Four Weddings* does indeed begin with a chase – although it is Charles and his flatmate Scarlett (Charlotte Coleman) swearily speeding to church in her Mini, rather than Scottish junkies or Welsh joy-riders. It also features a gang, each of whom is looking to escape their circumstances. Although again, it is singledom rather than economic depression that is the problem, and they are not 'gang members' so much as landed gentry: more Peter's friends than Renton's.

Despite being set among the upper/upper-middle classes, Curtis's script is, in other respects, unusually inclusive. Charles' brother David (David Bower) is deaf, as is Bower himself, providing the film's (silent) voice of reason through sign language; a nice touch. Gay couple Gareth (Simon Callow) and Matthew are the best-suited pair of the lot, although you do not need to be Inspector Rebus to work out which one will not make it to the end credits. [5] *Four Weddings* also has a noteworthy soundtrack, although it is the ceremony-friendly Elton John and Wet Wet Wet[6] rather than Iggy Pop and Underworld.

The Conservatives, under the moderate but much-mocked John Major, clung on to power until 1997, but as *Guardian* writer Tim Adams notes, there is something of: 'New Labour's shiny, happy geography in what we have come to know as Curtisland [...] an apolitical place, full of can-do possibility, obsessed with the educated middle class, perfectly relaxed about the filthy rich, much more in love with sentiment than ideas, and insatiable in its optimism' (2009).

Adams may be overstating the latter quality, but the film is consistently funny. At the opening wedding, Charles and Carrie are interrupted by the hapless John (Simon Kunz). 'How's your gorgeous girlfriend?' asks Charles. 'She's no longer my girlfriend...' John begins. 'Ah, dear. I wouldn't be too gloomy about it...' says Charles, before making a joke about her rumoured infidelity. 'She's now my wife', finishes John, suitably deflated. Later, Charles introduces himself to a dotty old man (Kenneth Griffith), only to be told, 'Don't be ridiculous, Charles died 20 years ago!' Charles, clearly not deceased, ventures, 'Must be a different Charles, I think.' Which only enervates the man more. 'Are you telling me I don't know my own brother?!' he harrumphs. 'No,' agrees Charles, too polite to argue his own existence.

In these scenes, Grant pitches his performance perfectly, making the most of Curtis's finely honed material. As the actor told the BBC's Sian Kirwan, 'The reason I turn down 99 per cent of a hundred, I mean a thousand, scripts is because romantic comedies are often very romantic but seldom very funny' (2014).

But *Four Weddings* is not just funny, it is moving, that one funeral proving as crucial as any of the other gatherings. For reasons Curtis never quite explains, Carrie marries Hamish (Corin Redgrave), a Scottish politician old enough to be her father, but during the reception Gareth drops dead of a heart attack, as if in protest. At his funeral, Matthew is introduced as Gareth's 'closest friend', seemingly without euphemism, and reads Auden's *Funeral Blues* as a desolate but dignified eulogy: 'Pour away the ocean and sweep up the wood / For nothing now can come to any good.'

Hannah's bitten-lipped dignity almost steals the show here, but credit should also go to Kristin Scott Thomas. As the vampish Fiona, she expresses a lifetime of longing in a few brittle words, when she admits her unrequited feelings for Charles. More cynical viewers might question why Charles has never shown a romantic interest in Fiona when (a) she is both intelligent and attractive; (b) he has slept with most of the female cast; and (c) her brother, Tom (James Fleet), is the seventh richest man in England. Still, if these are the rewards of true love, the film seems to argue, who needs it? Besides, the most enduring romances – from *Brief Encounter* (Lean, 1945) to *Casablanca* (Curtiz, 1942); *Before Sunrise* (Linklater, 1995) to *Brokeback Mountain* (Lee, 2005) – are the ones that remind us that love, rather than being all around, is painfully fleeting.

Four Weddings has been criticized – often retrospectively – for depicting a rarefied England full of daffy aristos, drippy Deirdres and bonking Bernards. But perhaps it is best thought of as a stepping stone from John Major's 'country of long shadows on cricket grounds, warm beer, invincible green suburbs, dog lovers and pools fillers' (1993) towards the more contemporary representations of UK life found in Britpop cinema. 'It's not Merchant Ivory,' Working Title's Tim Bevan told journalist Annie Thompson, '[Nor the] angst-ridden streets of London. While it's slightly old-fashioned, the first ten words in the film are fuck, which helps get the audience into it' (1994).

Four Weddings is also sadder than it seems. This is, after all, an England where even the fortunate are crippled by social expectations, shackled to the same tired institutions of school, church and marriage, and encouraged to join the pantomime of obsessive coupling, or be branded a 'lesbian' like Fiona, or a 'slut' like Carrie. Yet those institutions are no longer to be trusted.

The film's most questionable line, one that would not pass today, belongs to the drunken wedding boor (Rupert Vansittart) who tells Charles, 'I was at school with his [the groom's] brother Bufty. Tremendous bloke. He was head of my house. Buggered me senseless. Still, it taught me about life.' Say what you like about declining educational standards, but few Old Boys, you would hope, go misty-eyed for the halcyon days of institutionalized sexual assault.[7]

Religion, meanwhile, is shown to be an utter ass, thanks to the bumbling Father Gerald (*Blackadder*'s Rowan Atkinson) and his 'holy goat' – although everyone *still* prefers the church to the registry office. Even marriage comes under repeated attack. Tom claims, 'It worked for my parents. Well, apart from the divorce...'; Charles jilts poor Henrietta (Anna Chancellor) at the altar; and Matthew says of Gareth that, 'He used to prefer funerals to weddings. He said it was easier to get enthusiastic about a ceremony one had an outside chance of eventually being involved in.' Had Gareth lived, he and Matthew would have had to wait until 2005 for a civil partnership, or 2013 to get married. Even then, you sense the residents of Gareth's home town – a bleak industrial nowhere of council estates and belching chimneys, and the film's one acknowledgement of working-class England – would hardly welcome them with open arms.

And what are we to make of Carrie herself, perhaps the film's major stumbling block? Throughout, her behaviour seems clumsy, bordering on cruel. Having seduced and deserted a clearly smitten Charles at the first wedding, she takes him back to her hotel at the end of the second, despite the fact she is engaged. Then she invites him to the third wedding – her own – although they have only met twice, and offers the following crumbs of comfort during her speech, 'Someone told me here that, if things with Hamish didn't work out, he would step in. I just wanted to say thanks, and I'll keep you posted.'

If inviting Charles to go wedding dress shopping seems crass, turning up at his wedding to 'keep him posted' that she is newly available seems unspeakably calculating. And the sense that Carrie is toying with Charles is only encouraged by the diffidence of MacDowell's performance. This is most notable at the climax, when Charles declares his love to Carrie during a downpour and she replies, rather damply, 'Is it still raining? I hadn't noticed.' Though her reading has come in for much criticism over the years, the actress remains bullish. 'I think the scene is gorgeous,' she told journalist Alasdair Glennie, 'If people enjoy making fun of that line, that's fine [...] The character was so in love, she wasn't thinking about the fricking rain' (2013: n.pag.).

'There are catastrophic cycles in the history of British film,' wrote *Riff-Raff* producer Sally Hibbin in 1998, 'This is how they run: British movies suddenly become internationally popular; the Americans arrive and buy up everything they can; some years later they pull out; our industry collapses in the wake' (Miller 2005: 43). As evidence Hibbin points to the ripple effects caused by *Tom Jones* (Richardson, 1963), *Chariots of Fire*, *The Crying Game* (Jordan, 1992) and, of course, *Four Weddings*. It is certainly an irresistible way to read the movie: with the relationship between Charles and Carrie mimicking the lopsided love affair between the British film industry and Hollywood.

In the red, white and blue corner, Carrie is glamorous, worldly and completely in charge, swooping into England to do as she wishes whenever it suits her. If that inspires snobbery from the locals – as in this exchange between Charles and Fiona – so be it.

> Charles: Any idea who the girl in the black hat is?
> Fiona: Name's Carrie.
> Charles: Pretty.
> Fiona: American.
> Charles: Interesting.
> Fiona: Slut.

Eventually, it is implied, they will come around; such as when Scarlett turns on a dime from calling Americans 'dull as shit' to deciding that Chester (Randall Paul) is, in fact, 'lovely'.

Keeping the British end up, or trying to, Charles is keen to start a relationship with Carrie, shocked at how 'experienced' she is, and roundly terrible at marketing himself. When they first get together, she loves him, leaves him, then marries someone wealthier. Even during the film's supposed 'happily ever after', the pair are pointedly non-committal. 'Do you think not being married to me might maybe be something you could consider doing for the rest of your life?' asks Charles, in that hard-to-notice downpour. 'I do,' says Carrie, the implication being: for now.

Despite its ever-so-British setting, *Four Weddings* was released in the United States to begin with, which tells us a lot about the UK film industry's lack of confidence. As PolyGram's Michael Kuhn wrote:

> This was not an easy decision, but eventually it was thought that if we failed in the US we might still succeed in England whereas the opposite was not true. On the other hand, if we succeeded in the US, the outlook for the UK was very good.
>
> (2003: 60)

Kuhn had spotted what the British film industry had missed: that it was distribution, not production, which brought home the big bucks. By taking smaller films like *Four Weddings* to the global market without help from Hollywood, PolyGram, as a subsidiary of an international music company, could achieve what Film4 et al. could not hope to. Set up like a record company, PolyGram left creative control in the hands of filmmakers such as Newell, Curtis and the Working Title team, or later Danny Boyle, John Hodge and Andrew Macdonald. It was, says Kuhn now, about picking the right people 'and believing in them until they failed'.

Crucially, however, once the films were made, PolyGram took care of the marketing and distribution centrally – areas the British film industry had been traditionally poor in. Says Kuhn:

> In Britain you made a film because you made a film. You never thought about who was going to see it, or why… [But] if you have no idea about marketing, you start off with a terrible disadvantage. If you only listen to marketing, you keep making the same crap you made before.

In short, just as the major music labels pushed tiny Britpop bands to the top of the charts, PolyGram made interesting indie films, but sold them like massive studio titles. It was the best of both worlds, and one of the main reasons Britpop cinema became such a phenomenon: people had actually heard of the films.

Which is not to say the system was perfect. Gramercy Pictures, PolyGram's US distributor, wanted to change *Four Weddings*' title. Suggestions ranged from the lame – *Skulking Around, Tales of True Love and Near Misses* – to the quasi-pornographic – *The Pleasures of Merely Circulating, Loitering In Sacred Places.* Thankfully sense prevailed. PolyGram went to the 1994 Sundance Film Festival with two UK releases: *Backbeat* (Softley, 1993), the story of the fifth Beatle, Stuart Sutcliffe (played, naturally enough, by American actor Stephen Dorff), and *Four Weddings*. Though the former started out the favourite, the opening night film was *Four Weddings*, and it received a rave review from *Variety*. 'I could probably still quote the first paragraph,' says Kenworthy now. 'If we'd written it ourselves, we wouldn't have dared be as glowing in our praise.'

With the confidence that comes from US encouragement, *Four Weddings* was released, at first in New York and LA, with PolyGram spending $11 million – three times the film's budget – on marketing to keep word of mouth snowballing. 'That was one of those big calls made by Michael Kuhn. I mean, real balls-on-the-table stuff,' says Kenworthy, 'If it hadn't worked he'd have been fired instantly, I'm sure, it was a tremendous gamble. Would I have taken it? Probably not.'

PolyGram's chutzpah, it seemed, knew no bounds. When it transpired that *Four Weddings* was being shown on the smallest screen of a New York multiplex, where it had sold out, something had to be done. According to Kuhn:

> [Local rep] Linda Ditrinco did a deal with the cinema manager to swap movies so that we had a big house at the evening show when most of our audience could come. Since the competitor's movie was on the big screen at an earlier show, hopefully no one would find out. Nobody did. On that single initiative hinged much of the subsequent history of *Four Weddings*.
>
> (2003: 65)

Subsequent history, in this case, meant kickstarting the Britpop cinema boom, plus Oscar nominations for Best Picture and Best Screenplay. Not bad for a little British film that, for the sake of £5,000, almost lost its leading man.

Marketed in the United Kingdom as 'America's number one smash hit!', *Four Weddings* made £27.8 million at the box office (BFI 2017a) and represented, as Kuhn put it, 'a significant turning point' for all concerned:

> We [PolyGram] had built up our own distribution system from nothing and, with our own movie, had reached No.1 at the US box office. This was the first time a company run from England, or anywhere outside the US, had achieved such a feat – certainly since the Second World War.
>
> (2003: 67, 88)

In other words, 'We were in charge of our own destiny'. Soon the rest of the UK film industry would feel the same way, realizing that success involved emphasizing, rather than eliminating, a film's Britishness. 'The movies that preceded *Four Weddings* aimed for commercial success by imitating American movies; trying to out-American America, there was even one with America in the title,' recalls Kenworthy, most likely referring to *The Young Americans*:

> But Richard showed that all you had do to get a worldwide audience is to have a small conversation about things you know about – weddings and funerals – and if you get it right everybody will connect to it. It isn't just American culture that can travel round the world, it's films that give audiences what they want.

Connecting with audiences without sacrificing a film's unique character would become one of the key factors in the Britpop cinema boom that followed. 'It's obviously not for me to say this, but I'll say it anyway. I think *Four Weddings* kicked that off,' says Kenworthy, 'For a brief moment in the 1990s, British movies were where it was at.'

At the 67th Academy Awards on 27 March 1995, Kenworthy and Curtis nervously awaited the result of the Oscar for Best Picture – a ruthlessly strong field, including *Pulp Fiction* (Tarantino, 1994) and *The Shawshank Redemption* (Darabont, 1994). 'And the winner is…' began Al Pacino, presenting with Robert De Niro. When the first syllable that came out of his mouth was, 'Fff…' they thought: could it be? Well, no, recalled Curtis, 'It was *Forrest*

Gump' (Lamont 2014). Still, though they would have been far too polite to say it, it was nonetheless true. No matter that our American sweetheart might run off in the morning: the British had, finally, come.

What Happened Next…

The National Lottery… On 19 November 1994, some 22 million people tuned in to watch the UK's first lottery draw, run by Camelot. Seven of them shared a jackpot of just under £6 million (Kelly 2014), and British film would soon be another benefactor jostling for the top prize. In 1995 the Arts Councils of England, Scotland, Wales and Northern Ireland were employed to distribute lottery funds to UK films. This boosted production numbers – artificially, some might argue – making the British film industry seem investible again.

Richard Curtis and Duncan Kenworthy… Explored the intricacies of UK/US relations even further – and even more profitably – in *Notting Hill* and *Love Actually* (Curtis, 2003). The former starred Hugh Grant as a humble bookseller in love with Hollywood actress Julia Roberts. The latter cast him as a Tony Blair-alike prime minister tussling with the American president (Billy Bob Thornton) over the affections of cleaner Martine McCutcheon, rather than, say, the legality of the 2003 Iraq War. The American-actress-in-London subgenre flourished with *Sliding Doors* (Howitt, 1998), *Martha, Meet Frank, Daniel and Laurence* (Hamm, 1998) and *Bridget Jones's Diary* (Maguire, 2001).

Mike Newell… Directed the bleak *An Awfully Big Adventure* 1995) starring Grant before heading to Hollywood. Here he made the excellent, if uncharacteristic, gangster film, *Donnie Brasco* (1997), before returning home for *Harry Potter and the Goblet of Fire* (2005), perhaps the highlight of the series. He has never revisited the rom-com, because, he says, 'I've yet to find another one which was surprising enough to do' (IMDB 2018d).

Hugh Grant… Made quite a splash at the *Four Weddings* premiere, to which his girlfriend Liz Hurley wore a Versace dress held together by safety pins. Despite becoming a major Hollywood star, Grant has expressed antipathy for the acting profession, not least the unwanted/illegal media attention it brought. His best work is probably the Nick Hornby adaptation *About a Boy* (Weitz brothers, 2001), in which he stretched himself as an emotionally immature London playboy, and *Paddington 2* (King, 2017), in which he stole the show as an ageing ham.

Working Title… First with PolyGram, then with Universal, Working Title became one of the great success stories of the UK film industry, repackaging what it meant to be British for worldwide audiences in films as varied as *Bean* (Smith, 1997), *Elizabeth* (Kapur, 1998) and *Billy Elliot* (Daldry, 2000).

PolyGram… Became the largest indigenous investor in UK film, with a hand in most of the biggest Britpop cinema hits, including *Shallow Grave* (Boyle, 1995), *Trainspotting* (Boyle,

1996), *Twin Town* (Allen, 1997) and *Lock, Stock and Two Smoking Barrels* (Ritchie, 1998). But, says Kuhn, 'If we hadn't had *Four Weddings* it would have been a different story.'

Notes

1 Palace Pictures was responsible for explicit, esoteric works like *The Company of Wolves* (Jordan, 1984), *Scandal* (Caton-Jones, 1989) and *The Crying Game*. Goldcrest Films was known for ambitious prestige pictures such as *Chariots of Fire*, *Gandhi* and *Absolute Beginners* (Temple, 1986).

2 Apparently, it was *Bridget Jones's Diary* author Helen Fielding, a friend of Curtis's from their time at Oxford University, who suggested the funeral. He had originally envisioned it as *Four Weddings and a Honeymoon* (Lucas 2009).

3 This famous dictum by William Goldman can be found in his essential memoirs *Adventures in the Screen Trade: A Personal View of Hollywood and Screenwriting* (Goldman 1983) and *Which Lie Did I Tell? More Adventures in the Screen Trade* (Goldman 2000).

4 Grant is likely referring to *The Remains of the Day* (Ivory, 1993), in which he appears as the godson of James Fox's Nazi sympathizer. Previously Grant had played arty types such as Chopin – twice – in *Impromptu* (Lapine, 1991) and *Nocturnes* (Aubry, 1988), and Lord Byron in *Rowing with the Wind* (Suárez, 1988).

5 Created by novelist Ian Rankin, Edinburgh detective John Rebus was played on TV by John Hannah, and then by *Shallow Grave*'s Ken Stott. Hannah originally wanted the role to go to Peter Mullan, also from *Shallow Grave*.

6 Wet Wet Wet's theme song, a cover of the Troggs' 1967 hit 'Love Is All Around', topped the UK charts for 15 weeks in 1994. It was later voted the worst song of the decade by the *NME*, and spoofed in *Love Actually* as 'Christmas Is All Around'.

7 By way of comparison, in *The Heartbreak Kid* (Farrelly brothers, 2007), Ben Stiller's character jokes that he lost his virginity on a baseball diamond when 'a couple of the older kids pushed me down and…' It meets with stunned silence.

Chapter 2

Do You Remember the First Time?

Starring: *Shallow Grave* (Boyle, 1995)

Chapter 2: Do You Remember the First Time?

How Danny Boyle and co took on America at its own game

Alex Law (Ewan McGregor): It's not every day I find a story in my own flat.
Juliet Miller (Kerry Fox): It's not a story, Alex. It's a corpse.
Shallow Grave

It begins in primary colour. An arrogant, Argento red that fills the screen. Soon there will be a voiceover, in stark, middle-class Scots. Then David (Christopher Eccleston), staring impassively up at us, as the camera spins and Leftfield's score starts to jitter and swell. Seconds later, as we whizz through the streets of Edinburgh's New Town, David will inform us: 'This could have been any city, they're all the same…' But it could only be here, only now. And as we stare at that indelible red – the colour of the Film4 logo, of stop signs, of danger – it is really saying two words: fresh blood.

When director Danny Boyle, screenwriter John Hodge and producer Andrew Macdonald unleashed their stunning debut, Scottish noir *Shallow Grave*, on 6 January 1995, UK pop culture was in the recovery position. In April 1994, the suicide of Nirvana singer Kurt Cobain[1] seemed to symbolize the end of the US's musical dominance. That summer, Oasis and Blur, who almost called their previous album *England vs. America* (Harris 2003: 80), were taking back the charts from the likes of Bon Jovi, singing about pigeons and package holidays in their own accents. In the art world, Young British Artist (YBA)[2] Damien Hirst was shocking his way towards the 1995 Turner Prize with his half-cow-and-calf sculpture *Mother and Child (Divided)* (1993). 'It was', he noted, 'amazing what you could do with some imagination and a chainsaw' (*The 90s, 10 Years that Changed the World* 2015). Yet nowhere was the UK's new-found swagger less evident than the film industry.

Across the Atlantic, Quentin Tarantino was winning Oscars and adulation for *Pulp Fiction* (1994), a three-hour treatise on drugs, burgers and trash culture – the nerd holy trinity – dressed up in the cool, contemporary garb of a gangster flick. In the United Kingdom, the big success was *Four Weddings and a Funeral* (Newell, 1994). Capturing hearts rather than the zeitgeist, it was a film that could have been made any time in the previous twenty years.

Such was the dearth of up-to-date entertainment, it was entirely possible for switched-on Brits to listen only to UK indie music and watch only US indie movies. Indeed, surveying what was on offer, they might have been advised to.

Attempting to recreate *Mad Max* (Miller, 1979) within the M25, *Shopping* (Anderson, 1994) was inspired by the ram-raiding craze sweeping the North but proved, if anything, a little less subtle. It starred soon-to-be-familiar faces Jude Law,[3] Sadie Frost and Sean Pertwee as tearaway car thieves with no time for rules or consumerism (at one point Frost throws a box of Ferraro Rocher – not usually considered a travel snack – out of a car window in disgust, calling it 'yuppie food'), but plenty of time for racing around industrial estates shouting and for postmodern posturing. 'I know my rights. I watch *LA Law*,' says Law to policeman Jonathan Pryce. 'Is that supposed to be funny?' asks Pryce. 'No,' says Law, 'more like comedy-drama.' Unfortunately, *Shopping* contains more of the former.

'We were all into the idea of making multiplex films for the modern generation,' says Pertwee, now. 'There was,' he concedes, 'a great deal wrong with it, but it certainly looked amazing and it caught the eye of the Hollywood studio bosses' (2016). If *Shopping*'s main mistake was to sacrifice its true-to-life British roots for a more generic, internationally friendly setting, it did not hinder director Paul W.S. Anderson. His next job was the US video game adaptation *Mortal Kombat* (1995), which fitted his crash-bang-wallop sensibilities perfectly. Says Frost: 'At that point in Britain people didn't let you do something different, for a different audience, a youth film, you'd just get annihilated. And that's why the filmmakers went off to work in America' (2016).

In the mid-1990s, 'People would go a long way to avoid watching British movies...' says David Aukin (2016), then head of film at Channel 4, which funded *Shopping*. 'That's what we had to reverse: we had to make English films appealing.' *Four Weddings* may have made Film4 a lot of money, but, he says:

> The one that gave us confidence was *Shallow Grave*, that's the one that really got things going. First of all it was a unique voice, and it did that other wonderful thing, culturally. It divided the generations. Young people loved it, people over 40 didn't get it. You know if you can hit that nerve you've got something special.

From that first crimson frame, *Shallow Grave* is cool as can be; and the filmmakers come out fighting with a combination of beginners' passion (Hodge, Macdonald) and hard-won experience (Boyle). Brought up on Bond flicks and glam rock in working-class Greater Manchester, Boyle was bound for the priesthood,[4] until drama turned his head. After university, he became a theatre director at Joint Stock (with Aukin), the Royal Court and the Royal Shakespeare Company, before producing/directing one-off TV dramas for BBC Northern Ireland. Of these, the most enduring is *Elephant* (Clarke, 1989b).[5] A response to the violence of The Troubles, it is a brutal – and brutally simple – film, 39 minutes of senseless, dialogue-free killings captured, without comment, in a series of extraordinary tracking shots. Though the political outrage was impossible to ignore, it was the sense of constant motion, the confidence of that ever-roving camera, that Boyle would make his directorial calling card.

Confidence was hardly in short supply as *Shallow Grave* coalesced. At the 1990 Edinburgh Film Festival, Hodge met producer Andrew Macdonald, grandson of the mighty Emeric Pressburger,[6] who encouraged him to put pen to paper. At the time, Hodge was working as a hospital doctor and it showed in his script, which was pared to the bone, casually corporeal and in possession of a mortician's wit. 'I was very confident in the type of film I wanted to make,' says Macdonald, '[Something like] the American independent film, which was accessible and smart and, I thought, in Britain at that time, didn't exist' (2016).

Originally titled *Cruel*, the script did the usual rounds, and the pair plotted to sneak it to Aukin. Recalls Macdonald:

> We were at this screenwriting conference in Inverness. I knew I had to get the script to David, so I gave it to his minicab driver and slipped him a fiver – a lot of money 20 years ago – to give him the script, which he did. Years later, David told me that he'd lost his newspaper, and needed something to read on the flight from Inverness to London and it was our script.

Aukin was impressed, Film4 came on board to the tune of £1 million and Hodge and Macdonald started auditioning directors, including Boyle, who recalled:

> I was very honest with John and Andrew, the script was way better than anything I'd read. I was astonished at how good it was. I also said a lot of *Shallow Grave* was stolen from the Coen brothers, to which they could say very little. It was a case of honour among thieves. (Raphael 2013: 50)

The trio were soon as thick as thieves as well, high on 'the mixture of naivety and arrogance you have to have when you're making something – and at that age you've got plenty of it', as Macdonald says. The producer was in his late twenties; Hodge in his early thirties; Boyle a few years older. Still, 'For us to actually be sent off to Scotland to do as we pleased for five weeks [was] unbelievable really,' said the director (Raphael 2013: 51). Aukin, for one, had faith in his charges. 'It all changed with John Hodge, Danny Boyle and Andrew Macdonald', he says now. 'That was the changing of the guard.'

Shallow Grave tells the story of upwardly mobile Edinburgh flat-sharers Juliet, a doctor, Alex, a journalist, and David, an accountant, a trio so tight-knit they are practically incestuous. We first meet them searching for a new flatmate (though we never hear what happened to the previous one), weeding out the weak with casual cruelty. 'What on earth could make you think that we would want to share a flat like this with someone like you?' Alex asks poor Cameron (Colin McCredie). 'I mean, my first impression, and they're rarely wrong, is that you have none of the qualities that we normally seek in a prospective flatmate. I'm talking here about things like presence, charisma, style and charm.' Luckily, McGregor has enough of each to keep Alex just the right side of obnoxious.

Eventually they let the room to the mysterious Hugo (Britpop cinema mascot Keith Allen), a man who seems terminally incapable of giving a shit about anything. He is trying to write a novel 'about a priest who dies'. But when Juliet looks unimpressed, he changes it to 'some guy who's not a priest, who doesn't die. You see, it's better already.' No saint himself, Hugo *does* die, leaving behind drugs, a bag full of money and a dilemma. Should the trio report his death to the police and lose the cash, or keep the money and dispose of the corpse? No prizes for guessing which they pick, where Hugo's body ends up, or what the fallout does for flat harmony. Bright and breezy it may be, but this is still film noir. And as crime writer James Ellroy put it, 'The central theme of film noir is: you're fucked' (Guillen 2008). Said Boyle:

> It's interesting because, although it's completely sealed as a film – it's about three people in a flat – it's really about British society at the time [...] It's not a directly political film, yet it's deeply embedded in post-Thatcherite decay in Britain. Greed, aggrandizement, pleasure, selfishness, individualism. And nothing is worth worshipping other than money.
>
> (Raphael 2013: 49)

Boyle, Hodge and Macdonald had become Britpop cinema's first proper gang. Now they needed another. In the early scenes, the characters act as jealous gatekeepers to their own exclusive club and, by extension, the yuppie dream. To engender a feeling of togetherness among the actors, Boyle shared a flat with them for a week prior to filming. By way of rehearsal, they interviewed members of the crew as if they were prospective flatmates. Fox, an established Kiwi actress, had worked with the director on the TV mini-series *Mr Wroe's Virgins* (1993), along with cinematographer Brian Tufano,[7] one of the unsung heroes of Britpop cinema. Unlike their leading lady, relative newcomers McGregor and Eccleston were screen-tested for their roles.[8] While Fox and McGregor were allowed to speak in their native voices, Eccleston, a Mancunian, put on an impressive Scottish accent, plus owlish glasses inspired by a pair worn by Canadian director David Cronenberg (who he would later work with, in *eXistenZ* [Cronenberg, 1999]). McGregor, meanwhile, described his first encounter with Boyle, Hodge and Macdonald as 'like meeting a rock band' (Raphael 2013: xviii).

Shot on a budget so tight that Macdonald had to keep extra film stock locked away in a drawer to minimize wastage, the film's one extravagance was its magnificent set, built in a former furniture warehouse in Glasgow. Says Tufano: 'We agreed very early on that the actual set itself, the apartment, was in fact another character in the film' (2016). And not only did this character have to be big – at one point Alex rides a bike round the living room – it had to be beautiful.

To render the apartment more cinematic, the walls were made 30cm larger than life-size, then shot with a special Zeiss camera lens that Boyle adored because it 'makes Britain look bigger than it really is' (Raphael 2013: 69), which could practically be Britpop cinema's slogan. Inspired by Hopper and Caravaggio paintings, production designer Kave Quinn filled the rooms with great swathes of colour, 'To get away from that slightly drab British realism', explained Boyle in his DVD director's commentary, 'to kind of smash it up a bit' (2009a). Hereafter, Britpop cinema apartments would be unfeasibly large and all the colours of the rainbow. The protagonists of *Shooting Fish* (Schwartz, 1997), for example, live in a disused cooling tower, while a crummy flatshare in *This Year's Love* (Kane, 1999) seems to occupy half of Camden.

Of *Shallow Grave*'s many virtues – committed performances, witty dialogue, a delicious sense of enveloping darkness – perhaps pace is the key. Shorn of all but the most essential stage directions, Hodge's script could be read in 45 minutes. And, in Boyle's hands, it gets off to a suitably breathless start. During David's opening monologue about friendship and trust, the first shot is the tarmac blurring beneath a speeding car – Hugo's, as it happens. Recalls Tufano:

> The camera was on a low platform on the front of a camera car and undercranked at about six or ten frames per second [FPS]. It's like in the old silent movies, which were hand-cranked to about 16-18FPS. When you run them at the conventional 24FPS, they look speeded up and you get that jerky movement. Of course, that's exactly what Danny wanted for the start of *Shallow Grave*, to give it that energy.

Said Boyle:

> Film as a mechanical process is about momentum. The film moves through the camera and then through the projector, and it's moving at staggering speeds: 24FPS is quick! Film's origins were about motion and the capturing of motion [...] no matter what a film may be about, I love making it look and feel like an action movie.
>
> (Raphael 2013: 126)

Increasing the sense of urgency is the fact that the opening shot of David comes not from the beginning of the film, but the end, when his dead body is about to be shut in a mortuary drawer. By concertina-ing screen time in this manner, Boyle and Hodge make every moment into a thrilling now, adding to the forward rush.

Less visible, but no less effective, is the way Boyle makes his mark even in throwaway moments. Following a drunken dinner where David asks Hugo if he has ever killed a man, we cut to two thugs, Tim (Leonard O'Malley) and Andy (*Trainspotting*'s Peter Mullan), who are searching for Hugo – and the money. In the script, the scene is suspensefully placed to make us question Hugo's backstory, but otherwise straightforward: a man (David Scoular) takes a beating at an ATM machine. In Boyle's hands, however, it becomes surprising and subversive, a slice of pure Britpop cinema.

Helpless, we watch events from inside the cashpoint; the ATM instructions spelled backwards across the screen, adding an ironic commentary. 'Take Your Cash!' one warns, as the heavies attack. 'Thank You,' it continues, as they dole out more violence. 'Next Customer Please,' it finishes, as blood dribbles down the display and, in the distance, a double-decker bus speeds past.

This witty sequence is so much better than it needs to be. Indeed, throughout the film, the action (read: violence) feels both imaginative and real. Hugo's corpse, which the trio wrestle down the stairwell wrapped in black plastic, has the dead weight of a crash-test dummy (which it was). McGregor had to dig a genuine (though shallow) grave. When David draws the short straw and has to saw off Hugo's hands and feet, Eccleston was hacking at a joint of lamb. Next, when he removes Hugo's teeth with a hammer, the actor was actually hitting a melon with a face drawn on it. Hodge, it transpires, has a medicine man's flair for the mundanely painful. When Tim and Andy finally reach the flat, poor Alex endures a vicious pipe blow to the shins, inspired, according to Boyle's DVD commentary, by an injury sustained by Tottenham footballer Nicky Barmby (2009). Later, it is hard not to wince when a car door swings shut on his still-recovering legs.

An early scene of Tim and Andy's interrogations gives us another ingenious Boyle set-up. First the screen flashes red, then a face breaks the surface, and we realize we are looking up at a man (Grant Glendinning), being drowned in bloodied bathwater. It only now becomes clear that the film's first crimson frame was diegetic – part of the world the film takes place in – rather than a trick to get our attention. Plus, by flashing us back to the start, Boyle closes the gap between past and future, crime and punishment, so they feel connected, inevitable. It also reminds us that, like Macbeth, another upwardly mobile Scot, the flatmates are 'in blood stepp'd in so far' their only option is to keep wading.

As events quickly spiral out of the control, Boyle keeps a tight grip, working from a script without an ounce of fat on its bones. Traumatized by what he has done, the increasingly disturbed David decides to take up residence in the attic. Tim and Andy attack the flat and are dealt with, again by David, when they venture up to retrieve the money. Their bodies are dismembered and buried in the woods, although this time there are tattoos to be removed, too, something the film only hints at. Soon, the graves are discovered, bringing the unwanted attention of Inspector McCall (Ken Stott) and DC Mitchell (Hodge, cameoing).

It is about this point that relationships between the flatmates break down completely. Juliet plans to abscond to Rio with the money but, at the climax, David stops her, and the three turn on each other. A vicious tooth-and-claw fight sees them destroying the flat – the symbol of their soured greed – and each other, with knives, toasters, even the fridge (stocked with champagne, of course), until their yuppie playground has become a battlefield. The final reckoning sees David dead, Alex pinned to the floor by a kitchen knife, and Juliet at the airport, in tears, her case weighted down with newspaper cuttings that Alex substituted for the cash.

But even this brutal ending proves darkly humorous rather than downbeat. In a twist thought up by Boyle, Alex has squirrelled the money away under the floorboards, and may get to keep it. As Alex smiles,[9] Juliet screams and David is laid, belatedly, to rest, Andy Williams' 'Happy Heart' (1969) offers a burst of aural sunshine on the soundtrack. Next, we see a freeze-frame of the trio laughing in brighter times, Hodge's professional pessimism leavened by Boyle's positivity. It is a heady mix, allowing us to reframe the horrors we have just witnessed as a blast of black-hearted fun. Think of the scene where Alex, having pushed Hugo's car into a quarry, lets out a roar of delight. It is the sound of a man overjoyed to be alive, however long that may last, and a beautiful example of Britpop cinema's ebullience. Any director could have made the scene tense, but only Boyle could make it sing.

Although references to Hollywood films abound – the red-hued woodland burial is straight out of *Goodfellas* (Scorsese, 1990); the shafts of light piercing the attic darkness from *Blood Simple* (Coen brothers, 1984); and the dead man's voiceover is pure *Sunset Boulevard* (Wilder, 1950) – they speak of confidence rather than kowtowing. *Shallow Grave* may have been inspired by American indie movies, but it is loudly, proudly British. Chris Tarrant is on the box, entreating contestants to try and *Lose a Million*, just as David and Juliet will. Cans of Irn-Bru, Scotland's favourite soft drink, replace Coca-Cola as the product placement of choice. Meanwhile, pagan horror *The Wicker Man* (Hardy, 1973), perhaps the last truly iconic Scottish film, plays on the telly. It is a reminder of how far the country has come since the dark days of the 1970s, *Braveheart* (Gibson, 1995) be damned.

'One of the constant dangers of filmmaking here is the temptation to imitate America,' said Boyle (Raphael 2013: 66). Yet it is not guns the characters buy, but DIY tools, and whatever glamour they possess is not borrowed from another culture, but from their own, sometimes staggering, self-belief. That such a low-budget film would have, at its centre, the ultimate symbol of largesse – a bag of real money, £1 million in fact, that the production team had to hire especially for the close-ups – speaks volumes. Boyle and co were shooting for the moon.

Originally Macdonald confessed to having doubts about hiring Boyle because his work was too arty, but, he says:

> What I didn't realize was that it was the art, or whatever you want to call it, that Danny brought to the film was what made it really great, rather than just throwaway. If 20,000 other people had directed *Shallow Grave* it wouldn't have been as good.

Nor, suggested Boyle, would more resources have helped, no matter that the crew had to auction off furniture from the set in the last days of the shoot. 'One of the wonderful things about having very little money is this, if you all work together there's almost a siege mentality. We did it our way and we'd stand or fall by it' (Raphael 2013: 73).

As it happens, they nearly fell at the first hurdle. Recalls Macdonald:

> I remember being very keen that Danny made sure the film was violent enough. I was very keen that it was very violent and shocking, which we almost paid for at the end,

> when Channel 4's Michael Grade saw it. We were all very proud of it, so was David Aukin, but Michael just thought it was terrible.

Recalls Aukin:

> When I first saw it, I thought it was wonderful, loved it, then I showed it to my colleagues at Channel 4, including Michael Grade, my boss, and he hated it. He was genuinely upset. He said, 'You've made a film I can't possibly transmit on my channel, what do you think you're doing?' I figured at that point that my contract was not going to be renewed. Fast-forward six months and we're at the Dinard Film Festival, Michael is guest of honour and he has to present the prize for the best film to... *Shallow Grave*! He turned to me and said, 'OK, I knew nothing about the film, you're in charge, do whatever you want, I trust you.' Not only that but he doubled the Film4 budget! It was a great turning point.

The filmmakers, meanwhile, credit PolyGram for realizing that British films could be marketed like American films – that is, mercilessly. This included posting spades to journalists to remind them of Hugo's grisly fate. Says Macdonald:

> They sent them all wrapped in black, like when they were carrying the body, the idea being that people would think, 'What the fuck is this? Who's Danny Boyle? Who's Ewan McGregor? Who are these people?' And it kind of worked. I've still got mine.

In fact, it worked a treat. According to Boyle:

> PolyGram had an idea that what we needed in this country was to sell films for people to watch on a Friday night. After a tough week at work, the films they could either unwind with or get fired up by didn't have to feature Tom Cruise or Harrison Ford – they could actually be British films.
>
> (Raphael 2013: 74)

And, with the advent of Britpop cinema, for the first time they were. Says Macdonald:

> Without PolyGram there wouldn't have been that British boom. They were ultimately so hungry for success, they needed product, and they found and fostered these films. And, of course, they fostered Richard Curtis and Danny, who are probably the great voices of that generation. If they'd been around ten years before, they would have gone to America, like Alan Parker and Ridley Scott had to, or Hugh Hudson, there just wasn't enough going on in the UK. But PolyGram knew how to sell the type of films we wanted to make, films that were similar to records, you know, aimed at young people; populist but still with an edge.

Appropriately enough for a tiny film about a massive windfall, *Shallow Grave* would become the highest-grossing British release of the year, making just under £5 million at the UK box office, and $20 million worldwide (IMDB 2018f). But more than that, says Aukin:

> It was the first British film to recoup its cost at the UK box office alone in ten years. And because it sold around the world, relative to its size, I mean, it made a huge amount of money, so Film4 suddenly had real confidence. It was there to support British film 100 per cent.

With Film4, PolyGram and a trio of new talents firing on all cylinders, the foundations were laid for the Britpop cinema boom. Indeed, in 1996, Aukin gave the movement its mantra. Referring to *Shallow Grave*'s runaway success, he said: 'The conclusion I draw is that we can make films for ourselves' (Murray 2015: 55). And how.

What Happened Next...

Christopher Eccleston... Became one of Britain's best screen actors, with notable appearances in *Jude* (Winterbottom, 1996), *Elizabeth* (Kapur, 1998) and *The Others* (Amenábar, 2001), which ends with a Keith Allen cameo. His most iconic roles have been on TV, for example as the Ninth Doctor in *Dr Who* (2005–present, UK: BBC) and Nicky in Peter Flannery's sprawling, state-of-the-nation masterpiece *Our Friends in the North* (1996, UK: BBC), which Boyle was asked to direct. A shocking episode of Jimmy McGovern's *Cracker* (1996–2006, UK: Granada) saw Eccleston's character DCI Bilborough murdered by a Hillsborough survivor/skinhead played by future Begbie, Robert Carlyle.

Kerry Fox... Continued her career as an international character actress. She was nominated for a Canadian Genie award for her role in *The Hanging Garden* (Fitzgerald, 1997) and won a Silver Bear in Berlin for *Intimacy* (Chéreau, 2001). Her most visible UK role was in *Bright Star* (Campion, 1999), a biopic of John Keats.

British youth movies... Remained in short supply. The most watchable were *Boston Kickout* (Hills, 1995) and *Blue Juice* (Prechezer, 1995). The former, starring the ever-reliable John Simm, tackles teenage ennui in suburban Stevenage. It begins with a backyard scramble (the Boston kickout of the title) and features tracks by The Stone Roses and Oasis, and brief snatches of visual dynamism. But it is more coming-of-age drama than true Britpop cinema. *Blue Juice*, meanwhile, is set in what writer Jacques Peretti called 'the crazy teashop scene round St Ives' (2000). It stars Sean Pertwee as a surfer getting into various scrapes with his mates, including unlikely cockney Ewan McGregor,[10] to save their favourite café. It is hardly *Point Break* (Bigelow, 1991). Nor, Keith Allen cameo aside, is it Britpop cinema.

Danny Boyle and co... Stayed together for their next project, an adaptation of Irvine Welsh's cult 1993 novel *Trainspotting*. Of *Shallow Grave*, Welsh says, 'I loved the action and the pace of it, but I wasn't mad keen on the characters. I thought they were a bit kind of posh and cold basically. But I figured if you can have that action and that whole cinematic sense, and marry it to my characters, storylines and situations, you've got something fucking great you know?' (2016).

Notes

1 Deciding that, as he wrote in his suicide letter, 'It's better to burn out than to fade away,' Cobain was found dead at his home in Seattle on 5 April 1994 with heroin and Valium in his bloodstream and a shotgun wound to the head.

2 The YBAs were a loose group of 1980s/1990s Goldsmiths graduates, including Hirst and Tracey Emin, known for their controversial works and media savvy.

3 Future *Trainspotters* Ewan McGregor and Jonny Lee Miller auditioned for Law's role, as did *Lock, Stock and Two Smoking Barrels* star Nick Moran – in a full Geordie accent.

4 Boyle wasn't the only one. Martin Scorsese, John Woo and M. Night Shyamalan all trained to be priests. 'There's something very theatrical about it [directing],' said Boyle. 'It's basically the same job: poncing around, telling people what to think' (Kelly 2009).

5 Alan Clarke brought a sense of the cinematic, the dangerous, the unseen or unspeakable to social-realist TV films such as *Scum* (1977), *Made in Britain* (1982) and *The Firm* (1989a).

6 Producer Emeric Pressburger and director Michael Powell were perhaps Britain's greatest filmmaking partnership, responsible for *A Matter of Life and Death* (1946), *Black Narcissus* (1947) and *The Red Shoes* (1948) among other classics.

7 Tufano was the cinematographer on *Quadrophenia* (Roddam, 1979), and brought a lightness of touch and thrilling sense of movement to *Trainspotting* (Boyle, 1996), *A Life Less Ordinary* (Boyle, 1997) and *Billy Elliot* (Daldry, 2001).

8 Ironically, Robert Carlyle turned down the part of Alex, while Eccleston was initially considered for the role of Begbie.

9 Some viewers – the author included – presumed Alex must be dead, especially as Inspector McCall just stares at him when he says, 'Hello officer!' After all, we've already heard David 'speaking' in voiceover from the mortuary slab. Alex's line was added during post-production to clarify the issue.

10 McGregor, apparently, enjoyed the *Blue Juice* experience. 'What a mad time,' he told *The Independent*'s Mark Kermode, 'I loved it. I made a film with four of my mates, went surfing, and got a disease in the nose! Fucking brilliant!' (2002).

Chapter 3

The Day We Caught the Train

Starring: *Trainspotting* (Boyle, 1996)

Chapter 3: The Day We Caught the Train

Danny Boyle and co rip up the rulebook

Renton (Ewan McGregor): People think it's all about misery and desperation and death and all that shit, which is not to be ignored, but what they forget is the pleasure of it. Otherwise we wouldn't do it. After all, we're not fucking stupid. At least, we're not that fucking stupid.
Trainspotting

Before they even knew what it was, the Britpop generation knew they were going to see *Trainspotting*. No matter if they had not read the book, or did not understand the title: the teaser trailer had them hooked. In it, Renton, lying on the railway tracks, dispenses advice on the dangers of drink and drugs. Though the rumble of an encroaching train hints at the severity of his predicament, his voice retains that sly, self-mocking tone. 'Most of all', he concludes, 'don't let your mates tie you to the railway track.' As the rumble becomes a scream, he braces for the inevitable impact, but too late. There would be no stopping this juggernaut…

As 1995 slipped into 1996, the Britpop cinema boom began in earnest. The previous, sweltering summer had seen the Battle of Britpop rage between Blur and Oasis, who both released singles on the same day, reaching No.1 and No.2 respectively.[1] James Bond was back from hiatus in the glossily rebooted *GoldenEye* (Campbell, 1995), with Pierce Brosnan's Teflon charms banishing the memory of the dreary Timothy Dalton years. Meanwhile, thanks to lottery funds, increased American interest,[2] and a smattering of hits such as *Four Weddings and a Funeral* (Newell, 1994), the UK film industry was back from the brink. Investment in features rose from £169 million in 1992 to £560 million in 1996 (Todd 2005: 17), with 128 UK films produced in 1996, compared to 30 in 1989 (Dyja 2010: 121). Still, nobody could have predicted that it would be an adaptation of Irvine Welsh's controversial *Trainspotting*, about heroin addicts in 1980s Leith, that would capture the imagination of a generation.

'There's something very special about that time, and to have been a part of it,' Ewan McGregor told *Total Film*'s Jamie Graham. 'The movie version of Britpop was *Trainspotting*.

I have a real nostalgia for that. I hear [Oasis single] "Wonderwall" come on the radio, and I'm like, "Fucking take me back. I want to go back!"' (2016: 123).

What was most surprising, however, was not that *Trainspotting* became, in the words of historian Alwyne W. Turner, 'one of the defining cultural artefacts of the decade' (2013: 125), but that it was made at all. Says producer Andrew Macdonald:

> Yeah it was risky, but you have to remember that, in effect, *Shallow Grave* had made Danny, and certainly Ewan, a star in the UK. I think the riskier thing was us making a film that sounded so unappealing to the box office.
>
> (2016)

PolyGram's Michael Kuhn, who distributed the film, agrees:

> It could have been horrible. Very dark, all the drug taking… if someone pitched it to you now you'd think, 'Oh bloody hell!' But we just believed in the people. They'd done *Shallow Grave*, they knew what they were doing, we just had to shut our eyes and hope for the best.
>
> (2016)

David Aukin recalls:

> PolyGram wanted to fully finance it, they didn't want Channel 4 involved, and they wanted to cut the famous toilet scene. But that's what Film4 existed for, editorially, to take the risks and accept the responsibility for what the industry felt was going too far. So we kept our position in the film, PolyGram came onboard as our partners, and we kept the scene.
>
> (2016)

McGregor, who would disappear down the aforementioned toilet in one of the film's filthier flights of fancy, was more upbeat:

> I thought, 'Yeah, we're going to fucking nail it!' I could just feel it. To tackle a book about heroin addicts in Leith was probably as dangerous as you could imagine doing. And I loved it. I loved the spirit of, 'Yeah fuck it. Let's go!'
>
> (Graham 2016: 123)

Inspired by punk rock,[3] and spiked with gutter poetry, Welsh's scattershot prose was awash with heroin, hopelessness and black humour. As a novel it was a masterpiece, but as a potential film project it looked a mess. Somewhere amid the overlapping voices, most speaking in scarcely penetrable Leith dialect, was the tale of Mark Renton who, despite the best efforts of his friends Sick Boy, Spud and Begbie, not to mention his own apathy and drug addiction, chooses life, or something like it, by running off with £16,000 in stolen drug money. The story was in there all right, but it would take one hell of a screenwriter to extract it.

A cult success from the off, *Trainspotting* was quickly adapted for the stage. Written by Harry Gibson and directed by Ian Brown, it opened at Glasgow's Citizens Theatre in May 1994 before touring the world. Starring Ewen Bremner as Renton, who had impressed Welsh in *Naked* (Leigh, 1993) and would play Spud in the film, it was 'the best bit of acting I've ever seen', according to *Lock, Stock and Two Smoking Barrels* star Nick Moran, 'Just extraordinary. A mad, mental, disgusting ensemble piece of fucking filth' (2016). But it was also a series of scabrous monologues, a work that cohered by cumulative effect. Said Bremner:

> I knew the material really was hitting a nerve and I was confident the film was going to be a strong piece and people were going to respond to it because I was seeing it every night on stage. But none of us had any conception of the scale, the profound effect and impact that it was going make on the culture.
>
> (*The Graham Norton Show* 2017)

It was Macdonald who first gave a copy of *Trainspotting* to John Hodge. 'Suitably stunned', wrote Hodge in his introduction to the published screenplay, 'I handed it back' (1996: ix). But by cutting out extraneous characters to concentrate on Renton,[4] transposing the anarchic voice of the book into a galloping, go-anywhere structure, and softening the often-startling violence[5] without declawing it completely, Hodge delivered a script that was breathtaking in its brevity. 'You need somebody to tear the whole thing up,' says Welsh of the adaptation, 'John's an ex-doctor, he wields a very ruthless and cruel scalpel. You have to have that in adaptations' (2016).

Nor did Welsh mind that, in the filmmakers' hands, *Trainspotting* would shift from punk-rock polemic to Britpop cinema manifesto:

> There's a lot of people who wanted to do it as a kind of Ken Loach social drama thing, and I love Ken Loach, but I just didn't think this was the world for him. It had to be big and brash and cinematic, not seeing the characters as victims of society, because my view of it is that they weren't. They were people in a transition, who got the shitty stick in de-industrialisation, but still had their humanity and were still trying to get on and do something. I saw the heroin as basically just something people were doing in the absence of anything else to give their lives compelling drama; to give their lives, ironically, some kind of fucking structure. So I didn't see them as being victims, that was really important, and Danny and John and Andrew didn't see that either, you know, so were on the same page from the off.

Said Boyle:

> We met a lot of real junkies. That was really, really depressing. Suddenly there didn't seem to be any real energy to build the film on other than the book. When you meet the real things it's like all the life has been taken away and there's nothing left but victims, and

> you don't want to make a film about victims. It's a debilitating experience rather than something that gives energy and life.
>
> (Pennington 1996)

Much has been written on the making of *Trainspotting*. Yet, more remarkable than the on-set tales of McGregor almost, but not quite, trying heroin, or Jonny Lee Miller (Sick Boy) rollerblading with then-wife Angelina Jolie, is how the film effectively started its own genre.

Trainspotting, like the best of Britpop cinema, begins at a sprint. To the irresistible thump of Iggy Pop's 'Lust for Life', a 1977 punk anthem reappropriated for the new era, Renton and Spud race towards us, their feet pounding the Princes Street pavements. As shoplifted goods spew from their pockets and security guards (including Hodge) give chase, Renton's voiceover sets the pace. A stream-of-consciousness, anti-everything screed, it mocks those who: 'Choose life, choose a job, choose a career, choose a family, choose a fucking big television…'

The blur of narrative information here is so swiftly delivered it is less about absorbing it than being engulfed by it. Before 90 seconds have elapsed, we see Renton offering a sickly grin as he gets hit by a car; meet his friends, and witness their foibles, at five-aside football; and watch him swoon in opiated bliss in a squat.[6] 'Who needs reasons when you've got heroin?' he asks us. Who indeed?

It makes for an extraordinary intro, an entire way of life conveyed at lightning speed. But even Welsh's most iconic prose has been trimmed for purpose – it begins 'Choose us…' in the book (2013: 21) – not to mention moved to the front of the narrative. 'We were adamant that the film should explode into life,' said Danny Boyle to writer Alan Morrison. 'That speech was originally in the middle of the film [… but] John moved it forward. It's one of those moments when you can feel the film kick into life at script stage' (2003: 118).

The shot was first attempted on a quad bike, but the filmmakers almost ran Ewen Bremner over in the process. 'That's when we realized the quad bike was probably not the best way of doing it,' says cinematographer Brian Tufano (2016), who found himself strapped to a souped-up motorbike-and-sidecar instead. Says Macdonald:

> It was sheer naivety. There was no crowd control so we were riding along Princes Street with pedestrians everywhere jumping out of the way, and a cameraman in front partially obscuring the view. It was crazy, we could have killed someone.

Safety issues aside, it remains one of cinema's most exciting openings. Says Tufano: 'I've always worked on the principle that you grab the audience by the balls in the first five minutes, and once you've got them on your side, you want to make sure they stay there.'

Indeed, the film rarely lets up. Even the slower moments are animated with the constant rat-a-tat of Renton's running commentary, which is doing far more than it appears. Not only is it darkly funny – such as when he admits, with dawning horror, 'I am no longer constipated' – it highlights the tension between his actions (cheating, stealing, relapsing, then repeat) and the excuses he tells himself: 'The truth is that I'm a bad person.' As in *Alfie* (Gilbert, 1966) or *Goodfellas* (Scorsese, 1990), experiencing the character's sins through their own amoral filter encourages us to enjoy, rather than condemn, what they do, if only in the moment.

In *Trainspotting*, however, that moment lasts almost the entire 90-minute joyride. No matter how repetitive the junkie lifestyle, Renton's omniscient voiceover allows the story to leapfrog back and forth in time, through flashbacks and freeze-frames, without forgetting that, as Welsh puts it, for the addict, 'nothing exists outside the moment'.

The scene where Begbie (Robert Carlyle) throws his pint glass off a pub balcony, for example, is extraordinarily nimble. First, Begbie narrates a (heavily fictionalized) anecdote about his pool-playing prowess, which unfolds, in flashback, as a broad comedy sketch. Back in the present, he hurls the glass over his shoulder, an act of chillingly indiscriminate, but entirely characteristic, violence. The glass freezes in mid-air, allowing Renton's voiceover to fast-forward a few days to when Tommy (Kevin McKidd) tells him – and us – the real story, a much sorrier anecdote. Then we cut back to that falling glass, no longer frozen, followed by screams from below, spilled blood and a full-blown pub riot which Begbie wades into with glee. 'Begbie didn't do drugs,' Renton informs us, a touch too late, 'he did people.'

Making Renton the watchful centre of the group, his voiceover providing a wry reality check, makes the heightened performances of the supporting cast seem amusing rather than monstrous. But it also makes a mockery of an observation in the book: 'Nae friends in this game. Jist associates' (Welsh 2013: 7). Indeed, it is a triumph of marketing, not to mention Britpop cinema optimism, that Renton and co seem like members of a band – a heroin-chic Supergrass, say, or a gone-to-seed Suede – even if it is one you would rather listen to than join.

Music plays a key part in the film's inclusive cool, with Boyle, Welsh and co endearingly keen to show off their record collections. 'If it hadn't been for The Pistols and The Clash I would never have written *Trainspotting*,' Welsh claimed (Munro 2013: 37); a sojourn to London sees our not-so-fab-four crossing the road like The Beatles on the *Abbey Road* (1969) cover; and noted heroin users Iggy Pop[7] and Lou Reed get name-checks.

It is not just music from the past, though, or freshly minted Britpop hits, but a selection of timeless songs with the power to transport. Opener 'Lust for Life' sounds completely of the moment but was already twenty years old. Closer 'Born Slippy', by Underworld, takes us into an unknown future with its tribal drums, aggro pill patter and trippily transcendent chords. The rest are just as hard to place. Sleeper's cover of Blondie's 'Atomic' is 1980s new wave by way of 1990s Britpop. Pulp's jaunty 'Mile End' looks back at the band's years of London squalor, sounding old but seemingly written for the film. Blur's woozily soothing 'Sing', meanwhile, is many steps removed from their usual bluster. There are even haunting bursts of diegetic song, such as when Spud performs Rolf Harris's 'Two Little Boys' at Tommy's wake or Diane (Kelly Macdonald) appears in Renton's cold-turkey nightmares trilling the words to Heaven 17's 'Temptation'. The overall effect is of a mixtape that never dates; not a score, but the soundtrack to someone else's life.[8] Said Boyle:

> We decided early on that we weren't going to score the film in a traditional way, so you look at the masters. You look at the way that Scorsese – particularly in *Mean Streets* – uses his music. One of the ways we can actually identify the period is to move from Iggy Pop through to dance music – [when] Renton moves to London and goes to a rave – right up to Pulp, Blur, Sleeper and Elastica. The film's timespan is impossible because Renton doesn't age and they don't cut their hair, but you feel you've moved through a period of time on a sensual rather than documentary level.
>
> (Morrison 2003: 118)

Boyle's use of music is never more sensual than when Renton accidentally overdoses to the strains of Lou Reed's rueful 'Perfect Day' – a rare moment of peace amid the film's stylized *Sturm und Drang*. Already a denizen of the floor, a low life, repeatedly filmed from ground level, Renton sinks through the carpet in smacked-out abandon, as the song's toy-town piano enfolds us with him in its narcotic embrace. It might seem a strange choice, particularly as Renton and Sick Boy have written off Reed's solo work as 'shite', but it is much less celebratory than it appears, the song's narrator seeking the same solace in nostalgia that Renton does in heroin. Like Boyle, Reed finds beauty in the mundane ('Just a perfect day, feed animals in the zoo…'); his childish couplets (park/dark, zoo/too) matching Renton's rather more literal regression. Gazing up helplessly through the red (read: labial) lips of the carpet/coffin, Renton is completely without agency, a baby. Dragged downstairs by his dealer, Swanney (Peter Mullan), past graffiti alerting us to the fact that these are, indeed, 'hard times', he is manhandled into a cab, onto a gurney, into hospital. Here he is revived, reborn, dragged gasping back to reality to face his demons, as Reed offers an elegantly threatening sign-off: 'You're going to reap just what you sow.'[9]

This stunning sequence crystallizes *Trainspotting*'s slightly ambivalent attitude towards drugs. 'Just say no' is the official party line, but the film's gorgeous colours and giddy camera movements make more impression than the narrative's cautionary notes; the sad beauty of Renton's stoned satiety lingering longer than the awfulness of withdrawal.

Although the deaths of Tommy (through toxoplasmosis) and, particularly, baby Dawn (through neglect) are horrific, Renton – and, by association, the film – soon shrugs them off. If anything, it is the grubby matter-of-factness of the deleted scenes that makes a clearer case for abstinence. In one, the ever-ebullient Swanney loses a leg after injecting into an artery ('Could have been worse, eh? Could have been my fucking dick…') and is reduced to posing as a war veteran and begging for change. Another sees Sick Boy boasting about how he pimps out addicts for a 'fiver a skull'. Viewed separately, you can see why these scenes would have been excised, but in context they offer a sense that, while Renton may have chosen life/a job/a career/a family/a big fucking television etc., others were less lucky. Says Welsh:

> *Trainspotting* is still a very dark film. Renton rips off his mates, but he's got a big smile on his face at the end as he walks over the bridge. There's a lot of nasty, amoral exploitation between people going on, and a lot of despair. While the book has that too, it also has a lot of exuberance and it bounces along at a fair old rate as well. I can't really accuse them [the filmmakers] of doing anything that I didn't do myself.

Except he can. In the book, after Renton has stolen the £16,000 from Sick Boy, Begbie and Spud, Welsh offers the inconclusive, 'If there was one person whom Renton would try to compensate, it was Spud' (2013: 429). The film, meanwhile, shows Spud actually receiving that compensation, thus ending 'not by stressing Renton's disloyalty to Sick Boy and Begbie, but his loyalty – even tenderness – to the harmless Spud' (Smith 2002: 43), an idea Hodge supposedly hated.

As in *Shallow Grave*, no matter how grim the situation, Boyle finds pops of bright beauty amid the wreckage. Think of Swanney's muralled, highly set-designed den; the lysergically coloured council flats Renton passes on the way for his 'final hit'; or, once Renton has escaped the 'worst toilet in Scotland', the morphine suppositories he attempts to retrieve glowing through impossible blue waters.[10] Said Boyle:

> The spirit of the book is irresistible [...] It cuts through that anaesthetizing effect of modern life. We tried to capture that same spirit in the film via music, voiceover, costume and boldness. Babies on the ceiling. Scenes in toilets. Writing a sign declaring: 'You're now in the worst toilet in Scotland.' The film was like a Jackson Pollock; you could throw all these things at it.
>
> (Raphael 2013: 83–84)

The film's visual pep is matched by a sense of changing eras; the deprivation of the 1980s viewed through an upbeat, if ironic, 1990s filter. In the real world, Thatcher was long gone, the Conservatives on their way out, and New Labour waiting in the wings. In the film, Renton witnesses rave culture taking off, participates in the London property boom as an estate agent and rejects drugs and poverty to become an unapologetic – if amoral – achiever. 'I'm going to be just like you,' he swears, striding towards us, his face blurring into anonymity.

If heroin was a Thatcherite drug – all buying, selling and stony self-interest – *Trainspotting* felt more like a product of the Ecstasy generation: endlessly chatty, in constant motion, in thrall to the music. Explained Boyle:

> Ecstasy was everywhere in the mid-1990s, and so it was the prism through which people saw drugs at that time. Which is a different prism to heroin in the 1970s. In a funny way, *Trainspotting* has a euphoria you associate more with Ecstasy than a drug like heroin, which just leaves you in a corner for 14 hours till you're ready to search out your next fix.
>
> (Raphael 2013: 87)

Welsh has his own theory:

> Heroin's not very filmable, it's not very glamorous, most of the interesting shit is going on inside of people's heads... until it all goes wrong and they're trying to break into places and rip things off and all that. The film was criticized because it was almost portraying heroin as hallucinogenic, which it isn't. But my idea was that guys were on lots of other stuff, such as speed. When you're on a lot of speed you get sleep deprivation; and sleep deprivation hallucinations are worse than any acid hallucinations I've ever had, and they come about when you're doing all sorts of drugs: uppers and downers. I saw it as moving into that kind of landscape, so it didn't really bother me, but one or two drug purists complained that it made heroin out to be more visually trippy than it is.

Whatever the chemical cause, the film makes use of what Murray Smith calls 'black magic realism' (2002: 75), a sense of fluidity and mobility more associated with the fantasy genre. Where heroin is concerned, Renton is able to swim down through the toilet U–bend into a fantasy underwater world, jump from a pub wall to land at Swanney's flat for another hit, then sink through the floor. Not only do these sequences, in Smith's words, reiterate 'the power of heroin to transform – temporarily – the most impoverished real existence into one of sensual richness' (2002: 79); the suggestion of blossoming possibility, of brave new worlds hidden behind the most mundane of facades, is utterly captivating. Said Boyle:

> I think it's one of the points of cinema – to be visceral rather than intellectual or reflective. The reflection can come later. It should be the sensation of experiencing 90 or 100 minutes of live imagery. It should be unstoppable. You shouldn't be able to walk away.
>
> (Raphael 2013: 15)

Anyone who has come across *Trainspotting* on late-night TV, and sworn to themselves, 'just five more minutes', will know exactly what he means. 'We wanted to make an exciting film', says Welsh, 'and not a film about drugs, really, a film about youth, about the vibrancy of youthful friendships and that time when anything's possible.'

A heroin film made by (and certainly for) the Ecstasy generation, who use substances to abandon their inhibitions rather than obliterate themselves, *Trainspotting* is ultimately about escape. It is there in the drugs and the music. It is there in the great outdoors, where Renton famously proclaims, 'It's shite being Scottish'; and the grim indoors, where paintings of paradise beaches look down from leisure centre walls or innocent bystanders get glassed in purgatory-hued pubs. It is there in Sick Boy's obsessive Bond fandom,[11] Tommy's sex tapes, Begbie's pleasure at administering pain. It is there in the football videos, the 'mind-numbing, spirit-crushing gameshows', the bingo and the betting shops, the cigarettes handed out like candy in the backs of cabs. It is there, most of all, in Renton, a character who is always running away, disappearing through the floor, testing the edges of his own reality. Having exhausted all the possibilities, he affects the ultimate escape, walking out of the film to become one of us, his voiceover continuing even as the screen blurs to black.

While few would dispute that *Trainspotting* was phenomenal, nobody could deny it was a phenomenon. 'It was absolutely one of the greatest marketing campaigns ever,' says PolyGram's Michael Kuhn, who 'marketed it like an album', something PolyGram knew quite a bit about. Having spent £850,000 extra on advertising – more than half the film's £1.5 million budget (Smith 2002: 10) – PolyGram put that iconic teaser trailer on the *Shallow Grave* VHS, and hired Stylorouge, known for its album covers, to design the posters. As writer Claire Allfree put it: 'If *Trainspotting* the film redefined British cinema then *Trainspotting* the poster redefined the way it was marketed' (Pickadolla 2010).

Above a bright bar of what we shall call Britpop cinema orange, the main characters pose in chic black-and-white, like rejects from an unruly fashion shoot. Instead of a group shot, the characters stand apart, suggesting a panoply of clashing voices. Like the famous Uncle Sam recruitment poster, each of their stances represents a form of direct address, an invitation to join the gang. Begbie's raised middle fingers say, 'Fuck you!' but his eyes are smiling; Diane and Spud seem to be daring/begging us to dance; while Sick Boy wields an imaginary gun, a cocky caricature of threat. Shivering and damp, Renton looks like the last man standing at a rave, rather than a junkie who has just climbed out of a toilet. 'Hollywood come in… your time is up' screams the *Empire* quote. Faced with such a masterpiece of misdirection, it was easy to believe the hype. Says Macdonald:

> It was a hugely confident campaign, like *Shallow Grave*. In those days you didn't even do TV advertising for films, unless it was a massive Spielberg movie. So it was a very big, what they call 'outdoor' campaign, billboards and posters and that orange colour; it was great. We had a relationship with PolyGram after making *Shallow Grave* and they understood. Even though they themselves would have made the film differently, dead babies and all that, they knew they had something to sell and they just went for it massively.

Released on 23 February 1996 amid a wave of posters, postcards and merchandise – ironic, given that, as Catterall and Wells put it, 'Renton's "choose life" monologue was simultaneously mocking advertising, while selling anti-authority to the masses' (2002: 258) – the film made a massive £12.4 million at the UK box office (Dyja 2010: 259), and a more than respectable $16.5 million in America (Box Office Mojo 2018i).

Even if Hollywood's time was not quite up, Britpop cinema's moment had come. A midnight screening at Cannes saw, as Macdonald recalled, 'Damon Albarn and Noel Gallagher […] facing off against each other, Noel regretting that he hadn't done a song, Damon saying – ha! – he had' (Morrison 2003: 121). Hodge's wife, who also cameos in the film as a nurse, found herself sat between Gallagher and the Secretary of State for National Heritage, Virginia Bottomley. 'I thought that was a good summing up of *Trainspotting*'s place,' said Hodge (Morrison 2003: 121). Gallagher admired the film for being 'real', like his band Oasis, while Bottomley told the press it reminded her of her own past, before adding that she'd been a magistrate for 12 years (Walker 2005: 235).

The critics were (near) unanimous in praise. The *Evening Standard*'s Alexander Walker compared it unfavourably to *A Clockwork Orange* (Kubrick, 1972): 'Kubrick's film made one think; Boyle's film simply made one puke' (2005: 237). But then he also watched the film *with* Kubrick himself, who, apparently, noted the films' similar trajectories. *Time Out*'s Tom Charity was closer to the pulse, stating: '*Trainspotting* is the movie we have all been waiting for, the first British film of the 1990s generation to speak to the way we live here and now' (1996). Showing rare insight, US presidential candidate Bob Dole claimed the film 'glorified heroin' (Ross 1996). He was right, of course, despite the fact he had not seen it. But then, *Trainspotting* glorified everything. It was precisely because of the film's lust for life that the British public took *Trainspotting* to their hearts. How could they not? It was a cinematic sensation that had been made and marketed especially for them.

As writer Amy Raphael put it: 'It's no exaggeration to say that, with both *Trainspotting* and its predecessor, *Shallow Grave*, Boyle woke British film up from a kind of post-Thatcher stupor' (2013: x). The director agreed:

> *Trainspotting* is, in part, about a Scottish city that declined to die despite Tory attempts to bring it to its knees. The people of Glasgow and Edinburgh said 'fuck you' to Thatcher. They didn't want her 'help'. You look at those northern cities now and they are relatively reborn.
> (Raphael 2013: 105)

But it was not just the film industry that awoke – soon the empty Glasgow factories where these films were shot would be turned into luxury flats, New Labour would spin their way to power and the country's cultural output rechristened as Cool Britannia. Says Macdonald:

> It was a moment. You had all these things that felt British. People were interested in and loved British culture, where most of it, particularly in movies and music, had been American. It was a real moment.

Boyle, Hodge and Macdonald had every right to be defiant. Their difficult second album had become Britpop cinema's first true masterpiece.

What Happened Next...

Cannes Film Festival 1996... The column inches may have belonged to *Trainspotting*, but among strong competition from *Breaking the Waves* (Von Trier, 1996), *Crash* (Cronenberg, 1996) and *Fargo* (Coen brothers, 1996), the Palme d'Or was awarded to a rather more modest Film4 release, *Secrets & Lies* (Leigh, 1996). Leigh's intimate, semi-improvised tale of adoption and rapprochement went on to win Best Original Screenplay, Outstanding British Film and Best Actress for Brenda Blethyn at the 50th Bafta Film Awards on 29 April 1997. The previous year, when *The Madness of King George* (Hytner, 1995) and *Sense and Sensibility*

(Lee, 1996) cleaned up, *Trainspotting* won only one of its two nominations, for Best Adapted Screenplay. While the quality of these films was beyond reproach, the industry clearly had some catching up to do.

Brian Tufano... Shot most of the era's best-looking films, including Britpop cinema efforts such as *Tube Tales* (various, 1999), *Billy Elliot* (Daldry, 2000) and *Late Night Shopping* (Metzstein, 2001). His last film with Boyle, Hodge and Macdonald was the ill-fated short *Alien Love Triangle* (Boyle, 2008), part of a portmanteau that never materialized. He remains sanguine about the vagaries of the business: 'I remember we were watching the *Trainspotting* rushes, the scene where Robert Carlyle's talking about the magistrate and says, "I knew that cunt was going to fuck some cunt." There was a long pause before Andrew Macdonald said: "I think we'd better be shooting *A Life Less Ordinary* by the time this is released otherwise we may never work again!" You make those kind of statements and you think, "Oh my god if only you knew what was going to happen."'

Danny Boyle and co... Made lovers-on-the-run flick *A Life Less Ordinary* (1997) with McGregor and Cameron Diaz. Transposed to America from its original European setting, the film proved an awkwardly transatlantic, Britpop cinema take on Tarantino. Hollywood blockbuster *The Beach* (Boyle, 2000), perhaps Boyle's least personal film, followed – with Leonardo DiCaprio replacing McGregor as leading man. It took until 2002's *28 Days Later* for Boyle to come home and regain his mojo. 'Having that second hit [*Trainspotting*] felt like, "Oh, that's it, easy,"' says Macdonald. 'But it was hard for us after that because of people's expectations. It was very successful in America up to a point, so everything changed.'

Ewan McGregor... Was anointed Britpop cinema's brightest star, quickly turning into one of our most exportable talents. He graduated from smaller British pictures such as *Brassed Off* (Herman, 1996), *Little Voice* (Herman, 1998) and *Rogue Trader* (Dearden, 1999) to American blockbusters such as the *Star Wars* prequels (Lucas, 1999–2005) and *Black Hawk Down* (Scott, 2001). His best post-Boyle work has been for Scottish director David Mackenzie, who lets him speak in his own accent and play blankly amoral characters, as in *Young Adam* (2003) and *Perfect Sense* (2011). After falling out with Boyle over *The Beach*, he returned to play Renton in *T2 Trainspotting* (2017).

Irvine Welsh... Became that rare beast: a celebrity cult novelist, releasing books that managed to be challenging and popular, such as *Maribou Stork Nightmares* (1995) and *Filth* (1998), while partying like a true *Trainspotter*. 'I'm glad it happened when it happened because if it had happened ten years earlier for me I probably wouldn't have survived,' he says now. 'Everything just changed in such an incredible way. It was a bit of white-knuckle ride at times.' He regularly revisits his best-loved characters, whether in sequel *Porno* (2002), prequel *Skagboys* (2012) or sidequel *The Blade Artist* (2016), and knows which two words will form his epitaph. 'If I just had a fiver for every time somebody went, "Choose life!" to me, I wouldn't need any royalties for anything else,' he says. 'I get that five times a day, but it's great. Still, it's going to be an ironic gravestone, isn't it?'

Notes

1 With a video by YBA Damien Hirst and co-starring Keith Allen, Blur's clever-clever 'Country House' won the battle, but Oasis won the war. Although their Status Quo-esque rocker 'Roll with It' only reached No.2, the ensuing album, *(What's the Story) Morning Glory?,* became the third biggest-selling of all time in the United Kingdom, just behind their heroes, The Beatles' *Sgt Pepper's Lonely Hearts Club Band* at No.2 and Queen's *Greatest Hits* at No.1.

2 American-funded UK films included *Sense and Sensibility*, which won star/writer Emma Thompson an Oscar for Best Adapted Screenplay, and *Braveheart* (Gibson, 1995), which won a less explicable five awards, including Best Director and Best Picture. Of the latter, historian Alwyne W. Turner wrote, 'Perhaps unsurprisingly for an American movie made by an Australian about Scottish history and filmed in Ireland, the English don't come out too well' (2013: 457).

3 When living in London, Welsh had played in a band called Pubic Lice, graduating from 'guitar to bass to fuck all' (Munro 2013: 36).

4 Of Renton's extended peer group, the film cuts out/combines the characters of Nina, Matty, Stevie, Kelly, Second Prize and Lesley, among others. Not to mention Renton's two brothers, Billy, a soldier who is killed in Northern Ireland, and Davie, who was born with severe learning disabilities, and doesn't live to adulthood.

5 In the book, Sick Boy kills a dog with a baseball bat; Begbie has sex with a woman having a miscarriage; and even Tommy, the group's conscience, is addicted to fighting.

6 This is called 'gouching'. According to NHS drugs and alcohol expert Cathy Smith, 'Gouching means you've had enough heroin and are feeling really high, but beginning to tip over into what's called a nod. At work, we'd regularly find someone face down in a bowl of cornflakes because they'd just had some heroin and we'd lift their head up and they'd come round really quickly' (2016). Also, Smith confirms, it's true, heroin does make you constipated.

7 Indeed, Munro, an old friend of Welsh's, suggests the name Sick Boy comes from the 1973 song 'Death Trip' by Iggy Pop and the Stooges, which contains the line, 'Sick boy sick boy baby now learning to be cruel.' Other inspirations were less cryptic. On the street where Welsh grew up, 'Among the family's close neighbours were a Mr Renton and a Mrs Frances Begbie' (Munro 2013: 41).

8 The original *Trainspotting* soundtrack sold 700,000 copies, and was voted the 7th best ever by *Vanity Fair* in 2007 (Reuters 2007). In 1997, the 'choose life' monologue was sampled on a dance track by PF Project featuring Ewan McGregor. It reached No.6.

9 Bizarrely, considering its association with heroin overdoses, the BBC used the song in a star-filled 1997 promo, featuring vocals from David Bowie, Bono and Reed himself. See Chapter 9.

10 There are even a few self-referential in-jokes crammed in there. When Renton asks Diane, 'Are these your flatmates?' it's hard not to think of *Shallow Grave*'s central trio. And Keith Allen's dealer exits the film with plenty of drugs and money, as if he is on his way to Edinburgh to become 'Hugo'.

11 Jonny Lee Miller is, in fact, the grandson of Bernard Lee who played M in eleven James Bond films from *Dr. No* (Young, 1962) to *Moonraker* (Gilbert, 1979).

Chapter 4

A Life Less Ordinary

Starring: *Brassed Off* (Herman, 1996), *The Full Monty* (Cattaneo, 1997) and *Billy Elliot* (Daldry, 2000)

Chapter 4: A Life Less Ordinary

Working-class heroes in Britpop cinema

Danny Ormondroyd (Pete Postlethwaite): I know there's a spot of bother at the pit, but that's something separate. This is music and it's music that matters.
Brassed Off

Durham Coalfield, 1984, reads the subtitle. The middle of the miners' strike. First we see the LP, then the needle on the record player, dropped with quivering fingers. 'I was dancing when I was 12,' sings Marc Bolan, 'I was dancing when I was aaah…' – a gasp of transgressive pleasure, of something that cannot be put into words. As the music plays, we see young Billy Elliot (Jamie Bell) bouncing on his bed in a lemon-yellow vest. Behind him, the explosions of colour on the wallpaper suggest faded fireworks, a bright future gone dun with disappointment. Still he bounces in an arc of unadulterated joy, his feet not seeming to hit the springs, a feat not so much of grace but of sorcery. Then you realize there is no ceiling, the sky is the limit…

During the Britpop cinema years, films about the working classes underwent a rebranding worthy of New Labour. Faced with the destruction of the coal and steel industries, the protagonists of *Brassed Off*, *The Full Monty* and *Billy Elliot* sought answers in, respectively, brass band music, stripping for cash, and ballet dancing, with upbeat, if bittersweet, results. Whether art could save them from poverty was not always clear – but it did not hurt the filmmakers. Ken Loach's *Riff-Raff* (1991), which starred Robert Carlyle as an unemployed builder, cost £750,000 and made £61,000 at the UK box office (Mather 2006: 31). *The Full Monty*, meanwhile, which starred Carlyle as an unemployed steelworker, cost £2.2 million and made £52.2 million at the UK box office (Dyja 2010: 99). Clearly there were other factors at play – not least the promise of nudity, and American distributor Fox Searchlight making a play for PolyGram's pot of gold. But there was also a sense that the ebullience of Britpop cinema was much better for business than social-realist browbeating; that soft porn might be a slightly easier sell than misery porn. Says *Full Monty* producer Uberto Pasolini:

> I wanted to make a film about the working class that the working class would actually go to see. I had an image of the guys at the end of *Riff-Raff* walking away from the burning building and in front of a Chippendales poster. So there and then I said, 'Let's try and make it as a kind of Ken Loach film if Ken Loach was drunk.'
>
> (2016)

The approach paid off handsomely, setting the template for stirring social comedies such as *Kinky Boots* (Jarrold, 2005), *Made in Dagenham* (Cole, 2010) and *Pride* (Warchus, 2014). Though the films in this subgenre were often retro – set in the recent past, but harking back even further to the community spirit of the Ealing comedies[1] – their chirpy new tone chimed perfectly with Britpop music's cartoonified class anxieties.

At one end of the spectrum this meant working-class bands such as Oasis, who were bullishly insistent on being authentic while indulging an acquisitive streak that would have made Gordon Gecko blush. At the other, it meant middle-class bands like Blur, who did their best to appear anything but. 'While Oasis's success led them into Bond Street boutiques,[2] Blur's triumphs often seemed to be accompanied by deliberate steps downmarket,' wrote Britpop chronicler John Harris, noting the latter's fondness for anything that gave off 'the odour of proletarian authenticity', such as the Walthamstow Stadium greyhound races where the band launched their 1994 album *Parklife* (2003: 216–17). Ever the outsiders, Pulp provided a riposte to such class tourism in their 1995 single 'Common People': 'Laugh along with the common people, laugh along even though they're laughing at you, and the stupid things you do, because you think that poor is cool.'

Elsewhere, the sense that the country was recovering from the ravages of recession was palpable. The economy was growing, unemployment falling and a new government on the way. Says *Brassed Off* writer/director Mark Herman:

> Although late 1996 might have seemed a safer space, it was still then – just – a Tory government. With the general election on the horizon the following May, I remember some murmurings about a possible delay in release in case the film influenced voters in any way. Nevertheless, despite it being screened at the Labour Party conference, and some local offices having 'Brassed Off with the Tories' as a poster slogan, we managed to get it released as planned. Perhaps the Tories were so on their way out that they didn't much care. Or maybe they thought only two fellas and a dog would see it so let's not worry.
>
> (2016)

It is worth noting here that, with its dynamic cinematography, bursts of non-diegetic music and magic realism, only *Billy Elliot* fully qualifies as Britpop cinema, although all three films share such similar DNA it seems expedient to examine them together. The most traditional of the bunch, *Brassed Off* also offers the least hope, ending with a show-stopping tirade against the government from bandleader Danny, a bitter rendition of 'Land of Hope and Glory', and details of continuing pit closures. By contrast, *The Full Monty* and *Billy Elliot* share a guarded optimism recognizable in the rhetoric of New Labour, who would sweep into power in May 1997. 'Arguably, that feeling of optimism was New Labour's major economic achievement in its early days,' wrote historian Alwyn W. Turner, 'Objectively, nothing much changed' (2013: 344). There is also something very New Labour about the idea that Billy Elliot, the son of a miner, might be better skipping off to London to learn ballet than staying in County Durham to slog away at a dying trade – surely the preserve of Old Labour? If this optimism felt a little manufactured, a question of presentation rather than fact, it was completely in-keeping with the mood of the country, and the spin of those who would soon be running it.

While Thatcher had claimed there was 'no such thing as society' (Keay 1987), Britpop cinema was keen to show otherwise. Hence the shifting solidarity of the striking miners in *Billy Elliot*, the cheeky group dynamics of Grimley Colliery Band in *Brassed Off*, and *The Full Monty*'s Gaz (Robert Carlyle) cajoling the citizens of Sheffield to join his unlikely stripping troupe, whether black or white, straight or gay, fat or thin.

Although *The Full Monty*'s cast bonded over a shared fear of performing naked, ironically the crew almost mutinied over pay, until they were mollified with the promise of more money. Recalls director Peter Cattaneo:

> About a month in, people are halfway through, they're thinking, 'Jesus this is grim,' and they just grumble. Uberto sent this memo out saying there were a certain amount of points that were going to be spread equally among everyone who'd worked for three weeks on the production. I remember the memo going out and everyone going, 'I don't want points,[3] I want money,' but, of course, it turned out to be a not-insubstantial amount. I still bump into people who go, 'I can't believe I still get cheques from *The Full Monty*!' And they love it.
>
> (2017)

As with most of Britpop cinema, these films are almost exclusively concerned with male issues. Besides the ingrained sexism of the industry, and the belief that women would watch films about men, but not vice versa, the 1990s were an unsettling era for the male ego. Wrote Turner: 'In 1997 the number of women in the national workforce exceeded that of men for the first time in the country's history' (2013: 55). In the media, meanwhile, TV shows such as *Men Behaving Badly* (1994–98, UK: BBC) and *Fantasy Football* (1994–2004, UK: Avalon), and magazines like *Loaded* ('For men who should know better…') suggested a state of arrested adolescence ill-suited to addressing the thorny issues of identity, esteem and employment. According to Pasolini, *The Full Monty* is:

> About confidence; about what it means to be a man, what it means to be unemployed when, especially as a Northern man, you have an image of yourself as the breadwinner of the family. What happens when, all of a sudden, you don't have a job anymore and

> your wife is instead the breadwinner? [Writer] Simon Beaufoy was particularly good at bringing that issue out, the issue of male disempowerment.

Says Cattaneo:

> I just loved the fact it wasn't political with a capital 'p', but a funny take on it. And it's about much more than that, about the nature of masculinity, the nature of being a man in post-industrial England. I connected with it really strongly.

The film begins with Gaz and Dave (Mark Addy) trying, and failing, to steal girders from the derelict steelworks. The local working men's club is full of women cheering on a male strip show, moaning about their husbands and peeing standing up. At the dole office, Gaz decides that men are, 'Obsolete… Dinosaurs. Yesterday's news,' telling Gerald (Tom Wilkinson), 'You're not our foreman anymore. You're just like the rest of us: scrap.'

Before they hit upon the idea of starting their own Chippendales rip-off, the male characters are not just redundant, but completely unmanned. 'It's like having your balls chopped off,' explains Pasolini, 'and what happens then? You either turn childish or you start to despair.' Gaz and co hardly help themselves. One scene sees them stuffed into tiny classroom chairs like oversized children; another has them holding Gerald's beloved gnomes hostage while he interviews for a new job – surely a better solution than stripping?

Throughout, Gaz proves himself a particularly pernicious character. He takes his young son Nathan (William Snape) stealing, reasoning, 'You don't get a criminal record till you're 16'; refuses work from his ex-wife Mandy (Emily Woof) despite being late on maintenance payments; and dismisses the Chippendales as 'poofs' and the women who watch them as 'tarts'. It is unclear how much we are meant to indulge this attitude, or – indeed – how much the collapse of the steel industry is to blame for where he finds himself. Later we hear he learned to sew in prison, a fact of which he is both ashamed and, as far as his actions are concerned, unrepentant. Whatever happens after the credits roll, criminal turned steel-worker turned stripper should make for an eye-catching CV.

Brassed Off's miners-come-musicians are equally out of time and infantilized. Danny's son Phil (Stephen Tompkinson), who wears a beanie hat – 1990s shorthand for despair – and moonlights as a children's clown – 1990s shorthand for having a screw loose – jumps on the back of his dad's bike like a schoolboy. As they wobble off to band practice, his wife Sandra (Melanie Hill) screams after them: 'You have a wife and four bloody kids here in a house nobody will bloody buy, mortgage up to the bloody hilt, loan sharks on our backs, no bloody money, no bloody job, and what are you gonna do? Fucking juggle?' She throws a plate – another unnecessary expense – and is dismissed by Danny with the line: 'Bit clumsy with the crockery, your Sandra!' But she also has a point. Says Herman:

> The crockery joke is actually an example of where serious issues are disguised by humorous language. The line from her: 'What are you going to do? Fucking juggle?' often

> gets a laugh when actually it's a very serious question. To go from that, and the hurling of a plate, to another line – ludicrously flippant in the circumstance – that also gets a laugh and which leads into an almost slapstick version of 'The Floral Dance', makes the audience think they're watching a fairly broad comedy.

If the laughs are easy, the answers are anything but. Later, in the film's most divisive scene, Phil tries to hang himself at the pit-head – in full clown costume – as Danny is hospitalized with the lung disease that will eventually kill him. This kind of tonal tightrope walk is not always successful, but it is always watchable, and suggests a confidence to match the political commitment of the script.

While these films are particularly indulgent of male fallibility, their attitudes to women are positively Victorian, if depressingly accurate. *Brassed Off*'s heroine Gloria (Tara Fitzgerald), the band's glamorous new flugelhorn player, who also happens to work for the coal board management, is openly leered at, and rechristened 'Gloria Stits'. The Women Against Closure protesters are dismissed by Andy (Ewan McGregor) as 'pissing in the wind'. Later, in hospital, Danny threatens a nurse who wishes to hush his band playing outside: 'You'll wind up in the next ward!' He means it as a joke, but the sense is that these communities of men are so fractured and fragile they must be protected at all costs.

Eventually *The Full Monty*'s strippers attempt to understand how it feels to be objectified, with Dave asking the rest, 'What if next Friday 400 women turn round and say, "He's too fat, he's too old and he's a pigeon-chested little tosser." What then?' But for the most part they remain cheerily unreconstructed, with Gaz and Dave openly sniggering when Lomper (Steve Huison) and Guy (Hugo Speer) reveal themselves to be lovers.

The exception here is *Billy Elliot*, written by Lee Hall. Though set even further in the past, during the 1984–85 miners' strike, its sexual politics are sweetly inclusive. When young Billy, having failed at boxing, joins a ballet class run by Mrs Wilkinson (Julie Walters) as the only boy, he is dismissed as a 'poof' and a 'wanker', even by the adults. But Billy is pre-sexual, interested in neither Debbie (Nicola Blackwell), Mrs Wilkinson's daughter, nor Michael (Stuart Wells), his cross-dressing friend, though he shares tender moments with each. When he complains to Mrs Wilkinson that he feels 'like a right sissy', she tells him, 'Well, don't act like one.' The point here, one that the characters above would do well to heed, is that it is not dressing up that unmans you, but giving up.

That the filmmakers manage to wring laughs from mass unemployment is remarkable, and says a lot about the topsy-turvy mood of the times. For Herman, finding the balance between comedy and tragedy was:

> Always tricky and always absolutely the hardest part of the job – a job that was made somewhat easier because it was possible to tap into and utilize the sense of humour which Yorkshire is renowned for. If it was simply an angry rant at Thatcher, I don't suppose the film would ever have been made. A pitch simply about suicidal trumpet-blowing

> miners wouldn't have freed up the money we needed to make it, so yes, the edges had to be softened. There was still the danger that adding the humour, even if it was dry, and accurate, might still be perceived as taking the piss, though, so none of this was risk-free.

Producer Olivia Stewart agrees:

> I think the reason why *Brassed Off* was so popular – and I got letters from miners from all over the world, so Mark and Steve [Abbott, producer] must have had thousands – was that it combined anger with the spirit of laughter in the face of adversity.
>
> (2016)

They did not have to search far to establish exactly what that face might look like: 'The Italian title for the film is *Grazie, signora Thatcher!*' says Stewart, 'which I think is even better.' 'We had all grown up under Thatcherism, so we had a lot to shout about,' says Cattaneo. 'It forced people to become storytellers.' Though this new generation did not necessarily come from industrial backgrounds, they had still seen the devastation first-hand. As a student in Sheffield, Cattaneo broke into shut-down steelworks for an art project, like Gaz and Dave. He recalls:

> We took lots of time-lapse footage of these barren, empty factories. Great details like the old clocking-in cards still sitting there. Then I actually found an old 16mm publicity film, obviously made in the early 1960s, quite Technicolor, on the floor, and I thought, 'There's my degree!' So I intercut the jolly-jolly old footage of the past with the ghost-town it had become. And that was the loose inspiration for the opening sequence of *The Full Monty*.

Herman, meanwhile, used to pass through Grimethorpe in Yorkshire, the inspiration for Grimley, while working as a bacon salesman in the 1970s:

> At that time, with the pit working, it was a thriving place. Later, as I drove through in the early 1990s, after all the pit closures, the place was long dead, shops boarded up, empty, derelict housing. Like most people, I knew a fair bit about the miners' strike a few years before but, again like most people, I was unaware of the devastation that the closures had caused. The strike was all over the news, but the knock-on effect of Thatcher's closure programme – the actual murder of these communities – seemed to have been conveniently 'overlooked'.

Billy Elliot producer Jon Finn *did* come from mining stock, although his grandfather 'would never let us go down the pit, saying, "No way you're going to be a miner."' Parts of *Billy Elliot* were shot in Easington Colliery, where Finn's grandfather had actually worked. 'It was really weird,' he says now. 'That corridor up and down the A19, where all the coalfields had been, was completely fucked' (2016).

When it came to filming in Grimethorpe, 'It was not a happy place,' recalls Herman:

> It's worth remembering that at the time we moved our circus into town it had been painted in a very bad light. There'd been a recent TV news piece where the reporters had allegedly paid local kids to chuck bricks through windows, so crews with cameras weren't particularly welcomed with open arms.

According to Postlethwaite:

> The pit was not only closed down, but destroyed, razed. They covered the pits up with concrete, burying a quarter of a million pounds' worth of equipment.
>
> (2012: 183)

Stewart remembers calling it:

> The Bermuda triangle, because there were no signposts to it anywhere. When you arrived, most of the clapboard houses had pre-fab metal grilles cemented onto the front so nobody could continue living there or squat there. Mark asked a bunch of kids what they were going to do for Guy Fawkes' Day, and they said, 'We're going to burn down the Co-Op.' And that's exactly what happened: we came back the following morning and there it was with smoke coming out of it.

All the same, says Herman:

> The more we witnessed the real Grimethorpe, and the devastation that had been wreaked on their community, the more the crew, and certainly the cast, became emotionally attached.

It worked the other way, too. Postlethwaite recalled drinking with Tompkinson, when they were accosted by an elderly local who said:

> 'Reet, so, let me get this reet. Thou's playing the bandleader, the father…' I nodded: 'That's right.' And then he looked at Stephen, who was sat next to me: 'And thou's playing his son.' He seemed to weigh up the possibilities of our unlikely family, before turning to Stephen: 'I bet thou's glad thou takes after tha mother, eh?'
>
> (2012: 179)

This is exactly the kind of gruff good humour *Brassed Off* excels at, but it is also a form of denial, of escape. Says Herman:

> I found the more time I spent in the area, during research, the more I could see that this dryness, the 'if you didn't laugh you'd cry' tone, was so often used as a defence mechanism. Especially when people there were telling stories of the rough recent past.

The main method the characters chose to escape, of course, is music. By turns raucous and reverential, *Brassed Off*'s score was composed by Trevor Jones and played by Grimethorpe Colliery Band, whose story closely – but coincidentally[4] – mirrors that of the film. For Danny and the residents of Grimley, the band's success at the national championships seems to represent the town's only hope in the face of crushing despair. When Phil suggests there are other things in life more important than music, Danny replies, 'Not in mine, there isn't.' It is only once they reach the finals, and the pit has closed, that the bandleader changes his tune. He rejects the winning trophy, telling the audience: 'Truth is, I thought it mattered. I thought that music mattered. But does it? Bollocks! Not compared to how people matter.' While the scene was being shot, wrote Postlethwaite:

> The band told us that in real terms they'd actually won the national championships and, two days later, their pit was closed. They said they wished they'd done what Danny did and turned down the cup. We felt proud to be among them.
>
> (2012: 187)

Upon release, the *Brassed Off* soundtrack was an unexpected hit, receiving a Bafta nomination and selling 60,000 units (Dyja 2010: 118). Danny's speech, meanwhile, was sampled by anarchist pop collective Chumbawumba[5] on their 1997 anthem 'Tubthumping'.

Appropriately, seeing as the two films are often mistaken for each other,[6] *The Full Monty* begins with a brass band interrupting its heroes' mid-theft. 'It's the works band,' says Dave. 'It's still going. About only thing round 'ere that is.' The rest of the soundtrack is built around 1970s hits by Hot Chocolate ('You Sexy Thing'), Donna Summer ('Hot Stuff') and Sister Sledge ('We Are Family'). Composer Anne Dudley won an Academy Award for Best Original Score, something of a surprise considering she had only written 'about 20 minutes' worth of music' (Fontaine 1998). Frankly the award may as well have been for persuading Tom Jones to cover Randy Newman's 1972 hit 'You Can Leave Your Hat On', which makes a memorable appearance in the film's climax. 'Have you gone a bit downmarket, Anne?' Jones asked, when she explained the plot of the film (Fontaine 1998). Whatever its awards credentials, the music brings some much-needed sunlight to Sheffield's drab industrial surrounds. Not least in the famous dole queue scene, which sees our heroes unable to stop themselves slipping into their dance routine when 'Hot Stuff' comes on the radio.[7]

This iconic sequence shows how music, the most abstract of pleasures, can elevate the everyday – a key Britpop cinema concern. But it almost went unfilmed. Recalls Cattaneo:

> Obviously it's a very low-budget film, so time is precious, 'Do we really need this scene?' was always the question. You know: 'Does it really further the narrative? If you cut it out, have we still got a movie?' But I was fighting for it because I knew how much I'd loved it on the page, and I'd seen it in rehearsals, so I was saying, 'It's fucking hilarious, we can't cut it!' But it got pushed and pushed back in the schedule, then we just smashed it out in about an hour. It was literally, do the queue, two takes, one wide, do it tighter. Then we

> just put Robert in the same lit area, clear out the guys, cheated the eyeline so he seems like he's looking down the room even though he's standing just where they were, and get a lovely reaction shot, which is Gaz thinking, 'Look what I've created.' That was it, bang.

To lose such a scene would be to singularly misunderstand the film's appeal – and not for the first time. One of the early drafts left out the final striptease. Says Pasolini: 'It was: the music starts, the guys go onstage and then we pull out of the building, and down the sad streets of windy, dirty Sheffield.' According to Pasolini, Film4's David Aukin, who read the first draft (ultimately dropping it in favour of *Brassed Off*), told him:

> 'Well, it's a lovely thing, but you've got to be joking! You have to have them strip and you have to have them strip on camera, you're completely mad!' I said OK, thinking we can always shoot it and cut it if it didn't work out. But the success was all down to that. Obviously, I don't have a commercial bone in my body.

When Cattaneo came on board: 'The draft I read ended with a full-frontal naked star-jump freeze-frame.' Which proved problematic to say the least. He considered shooting it from the audience's point of view, only for Austin Powers-style intrusions such as a fist in the air and a spontaneously thrown hat to spare the actors' blushes, but it felt too 'contrived'. Then, once he had visited various working men's clubs and actually been onstage, he had a brainwave:

> I thought, 'Oh yeah, we can shoot it from behind.' If we see a row of naked bums with the audience beyond we'll know they've done it. Besides, six bums are funny, six willies are a bit biological.

Come the day of the shoot, the club was full of extras from real Chippendales shows. Cattaneo recalls:

> The actors had said to me they were only going to take their thongs off once, that was the deal; so we kept shooting and stopping, shooting and stopping, getting to nearly-nearly-nearly and I'd go, 'Cut!' because we hadn't quite got what we needed yet. The room was electric. When that final shot happened it was just like, 'Wow!' you know, and you look at it, with that light on their butt cheeks, so perfect, you just knew it was magic.

Based on Lee Hall's experience growing up in working-class Newcastle wanting to be a writer, *Billy Elliot* was, if anything, even less commercial a prospect than a fully clothed *Full Monty*. 'It just sounded like a shockingly bad pitch on paper,' admits Finn. But the music, from the giddy sexual fluidity of T-Rex to The Jam's jittery fury, offers something for Billy and the audience to lose themselves in. 'I forget everything and sort of disappear…' Billy tells the audition panel at The Royal Ballet School, 'Fire in my body, I'm just there, flying like a bird, like electricity.' Not everyone in the film has such an outlet. Billy's dad (Gary Lewis), a widower and lifelong miner who cannot comprehend his son's love of dance, smashes the family piano for firewood. Mrs Wilkinson, meanwhile, 'feels unfulfilled, that's why she does dancing', according to Debbie. 'She does dancing instead of sex?' asks Billy. 'That's mental.'

While it pulls no punches in depicting the clashes between the strikers and the police, there is something irresistible in the contrast between mining and ballet, the earth-bound and the airborne, that brings the film to life. After Mrs Wilkinson and Billy's brother Tony (Jamie Draven) argue over his future, a frustrated Billy dances to The Jam's 'Town Called Malice' like an apoplectic, if pint-sized, Gene Kelly. He starts by smacking the backyard walls, as if rebelling against the very bricks themselves, art vs. industry, then kicks down the toilet door, breaking out of the box, both literal and figurative, he is stuck in. Then, like Renton and The Beatles before him, he jumps to freedom – landing painfully because life, even the Britpop cinema version, is never perfect – and races down the street, kicking a defiant football (also like Renton) that narrowly misses an old lady's head.[8]

Next, the film borrows a dose of *Trainspotting*'s 'black-magic realism'. Billy limps up the street while in the far distance, a sailboat – the ultimate symbol of escape – blithely bisects the ocean behind him, to be confronted by a solid barrier of corrugated iron. There is no way forward and, as if in sorrow, snowflakes appear, the world turned inexorably to winter. But even black-magic realism comes at a price. Says Finn:

> It was beautiful, because you'd be standing there on a nice summer's day, then step through the barriers and it would be completely white. But it was also a fucking disaster. The guys who did the snow were lovely, and they said, 'It's great because we'll just spray the snow everywhere and it just washes away.' Well, we covered a fair few streets in snow, only to find out that it didn't wash away quite the way we thought. I remember sitting with the local debt collector and explaining why we'd blocked her drains. It was the hardest negotiation I've ever done.

An earlier sequence features a chase of which Danny Boyle would be proud. To the tune of The Clash's 'London Calling', Tony, the union agitator, races from the police through the houses and streets, passing that 1980s standby, the space hopper, in one backyard, then pausing to steal a cheeky sip from a cup of tea in someone's kitchen. Although it ends in tears, with a severe beating and arrest, for a few minutes it feels like music and motion might be the answer to their problems after all.

As in the best of Britpop cinema, upbeat beginnings and uncertain endings proliferate. *Brassed Off* starts with the jaunty 'Death or Glory', as the miners' head-torches strafe the screen like James Bond's iconic gun-barrel graphic, and they emerge from the pit grubby but grinning. It is a happier image of mining life than we see anywhere else in the film – indeed, anywhere outside of *Snow White and the Seven Dwarves* (various, 1937) – but the conclusion undercuts the championship win by emphasizing the death of the industry, even as Gloria and Andy kiss and Phil and Sandra tentatively make up. Drawing the disparate plot strands together requires some extremely deft writing, but, as Mather noted, 'The film is seemingly aware that its real subject is, perhaps, what comes after the end of the story' (2006: 33). Critic Alexander Walker was even more cynical, claiming:

> It was a sentimental victory, though, rather than a dialectical one… The pits might have closed [but] in the rousing music their brass bands made, the myth of a deeper, darker England lingered on. One could shed an honest tear.
>
> (2005: 280)

Yet perhaps this is disingenuous: how else to end a comedy-drama than with a sense of the characters' yoyo-ing fortunes? Phil and Sandra are heading back to face certain poverty, at best together; Gloria and Andy are young and without ties – in other words, they can start over somewhere new; and Danny is heading home to die, so it is hardly *The Shawshank Redemption* (Darabont, 1994). Says Herman:

> The truth is, you want people to be laughing, enjoying the fun, but you also want to pull the rug from under those people's feet and wake them up to some harsh reality. The comedy disguises the polemic, that was always the intention.

Inspired by the publicity films Cattaneo found in his extracurricular explorations, *The Full Monty* booms into life courtesy of a clip from the absurdly chipper (and seemingly genuine) film *Sheffield, City on the Move*! With a narrator whose clipped tones recall *Harry Enfield & Chums*' 1930s newsreel announcer Mr Cholmondley-Warner,[9] the city is introduced as 'the beating heart of Britain's industrial North' over images of such metropolitan delights as furnaces, roundabouts and Morris dancers. After a whistle-stop tour of the 'jewel in Yorkshire's crown', the film cuts to an empty factory, 25 years later, the promise of that space-age future long evaporated.

In terms of uncertain endings, *The Full Monty* pulls off a masterstroke of mixed messages. Having watched its heroes strip naked for a paying audience, recovering their pride and, just possibly, their relationships,[10] the film climaxes on a triumphant freeze-frame that does not even begin to answer the remaining questions. For a start, how does getting naked for money constitute a healthy form of empowerment? And what are they going to do next? The show is a one-off fund-raiser, and they will still be unemployed in the morning. But the freeze-frame is a tricksy device, inviting us to leave the characters at the peak of their happiness, with their hats on and their illusions intact.

'My father always said it was the saddest thing he'd ever seen,' says Pasolini, who might, on that basis, want to give *Requiem for a Dream* (Aronofsky, 2000) a wide berth:

> It's a film where positive things happen, of course, to the individual characters, whether it's a father holding on to his relationship with his son, a husband and a wife reconnecting again physically and emotionally, and someone else who accepts his own sexuality – there

are lots of personal stories that resolve positively, but the reality of their financial situation is not going to change at the end, it's not that all of a sudden they'll be rich.

Admits Cattaneo:

Initially I wasn't always 100 per cent comfortable with it. We even talked about picking up a scene where they hand out the money and pay the guy for the club, and are left with like £1.75 or something, because I never wanted it to feel like all their problems were over. But I think because the overall tone of the film has a sort of bitter-sweetness to it, that you just don't feel that; it's a moment for them to get their self-esteem back, a moment for them to rediscover the bond of the workplace outside the workplace. The problems are still there, the battle's not been won, but they're just stronger to try and deal with their problems.

Beginning with that joyful bed-bounce, against oversized walls that recall the *Shallow Grave* set,[11] *Billy Elliot* ends with suitable even-handedness: sending Billy off to London where he will thrive, while we watch Tony and Mr Elliot heading back down the pit, the strike over. Says Finn:

Yeah, they're fucked. That was always the most emotional bit for me as well. They were dinosaurs, lost in time. And actually they were lucky to be going down the pit because soon they wouldn't even be doing that.

So does art offer these characters a solution or just an escape? 'A solution?' says Herman. 'I think Danny answers that question in his final speech. "Does it bollocks!" If it offers an escape, it's only temporary.' Where *The Full Monty* turns that temporary escape into a freeze-framed success story, *Billy Elliot* suggests that only a privileged few can really take advantage of it. Perhaps what is most striking here is the slight disconnect between the filmmakers' intentions and how their works were received. For the writers, directors and producers, the jokes and songs represent an attempt to get a serious political message across in a populist manner, to sugar the pill. For the viewers, it is the sugar, rather than the pill, that sticks with them. Perhaps this is where Britpop cinema and Blairite spin intersect. As the new prime minister himself noted: 'It's the signals that matter not the policy' (Turner 2013: 404).

Upon release, each film performed impressively, both in the United Kingdom and abroad. Recalls Herman:

I seem to remember we had a pretty bad first weekend, so much so that we had a panic meeting with Film4 and [American distributor] Miramax about how to proceed. They decided to give it another week, and during that week the figures went against all expectations. Word of mouth was obviously huge. I think what happened was that expectations were very low – who wants to see a film about miners and brass band music? – but that people who went were impressed far beyond those expectations. That word of mouth continued to grow and, after a decidedly wobbly start, it slowly snowballed.

Brassed Off made its £2.8 million budget back in the United Kingdom (Walker 2005: 280), and almost the same again in the United States (Box Office Mojo 2018d). Not bad for a film with such a defiantly parochial pitch.

With the combined might of BBC Films, Working Title and Universal behind it, *Billy Elliot* did even better, making £18.3 million in the United Kingdom (Dyja 2010: 259) on its modest £3 million budget, and $109 million worldwide (Box Office Mojo 2018c). Originally titled *Dancer*, it was confused with the extremely harrowing *Dancer in the Dark* (Von Trier, 2000) at Cannes, necessitating a swift title change. When it was first screened, Finn was told, '"That's great, you've made a film for fags and old women." I went, "Oh well, there's quite a lot of those!"' The film received Academy Award nominations for Best Screenplay, Director and Supporting Actress, but won none. All the same, 'It was an amazing period for making stuff,' says Finn. 'Now you'd think, god that script is going to bankrupt and kill me. But then you could really put stuff together.'

Like *Four Weddings and a Funeral* (Newell, 1994) before it, *The Full Monty* was released in the United States first, making $45 million, then $257 million worldwide (Box Office Mojo 2018f). In the United Kingdom it made £52.2 million, becoming the most successful British film of the decade (Dyja 2010: 259), and remains among the 25 highest-earning films at the UK box office.[12] Says Herman:

> I remember someone saying – after *The Full Monty*'s huge success – that they wished we'd had the Grimley Colliery Band get their kit off at the Albert Hall Final. I assured them, if we had done that, nobody would have gone. They had a point though. The ending seems to suggest that you can solve all your problems if you just drop your kecks in public, whereas in reality, as far as I can see, it's not quite that simple. But that's why it was clever, that's why audiences lapped it up and went again and again. That kind of upbeat escapism will always win over a dose of reality.

Cattaneo thinks *The Full Monty* benefitted from a wave of political optimism and community spirit:

> It was the start of a new era. It opened the weekend that Princess Diana died, so we were quite nervous about that, but there was something in the air about people getting together, it was the end of Thatcherism, and it felt like New Labour were a new beginning, like Great Britain was culturally significant again, with Britpop and all these other factors combined.

At the 1997 Baftas, *The Full Monty* beat US favourites *Titanic* (Cameron, 1997) and *LA Confidential* (Hanson, 1997) to win Best Film, as well as Best Actor for Robert Carlyle. There was just one fly in the ointment. Because Film4 had backed *Brassed Off* instead, and Fox

Searchlight had put up all of *The Full Monty*'s budget, 'The praise went to Britain, but all the film's profits went to America' (Brown 2005: 33). 'And thus,' lamented Alexander Walker, 'the British film industry lost the biggest money-maker in its post-war history' (2005: 280). The United Kingdom may have proved itself great at making films, but as a great filmmaking nation there was much to learn.

What Happened Next...

Mark Herman... Returned with *Little Voice* (1998), an adaptation of Jim Cartwright's 1992 play mixing Northern humour, music-as-escape and Ewan McGregor once again. His next film, *Purely Belter* (2000), concerned two young Newcastle United fans going to great lengths to secure season tickets, and featured a cameo from footballer Alan Shearer, and songs by Britpop acts Shed Seven and Ian Broudie.

Peter Cattaneo... Went to the Oscars just 24 hours after the birth of his first child, then flew back empty-handed straight after. 'My American agent said, "You don't do that! When you get nominated for an Oscar you stay and you milk it, and you get every film you can possibly get!" But I said, "I've just had a newborn baby, I'm going home"'. He returned to the director's chair for prison musical *Lucky Break* (2001).

Stephen Daldry... Made Oscar-friendly fare such as *The Hours* (2002) and *The Reader* (2008). In 2005 he directed *Billy Elliot: The Musical* at London's Victoria Palace Theatre, with songs by Elton John and Lee Hall, and choreography, as in the film, by Peter Darling. The show finished in April 2016, and has been produced around the world. Finn describes the *Billy Elliot* phenomenon as, 'Like being the member of some very strange family.' Both *The Full Monty* and *Brassed Off* were also adapted for the stage.

Pete Postlethwaite... Became one of the industry's most in-demand character actors, dividing his time between American indies such as *The Usual Suspects* (Singer, 1995), Hollywood blockbusters like *Inception* (Nolan, 2010) and intimate British films such as *Among Giants* (Miller, 1998). Also written by Simon Beaufoy, the latter concerned electricity tower painters and was dubbed 'The Monty Pylon Show'. Postlethwaite's 2012 autobiography *A Spectacle of Dust* details his career up to the diagnosis of pancreatic cancer, which claimed his life on 2 January 2011. Anyone who makes it through the final chapter dry-eyed frankly did not deserve him.

Notes

1 In the post-war era, Ealing Studios produced a series of impeccably crafted but essentially knockabout social comedies including *Passport to Pimlico* (Cornelius, 1949), *The Lavender Hill Mob* (Crichton, 1951) and *The Ladykillers* (Mackendrick, 1955).

2 Indeed, singer Liam Gallagher would start his own upmarket clothes shop, Pretty Green.
3 'Points' are deferred payments that can be recouped once the film has gone into profit. Due to industry finagling, this almost never happens.
4 Mark Herman came up with the idea on his own. 'Obviously nobody believes this,' he says, 'but I wrote the story – basically a colliery band winning the national championships at the same time as losing their pit – a long time before learning that that's what happened to Grimethorpe.'
5 The group's second biggest claim to fame, after 'Tubthumping' reached No.2, was when founder member Danbert Nobacon (born Nigel Hunter) tipped an ice bucket over Deputy Prime Minister John Prescott at the 1998 Brit Awards.
6 Says Mark Herman: 'In some people's memory, the two films are pretty much wrapped into the same thing. I was introduced to a woman at a party not that long ago who told me *Brassed Off* was her favourite ever film, especially that scene… and then she started doing that dance they do at the dole office in *The Full Monty*. I pretended to be flattered.'
7 Prince Charles re-enacted the scene on a trip to Sheffield in 1998. 'I liked the film so much, I've seen it twice,' he explained (BBC 1998a).
8 This happened for real, and almost resulted in injury. 'Had the ball connected,' says Finn, 'it would have completely taken her out.'
9 Played by Jon Glover, and supported by his manservant Grayson (Enfield), Cholmondley-Warner was a regular feature of *Harry Enfield's Television Programme* (1990–92, UK: Hat Trick Productions) and *Harry Enfield & Chums* (1994–98, UK: Tiger Aspect Productions), presenting spoof vintage public information films such as *Women: Know Your Limits!*
10 It is hinted by Mandy's presence in the crowd, where she looks on not disapprovingly, that she has changed her opinion of Gaz, although it is hard to see why she would have come in the first place.
11 As in Boyle's earlier film, Billy's bedroom wall is much bigger than its real-world equivalent would be, and the splashes of citrus colour throughout the house seem to have been set-designed rather than, say, picked out by the rather dour Mr Elliot.
12 The list is largely made up of sequels, series and adaptations such as *Star Wars*, *James Bond*, *Harry Potter* and *The Lord of the Rings*. At the time of writing, *Avatar* (Cameron, 2009), *Titanic* (Cameron, 1997) and *Mamma Mia!* (Lloyd, 2008) are the only standalone films based on original material that beat *The Full Monty*, and even then on comparatively stratospheric budgets (BFI 2017).

Chapter 5

Staying Out for the Summer

Starring: *Spice World* (Spiers, 1997), Natural Nylon, *Shooting Fish* (Schwartz, 1997) and more

Chapter 5: Staying Out for the Summer

Cool Britannia and the Britpop cinema boom

Martin Barnfield (George Wendt): This is what our movie should be about. They're young. They're cute. They're hip. They're wacky.
Graydon (Mark McKinney): Yeah, but can they act?
Martin Barnfield: What? Act? Did anyone care if Marilyn Monroe could act? All they cared was, 'Was she in focus?'
Graydon: I've just got an idea. You're gonna love it. I see it very clearly. It's the Spice Girls. There's five of them, and they're singers…
Martin Barnfield: I love it. We pitch this afternoon.
Spice World

The 1997 Brit Awards ceremony was not just the usual industry backslap. Underneath the veneer, new battle lines were being drawn. In 1995, with Britpop in ascendency, Blur and Oasis faced off, and guitar music was the winner. In 1996, Pulp's Jarvis Cocker had seen off Michael Jackson's paedophilic pomp with a well-timed moon. But this year marked a cultural sea change. While *Trainspotting*, naturally, won Best Soundtrack, and George Michael beat Tricky, Sting, Mark Morrison and Mick Hucknall in a bizarre Best British Male contest, two sides emerged. In one corner were the earnest Manic Street Preachers, winning Best Album, with Ocean Colour Scene and Kula Shaker behind them. In the other: five-headed pop beast the Spice Girls winning Best Single for the aptly titled 'Wannabe'. Accepting the award, Sporty Spice challenged Oasis's Liam Gallagher to, 'Come and have a go if you think you're hard enough.' Truth is, none of them were.

If 1997 was the year Britpop cinema reached critical mass, it was also the year the British film industry started to resemble a conveyer belt, churning out product after product. The drought of the early 1990s had become a flood; our moment in the sun, an outbreak of mass sunstroke.

As was often the case with New Labour, the headlines sounded great even if the delivery underwhelmed. Within months of taking office, the party had appointed Tom Clarke as the first ever Minister for Film and announced a drastic restructuring of lottery film funding to the tune of £92.25 million plus a 100 per cent tax rebate for British films made for under £15 million (Dyja 2010: 41, 152).[1] Due to the spread of multiplexes, the number of UK screens swelled, cinema admissions were the highest of the decade so far (Dyja 2010: 64, 93–94), and thanks to hits such as *Four Weddings* (Newell, 1994), *Trainspotting* (Boyle, 1996), *The Full Monty* (Cattaneo, 1997) et al., British films' share of UK box-office receipts leapt from 11 per cent to 23 per cent (Watson 2005: 80).[2] Increasingly, though, these 'British' releases were international co-productions. And as 1997 wore on, it was possible to discern quality being sacrificed in the name of quantity. Says Film4's David Aukin:

> After the success of those films, everyone wanted in. The government created consortiums to handle lottery funding, and suddenly there was millions of pounds floating around and everyone grabbing it. The cream wasn't allowed to rise to the top – everything was cream. (2016)

All this took place amid the indignities of Tony Blair's most cringe-worthy initiative: Cool Britannia. In opposition – especially in opposition to John Major – Blair made a decent claim to seeming, if not cool exactly, then at least contemporary. At 43, he was the youngest prime minister of the century, he played electric guitar and made proclamations such as, 'I am a modern man. I come from the rock'n'roll generation: the Beatles, colour TV. That's the generation I come from,' without being openly mocked. Indeed, so contemporary was Blair, he beat Suede's Brett Anderson in a tabloid poll of UK hunks (Turner 2013: 132, 329).

Coming off the back of *Trainspotting* and Britpop, the idea of commodifying UK pop culture under one Labour-saving banner was inspired. Yet taking the name from a 1967 novelty Bonzo Dog Doo-Dah Band song[3] suggested a finger somewhat further from the pulse than might be desirable. In fact, Cool Britannia wasn't a question of harnessing creativity, but of branding. And the argument that the United Kingdom was, currently, the coolest place on the planet simply because a bunch of politicians and journalists said so would prove rather fraught.

As evidence, Blair and co brought out the big guns, inviting the likes of Noel Gallagher for drinks at No.10 Downing Street, where he hobnobbed with Vivienne Westwood and Ian McKellen, as well as such iconoclasts as Ross Kemp and Mick Hucknall. US society magazine *Vanity Fair* organized a 25-page Cool Britannia special featuring Liam Gallagher and his 'movie-star' wife Patsy Kensit in bed; Damon Albarn and Phil Daniels in a bar; the pioneering journalists of *Loaded* at work; and YBA Damien Hirst with his cronies Alex James and Keith Allen mid-bender. Sadly, a planned shot of Noel Gallagher, Paul Weller, Paul McCartney and Blair recreating The Beatles' *Abbey Road* – like the *Trainspotting* gang, and Blur in their 'Park Life' video – proved a wish too far. Ultimately, the Cool Britannia cover was only published in the United Kingdom (Harris 2003: 325, 343–44), but for a while the country seemed as keen as Blair to believe its own hype.

Formed in 1994, then signed by pop svengali Simon Fuller, the Spice Girls topped the charts in 37 countries (BBC 2003) with their 1996 debut single, 'Wannabe', and went on to become the most successful girl group of all time (Duta 2015). Combining high-street glamour with 'Girl Power', an extremely supple form of feminism, the group had nicknames – Scary, Sporty, Baby, Ginger and, perhaps the biggest leap, Posh – so fans could pick their favourite, like toy dolls, or the *Trainspotting* poster.

As proof of her patriotism – not to mention her self-promotional skills – Ginger (Geri Halliwell) wore an iconic Union Jack dress, stitched from her sister's tea towels, to the Brits. Although Halliwell had already pledged allegiance to Margaret Thatcher, calling her 'the first Spice Girl' (Turner 2013: 61), the dress became an icon of Cool Britannia, selling for a record £36,200 at auction in 1998 (BBC 1998b). Having won the nation's hearts, minds and hard-earned cash, the Spice Girls were arguably, if briefly, as big as The Beatles. So it was only a matter of time before they made a film, *A Hard Day's Spice* if you will. Says PolyGram's Michael Kuhn, who distributed it:

> *Spice World* was just, 'God, here's an opportunity. Can we get this film made now before they disappear up their own arses?' you know? That's also part of the music business, obviously you've got the auteurs, but a lot of it was, 'Let's just fucking ride this wave and hope we get home before it all disappears!'
>
> (2016)

Made quickly, cheaply and with a shiny cynicism that, if you squint (or are ten years old), might pass for fun, the film explicitly aligns itself with Cool Britannia, following the girls' Union Jack tour bus around a tick-list of London landmarks while they endure a breathless promotional schedule of rehearsals, gigs and stunts. Amid endless cameos from yesteryear musical stars such as Elton John, Bob Geldof and Meat Loaf, and scattershot skits on British tabloids, fashion and pop culture, the girls bicker, banter and have dress-up montages – anything to avoid actually singing or dancing. Indeed, rarely has needing the toilet proved such a reliable plot device.

Classic Hollywood references abound. Posh (Victoria Beckham) dresses as Honey Ryder from *Dr. No* (Young, 1962); Ginger dons a Marilyn Monroe frock and stands expectantly over an air-vent; and Sporty (Mel C, aka Melanie Chisholm) rappels from the ceiling like Tom Cruise in *Mission: Impossible* (De Palma, 1996), albeit to play Subbuteo. There are even some off-brand British cinema references. At a photo shoot, the girls discuss changing their trademark looks. 'What about bricklayer Spice?' asks Posh. 'Or, erm, *Trainspotting* Spice?' says Baby (Emma Bunton), although scenes of the girls shooting up, or styled as Renton, Sick Boy, Begbie and co are conspicuous by their absence. During the end credits, where the actors break character and the girls harangue the audience, Baby and Ginger introduce themselves to Claire Rushbrook, who plays Deborah, with the greeting, 'Alright sweetheart!', while Scary (Mel B, aka Melanie Brown) tries to remember where this comes from. In fact, they mean *Secrets & Lies* (Leigh, 1996), in which Rushbrook co-starred, an unlikely Spicebus favourite.

For the most part, the plot is so piecemeal it feels like the filmmakers are making things up as they go along. At times, we even get to see what the spitballing process might look like. As the girls race to a climactic Albert Hall gig, the chase is narrated by scriptwriter Graydon to manager Clifford (Richard E. Grant). In one sense he is pitching us the film we are already watching; in another a (real) terrible film becomes a (fake) terrible film narrated by its own (fake) screenwriter. Take that, Charlie Kaufman.[4]

At best inconsistent, and at worst extremely dubious, the film's sexual politics are perhaps its most interesting aspect. For all the talk of Girl Power, nobody seems exactly sure what it means. Paraded around like gobby ingénues, the girls are entirely at the mercy of their manager, his schedule and a shadowy, Blofeld-style overlord (Roger Moore); sexualized puppets as much as successful popstars. When the girls meet aliens, one grabs Scary Spice's breast by way of greeting; when visiting a child in a coma, Posh suggests, 'Maybe you should take your top off, Geri.'

Although the girls' Top Trump characteristics are constantly thrust to the fore, they feel more like product differentiation than personality traits,[5] just as Mel B and Mel C are allowed to be Scary or Sporty, but not have surnames. One photo-shoot has them dressing up as each other, thus proving effectively interchangeable. 'Blah, blah, blah, Girl Power, feminism, know what I mean?' mutters Mel B as Geri. Later Geri will disguise herself as Bob Hoskins, who offers the befuddling slogan, 'Girl Power, equalisation between the sexes.'

Perhaps such confusion should come as no surprise. The 1990s had seen the rise of ladette, defined by 'public drinking, recreational drug use, fantasies about promiscuous and anonymous sex... [which] had previously been thought of as behavioural traits of young men' (Turner 2013: 67); men's magazines ironized casual misogyny; and strong female characters such as *Tomb Raider*'s Lara Croft[6] could do all the archaeological adventuring they wished as long as they looked good in hot pants. However clumsily, *Spice World* tries to place the girls in the middle of this mess, projecting a teenager's idea of confidence or, in Geri's words, 'strength and courage in a Wonderbra', while making as much money as possible, quality be damned. 'That was absolutely perfect without being any good,' offers Jools Holland's musical director, a generous summary for a film that, like Cool Britannia itself, could be repented at leisure.

While the Spice Girls criss-crossed the capital like lost tourists, another ambitious group was coalescing in the newly Swinging London. Camden was Britpop's original epicentre, particularly The Good Mixer pub, and the so-called Primrose Hill Set kept the party going after hours in the loftier, leafier part of the borough they called home. Here actors such as Jude Law, Sadie Frost and Sean Pertwee rubbed shoulders with supermodel Kate Moss, while nearby Noel Gallagher and his neighbour Ewan McGregor played lightsabres on the lawn of Supernova Heights.[7] In Soho, Cool Britannia's carousing ground, the sense of possibility was palpable. Says Pertwee:

> The film industry had been such a closed shop for many years. It was a real breakout, an exciting time. When we used to go out mob-handed we'd meet the most extraordinary

> people, from Ray Winstone to Rhys Ifans to The Prodigy. I'm not name-dropping, it was just one of those times when everything came together on every level. It was the perfect storm, a combination of music, art, food and filmmaking. Soho was a small place and it was very exciting.
>
> (2016)

Inspired by United Artists, a studio founded in protest by Charlie Chaplin and friends in 1919, Pertwee, Law, Frost, McGregor and Jonny Lee Miller formed their own collective, Natural Nylon, with producers Bradley Adams and Damon Bryant, making the company official in 1997. The name combined two of the world's coolest cities, New York and London (NY-Lon), with the 'natural' added so everyone knew they intended to wear, rather than sell, tights. The idea, says Pertwee, 'was to have the opportunity to play parts we'd never be given the opportunity to play', and the group's flagship project was to be *The Hellfire Club*, about the debauched antics of Sir Francis Dashwood's eighteenth-century aristos, with Stephen Daldry mooted to direct. According to McGregor:

> We set up Natural Nylon to make movies in the way we wanted to make them. We didn't want to have to pander to the States, which is something I think causes a lot of British movies to suffer. After all, they don't try to make films that appeal to us, so why should we worry about them?
>
> (Kermode 2002: n.pag.)

It's an admirable Britpop cinema manifesto, and although Natural Nylon didn't make any films that could properly be classified as such, a selection of the actors appeared in *Final Cut* (Anciano and Burdis, 1998) and *Love, Honour and Obey* (Anciano and Burdis, 2000), semi-improvised efforts with a can-do approach that matched the confidence of the movement. Says Frost, the self-styled Yoko Ono of the group:

> There had been a lot of talking and not doing, and I think there was a young breed of filmmakers who just wanted to get on and do stuff, and that's why things like *Final Cut* and *Love, Honour and Obey* happened. We got a bunch of actors together, then just went off and did them, and at that time people didn't really do that.
>
> (2016)

A good deal less interesting than its own 'Making of', *Final Cut* sees Frost, Winstone, the directors and assorted pals – most using their own names – gathering for Law's funeral, at which is revealed his last film, a series of secret videos detailing NW1's incestuous goings-on. Mostly this means people in toilets taking cocaine and talking rubbish, although a sequence in which a man examines his own genitals in the mirror offers a swift visual summary of the project. Using footage not found so much as constructed, the film anticipates fly-on-the-wall reality TV shows such as *Big Brother* (2000–present, UK: Endemol) and could be seen as a clumsy correlative to the stripped-back aesthetics of Denmark's Dogme 95 movement.[8] The critics, needless to say, were not kind, with *The Guardian*'s Jacques Peretti calling the film 'physically unwatchable' (2000: n.pag.). It is certainly self-indulgent, like a celebrity home movie where everyone is having more fun than the viewer. Says Frost:

> People either loved or hated those films. *Final Cut* got a lot of criticism because it wasn't how you were so supposed to make films, but at that time it was a bit ahead of itself. We were the first people to do it in the UK, then people started perfecting that model. We were really kind of amateurish, I guess, but we did have a great time making them.

While Natural Nylon released *eXistenZ* (Cronenberg, 1999), a Canadian reality-bleed sci-fi starring Law, and *Nora* (Murphy, 2000), an international co-production telling the story of Nora Barnacle (Susan Lynch), wife of the Irish novelist James Joyce (McGregor), getting the group together proved easier out of hours. Their next project – not an official Natural Nylon production – was the semi-improvised gangster film *Love, Honour and Obey*. With gunfights, casual violence and the trappings of the genre to play with, its postmodern pleasures are slightly more obvious than those of *Final Cut*: Jude Law warning of the dangers of mixing friends with business; Jonny Lee Miller in full clown costume resembling Mr Chuckles from *Brassed Off* (Herman, 1996); Ray Winstone in horrible sportswear giving it both barrels, not something the era was exactly short of. Recalls Pertwee:

> Everyone in that film used to hang out in the pub next to my house in Primrose Hill. Ray [Winstone] and I were working on some other movie together and Dom [Anciano] said, 'Can you get this to Raymundo?' and I said, 'Of course.' And I just heard gales of laughter from Ray's trailer. The script was like 25 pages long, we improvised every single word of it.

Using a style honed on the sitcom *Operation Good Guys*[9] (Anciano and Burdis, 1997–2000, UK: BBC), the actors were encouraged to play off against each other as leaders of rival North and South London gangs. Says Pertwee:

> You just go in and see what happens, which is terrifying, especially when you're going up against Ray Winstone! It was always a really scary thing to do, like having a sort of acting colonic, quite frankly, but after the first day, it was like the best drug you've ever done in your life.

Winstone, it seems, had not always been so keen to improvise. According to actor Nick Moran:

> I had an interview with Mike Leigh for *Secrets & Lies,* worst experience I ever had, because he really gets involved, you start baring your soul, and he just goes, 'Yeah, life's tough isn't it? Anyway see you!' Ray Winstone had the same interview, and Mike wasn't

> getting anywhere with Ray. 'Tell me about your family,' 'What's it got to do with you?' 'How long have you been married?' 'None of your business.' Then Mike said, 'I want you to go outside and think of something that makes you really angry and then come in.' Mike came out 15 minutes later, 'Where's Ray?' The receptionist goes, 'Who?' 'The guy that came out?' 'He's gone home!' Ray is such a god among men, he's that candid. It just wasn't going to wash.
>
> (2016)

Although the self-indulgence levels are as vertiginous as *Final Cut*, and it is difficult to buy Law as a Cockney hardcase, *Love, Honour and Obey* does not lack Britpop cinema confidence. Says Pertwee:

> There's an extraordinary litany of talent in that movie. Rhys [Ifans] did it for a nice watch, because they'd run out of money by that stage. Noel [Gallagher] was a friend of ours so he wrote the soundtrack ['Force of Nature']. We were just pulling everyone in.

Aside from the Natural Nylon gang (minus McGregor), the film also features Kathy Burke and Laila Morse from *Nil by Mouth* (Oldman, 1997), TV presenter Denise Van Outen, and Perry Benson from *Quadrophenia* (Roddam, 1979) and *This Is England* (Meadows, 2007). According to Pertwee:

> There's a lot wrong with it, but I still think it's one of the funniest films. We get so many props from London cab drivers. It seems to be the cab drivers' favourite film of all time, they love it.

True fans could not only enjoy the film on DVD, they could listen to it as well. The cast's karaoke performances of Tony Williams and David Essex standards were released on a soundtrack CD, which Radio One DJ Chris Evans played on air. 'It almost put us into the charts,' says Pertwee, 'which was ridiculous, because none of us are singers.' Indeed not, but if anything summed up the giddy possibilities of the era, it is the idea that, by sheer force of personality, the Primrose Hill Set might be troubling the Top 10 as well as the cinema.

Things were changing behind the scenes as well. Since 1995, the UK Arts Councils had been subsidizing British film production with lottery funds, but picking winners often proved harder than predicting the jackpot, and a good deal less profitable. By 1997, only two of the 66 films part-funded this way had enjoyed a full UK release (Walker 2005: 271): *Crimetime* (Sluizer, 1996), a nasty psycho thriller from the director of the truly harrowing *The Vanishing* (1988) and its truly horrible US remake (1993); and *True Blue* (Fairfax, 1996) billed as '*Chariots of Fire* on water', but sinking somewhat faster. Under New Labour, the flow of funds – and films – increased. As critic Alexander Walker put it, 'Never before had film-makers had it so good, or made so many films that were so bad' (2005: 199).

Rather than squander resources on substandard efforts, the Arts Councils decided to spread a £92.25 million lottery windfall across three 'franchises' with proven track records: The Film Consortium, which included such old-guard luminaries as Mike Newell, Ken Loach and Stephen Woolley (late of Palace Pictures); the French-owned Pathé Pictures; and DNA, run by *Four Weddings* producer Duncan Kenworthy and *Trainspotting* supremo Andrew Macdonald (hence DNA, Duncan and Andrew). But the initiative was slow to bear fruit, and for every critical success such as *Ratcatcher* (Ramsay, 1999) there were plenty of duds like *Plunkett & Macleane* (Scott, 1999) starring *Trainspotters* Jonny Lee Miller and Robert Carlyle. Indeed, by 2000 only three lottery-funded films had made their budgets back at the UK box office (Dyja 2010: 153): *Billy Elliot* (Daldry, 2000), the slapdash caper movie *Shooting Fish* (Schwartz, 1997) and cynical, London-set rom-com *This Year's Love* (Kane, 1999).

Inexpertly policed, to say the least, the distribution of lottery funds led to ridiculous situations such as Miramax, a Hollywood studio, receiving £1 million to make *Mansfield Park* (Rozema, 1999) by Jane Austen, one of Britain's greatest writers – surely a feat that could have been managed without the public's financial aid (Thorpe and Barnett 2000). More problematically, the subsidies meant that profits could be made on films that were never released, leading to an excess of British films of variable quality gathering dust on the shelf. Despite receiving a £1 million grant from the Scottish Arts Council, and the presence of Colin Firth and *Chariots of Fire* director Hugh Hudson, *My Life So Far* (Hudson, 1999), another Miramax effort, was only released in America, and then several years later (Pendreigh 2000).

Aside from heritage hits such as *Mrs Brown* (Madden, 1997), most lottery-fund beneficiaries were, in Walker's words, 'Anxious at all costs to be modern, to create more overtly "entertaining" films, to include recognisable daily reality but not to seek out the miserabilism that daunted audiences and saw a downturn in box office receipts' (2005: 239). In other words, prime Britpop cinema territory.

Shot on a budget of £2.9 million, including £980,000 of lottery money, *Shooting Fish* was the first to pay back its loan, after bringing in £4 million at the UK box office (Dyja 2010: 154) – ironic considering its plot is a jumble of outlandish get-rich-quick schemes and pilfered windfalls. The film introduces us to transatlantic odd-couple orphans Dylan (Dan Futterman) and Jez (Stuart Townsend): the former slick, oversexed and American, the latter nerdy, earnest and English (though Townsend is Irish). They make their living conning big businesses with promises of talking computers, scamming members of the public over loft insulation and scoring freebies from skips. 'We're 1990s Robin Hoods,' claims Jez, but perhaps a modern-day *Plunkett & Macleane* (tagline: 'They rob from the rich… and just keep it!') would be nearer the mark. Together they plot to buy a stately home, and tussle for the affections of medical student/peer of the realm Lady Georgina (Kate Beckinsale), who comes along for the ride because… well, never mind. Plotting issues aside, the film is practically a ticklist of Britpop cinema tropes.

Swathed in the also-ran indie of Space, Strangelove and The Supernaturals, it begins with Dan's smartarse voiceover and features several chases, one of which sees Jez escaping thanks to his 'quick-release trousers', an item Renton might have benefitted from purchasing. The *Shooting Fish* logo borrows heavily from *Trainspotting*'s stylized titles, flashbacks are seen through green or purple filters, and an intimate scene between Jez and Georgie plays out in striking, but superfluous, yellow and blue neon – think Danny Boyle-lite.

Dylan and Jez first meet when they are hired to paint a cooling tower (needless to say, they cheat) and, by some strange form of domestic Stockholm syndrome, they end up living at the top of one as well. Kooky, colourful and cavernous enough to skateboard in, it is perhaps the ultimate Britpop cinema residence, full of dancing sunflowers, Coke machines and the sort of dayglo tat that would fit perfectly in a Blur video. As Georgie notes, admiringly, 'Not many people have a pond on their roof.' With realism far from the agenda, the freewheeling plot coasts entirely on wish fulfilment: the idea that anyone who wants it enough can own a very big house in the country. If only the protagonists' charms were quite so plentiful.

Whether telling Georgie, 'I want to pleasure you with my tongue,' or admiring her 'little sit-up breasts' while she is sleeping, Dan is obnoxious to the point of creepiness. Although slightly more appealing, Jez embodies that hoary movie cliché: the geek who is one haircut shy of looking like a model. 'You two are compulsive risk takers, you thrive on danger!' chides Georgie, but there is no rhyme or reason to the pair's schemes. 'I can't figure you out. You spend lots of time with a complicated computer scam. And that pays you what, say, 50 grand?' she continues. 'Then you work just as hard for £800.' The film never really explains itself either, relying instead on an extreme form of Britpop cinema breeziness to keep the hijinks coming. But with nothing at stake, it becomes a struggle to care what happens, as if the easy-come-easy-go economics of lottery funding have seeped into the film itself. Bluntly speaking, a £1 million subsidy might buy more filmmaking frills, but it will not necessarily make better films.

In time, the lottery franchises would produce such hits as Revolution Films' *24 Hour Party People* (Winterbottom, 2002) and DNA's *28 Day's Later* (Boyle, 2002a) but not before the system was overhauled again, with the creation of the UK Film Council in 2000. Says Aukin:

> It's an awful thing to say, but I think what happened is we got swamped with cash, and all sorts of things got made that shouldn't have been made. In one year we got into a situation where 120 or so British films were made, but were two British films a week going to be distributed through British cinemas? I don't think so. There was no demand.

On 31 August 1997, Princess Diana died as she had lived, hounded by the press, in a senseless car crash in Paris. Wrote historian Alwyn W. Turner:

> Cool Britannia did not long survive Diana. Her death seemed to mark the end of the brief period in which control of popular culture had lain in the hands of the anti-Thatcher generation, for that strange week allowed no space for the ironic detachment that had been characteristic of so much of the early 1990s.
>
> (2013: 383)

New Labour's appeal would soon fade with familiarity – as evidenced by a 14 March 1998 *NME* cover showing Tony Blair under the headline, 'Ever had the feeling you've been cheated?', a (mis)quote from The Sex Pistols' Johnny Rotten.[10] And the sense was that Cool Britannia and the 1997 surge of Britpop cinema was a pop-cultural wave that crested sharply, then crashed. Says Irvine Welsh:

> It was very limited, the idea that we had this culture we could continually sell to the rest of the world. But you can't. We were selling off the very essence of it, the very bones of it, and you can only sell it once. I also thought there was something sad about it, that Cool Britannia was like a requiem mass for British culture. The internet was going to be in ascendency, it was getting harder for culture to develop and incubate, and culture was going to become media culture, you know, you could see all that happening. So to me there was a kind of lament for British culture as well as a celebration of it.
>
> (2016)

Whether Blair or Britpop band, Primrose Hill Set or Spice Girl, perhaps the class of 1997 were simply fiddling while Rome burned down after all.

What Happened Next...

Shooting Fish alumni... Experienced various degrees of success. Director Stefan Schwartz makes top-line American TV shows such as *Fear the Walking Dead* (2015–present). Richard Holmes produced the critically reviled *Dead Babies* (Marsh, 2000), also set in a stately home, as well as more interesting UK efforts such as the hoodie horror *Eden Lake* (Watkins, 2008) and maternal thriller *Keeping Rosy* (Reeves, 2014). Of the cast, Kate Beckinsale has burned the brightest, becoming an international star thanks to the *Underworld* series (various, 2003–16).

The Spice Girls... Continued their quest for world domination, banishing blokey Britpop bands from the charts, and inspiring a new generation of girl groups, from All Saints to Sugababes. Geri Halliwell left in May 1998 to pursue a solo career and, having reached saturation point, the group went on hiatus in 2000. Their greatest gift to pop culture was not Girl Power, however, but the idea of, as *Guardian* music journalist Sylvia Patterson put it, 'the band as brand, of pop as a ruthless marketing ruse' (2016: n.pag.). All five Spice Girls have since dabbled with acting, although Halliwell has the most impressive resume, appearing in *Fat Slags* (Bye, 2004), based on the *Viz* cartoon, and *Crank 2: High Voltage* (Neveldine and Taylor, 2009) as Jason Statham's mother, despite being five years younger than him.

Natural Nylon... Went the way of the Spice Girls, albeit for different reasons. After a string of disappointing releases, from the Civil War drama *To Kill a King* (Barker, 2003) starring Tim Roth, to the SFX-heavy *Sky Captain and the World of Tomorrow* (Conran, 2004), starring Law, the company folded in 2003. 'Every single member of the acting company's career went stratospheric,' says Pertwee, 'Then, bang, that was that. It just became insane, there was too much attention. An unfair spotlight was shone on us, it became almost like an elitest group, and that was exactly what we weren't trying to do.' According to Frost: 'In a way the ambition was one of the reasons the film company finished. Everyone was so competitive that they couldn't actually work together because they were all leading men'. By 2002, when he left, 'No one was getting paid,' McGregor told journalist Miranda Sawyer, 'Maybe it felt to the others like a bit of a Renton-esque move on my part… to leave like that. I just fucked off and the company slowly fell apart' (2017).

Notes

1 Section 48 of the Finance (No.2) Act 1997 allowed qualifying British films to write off production expenditures against taxable income (Dyja 2010: 41).
2 The number of UK cinema screens increased from 1,685 in 1990 to 2,383 in 1997; while admissions went from 97 million in 1990 to 139 million in 1997 (Dyja 2010: 93–95).
3 The phrase 'Cool Britannia' appears to come from the opening track on Bonzo Dog Doo-Dah Band's 1967 debut album *Gorilla*. A 1996 Ben & Jerry's ice cream flavour shared the name. US indie band Death Cab for Cutie took their moniker from track seven.
4 Charlie Kaufman is an American scriptwriter known for meta masterpieces such as *Being John Malkovich* (Jonze, 1999) and *Eternal Sunshine of the Spotless Mind* (Gondry, 2004). His most strikingly self-referential work is *Adaptation* (Jonze, 2002), which dramatizes the struggle of one Charlie Kaufman (Nicholas Cage), to adapt Susan Olean's 1998 book *The Orchid Thief*.
5 In fact, it was *Top of the Pops* magazine, not Simon Fuller, who gave the girls their nicknames.
6 Lara Croft is the fearless yet feminine heroine of the *Tomb Raider* computer game series (1996–present) created by British firm Core Design. She was played by Angelina Jolie in the film *Lara Croft: Tomb Raider* (West, 2001) and its sequel (De Bont, 2003), then by Alicia Vikander in a 2018 reboot (Uthaug, 2018)
7 McGregor had just been offered the part of Obi-Wan Kenobi in *Star Wars: Episode I – The Phantom Menace* (Lucas, 1999). His uncle Denis Lawson had appeared in the original 1977 film. Supernova Heights was named after the Oasis song 'Champagne Supernova'.
8 Started in Denmark in 1995 by directors Lars von Trier and Thomas Vinterberg, Dogme 95 was an attempt to purify filmmaking by stripping away all artifice. Its ten commandments banned genres, non-diegetic lighting, music and sound effects, and superficial action such as murders, among other things. The first, and best, Dogme 95 films were *Festen* (Vinterberg, 1998) and *The Idiots* (Von Trier, 1998).
9 A fusion of sitcom and docu-soap, like the more successful *The Office* (2001–03, UK: BBC), *Operation Good Guys* was a BBC mockumentary set in a police station. The 'Stardust' episode (1999) features cameos from Jude Law and Jonny Lee Miller, introduced as, 'Jude

Law, a well-known film star, and Bobby Lee Miller… Jonny Lee Miller, also an actor.' Both *Trainspotting* and *Plunkett & Macleane* get name-checks. Other notable series cameos include gangster 'Mad' Frankie Fraser, footballer David Seaman and musician/actor Martin Kemp from Spandau Ballet and *The Krays* (Medak, 1990).

10 'Ever get the feeling you've been cheated? Good night!' said Lydon to the audience at the Sex Pistols' last ever gig, at Winterland Theater, San Francisco on 14 January 1978.

Chapter 6

The Drugs Don't Work

Starring: *Twin Town* (Allen, 1997) and *The Acid House* (McGuigan, 1998)

Chapter 6: The Drugs Don't Work

In search of the next *Trainspotting*...

Ewan Proclaimer (Tom Hollander): *Sick Junkie* is a comedy about a group of normal, ordinary kids – all heroin addicts, of course. Possibly Welsh, maybe Irish, probably Scottish. We see a week in their ordinary, mundane lives. They inject heroin into their eyeballs. They have babies in toilets. They get AIDS. They try and raise veins on their private parts in order to inject more heroin. They kill a social worker. They have anal sex in exchange for heroin, which turns out to be cut with bleach, and kills them. They have abortions. They're raped by gangs of English policemen.
Sam Bell (Hugh Laurie): Excuse me. Um, I just want to make sure I'm following this… This is a comedy we're discussing, is it?
Maybe Baby (Elton, 2000)

Glastonbury Pyramid Stage, 28 June 1997. It was always a risk. The last bands to headline here back in 1995 were the loveable outsiders Pulp, and Oasis, all swagger and sneer, with Robbie Williams guesting. But Radiohead are polar opposites – introverted, alienated, no style all substance – and singer Thom Yorke seems to come from another planet entirely: tiny, vulnerable, with the voice of furious angel. Taking the stage after retro Britpoppers Cast, Dodgy and Ocean Colour Scene, above a sea of mud, the band are a revelation. But as the music moves from fragile to fraught, they seem overwhelmed, with Yorke's knife-edge performance tipping towards panic attack. When things go wrong – monitors blowing, equipment failing – he fights the urge to run. Instead, he asks the crew to turn the lights on the crowd, less an act of showmanship than a cry for help. And 80,000 people cheer.

Cool Britannia stuck longer in the collective memory – or perhaps the craw – than it deserved. But as the manufactured pop of the Spice Girls and co increasingly colonized the charts, discontent was brewing. Soon, Britpop's sunniness was giving way to the claustrophobic futurism of Radiohead's *OK Computer* (1997), and the bands that remained, or remained relevant, made music of a darker timbre. Blur and Pulp recorded comparatively downbeat drug albums[1]; Oasis disappeared up their own noses; and the likes of Elastica, Sleeper and Menswear simply disappeared. Tellingly, the *NME*'s album of the year in 1997 was Spiritualised's *Ladies and Gentlemen We Are Floating in Space*, which came in a foil blister pack to resemble prescription meds.

Though many years behind the zeitgeist, Ben Elton's *Maybe Baby* contains a grain of truth. Starring Hugh Laurie and Joely Richardson as a middle-class London media couple desperately trying to conceive, the film – think *Bridget Jones's Fertility Diary* – features Tom Hollander as a Scottish writer/director/shock merchant called (yes, really) Ewan Proclaimer, complete with a shoddy goatee and shaky Glasgow accent. Clearly, and rather unfairly, inspired by Irvine Welsh, he's an affront to the goggle-eyed decency of Laurie's BBC drone. 'Well, I don't see it as the BBC's job to fund cynical tales about drugs and prostitution which purport to reflect everyday life in Britain just so that fashion junkies who make them can swank about at Cannes looking tough, then bugger off to the States the first chance they get,' huffs Laurie. But just as Elton was making a ham-fisted land-grab for Richard Curtis's throne, the British film industry was falling over itself to find the next *Trainspotting* (Boyle, 1996). And if it proved too hard make it, they would have to fake it.

With *Trainspotting* so deeply embedded in the national consciousness, it became practically a legal requirement for every British film that followed to mention its name somewhere in the marketing. Thus, the DVD for the unremarkable *South West 9* (Parry, 2001) bore the optimistic précis: '*Trainspotting* meets *Pulp Fiction*'; *24 Hour Party People* (Winterbottom, 2002) was described as '*Trainspotting* meets *The Fast Show*'; while *This Is England* (Meadows, 2007) was, simply, 'The best British film since *Trainspotting*.' No matter if the filmmakers approved or not.

Where Boyle's work had emphasized Scotland's countercultural credentials, swinging London films such as *Croupier* (Hodges, 1999) and *Wonderland* (Winterbottom, 1999) spoke for England, and Northern Ireland was still licking its wounds with darker, Troubles-centred dramas such as the Stuart Townshend-starring *Resurrection Man* (Evans, 1998),[2] Wales had yet to receive its Cool Cymru film. That changed with 1997's *Twin Town*, a scabrous tale of petty crime and corrupt policemen in Swansea, which was co-written and directed by Kevin Allen, brother of the ubiquitous Keith. Recalls the still-incensed writer-director:

> I made the movie then they went and marketed it as the Welsh *Trainspotting*, which was just an arrow through the heart. I mean, would you like your film to be called the Welsh *Trainspotting*? It's not the Welsh *Trainspotting*, it's a lie. It wasn't trying to be *Trainspotting*, it wasn't inspired by *Trainspotting*, where's the fucking connection?
>
> (2017)

An actor who had appeared in Ben Elton's TV sitcom *The Thin Blue Line* (1995–96, UK: Tiger Aspect) and *Spice World* (Spiers, 1997),[3] Allen knew Danny Boyle from the Royal Court

Theatre, and had a cameo in *Trainspotting* as one of the London drug-deal goons (the one with the big moustache). Together with Andrew Macdonald, Boyle helped Allen set *Twin Town* up with PolyGram, with the pair executive-producing. 'Which was great,' Allen concedes, yet both 'a blessing and a fucking curse.' Although he insists he hadn't seen *Trainspotting* at the time, there are more than a few thematic similarities. Like *Trainspotting*, *Twin Town* is quick to undercut any nationalist cheerleading; its tone combines nihilism with knockabout comedy; and its plot deals with drugs, boredom and rebellion. It might not be the Welsh *Trainspotting*, but at least the films belong on the same Britpop cinema shelf.

The tale of tearaway brothers Julian (Llyr Ifans) and Jeremy Lewis (Rhys Ifans), and their increasingly bitter feud with local kingpin Bryn Cartwright (William Thomas), *Twin Town* begins, not with a chase as such, but with a stolen BMW screaming through otherwise peaceful streets, a proper statement of the film's outlaw intent. Says Allen:

> Joy-riding, it's in the words: 'joy' and 'riding'. Imagine being a teenager and getting a two-litre Ford Escort and taking it on some waste ground, pretending you're Ayrton Senna, then burning it. I can't think of anything more fun than that.

In keeping with the film's rebellious streak, the BMWs were procured from what Allen terms 'local scallywags' and the joy-riding scene, he says now, was a one-off: 'We couldn't have done that on our regular below-the-line budget, so we got some cameras and made some cars take off and blew up a caravan… we broke a few rules, you know, it was all fairly subterranean.'

Dynamically shot by John Mathieson, a music-video director who would go on to film *Plunkett & Macleane* (1999) for Jake Scott, and *Gladiator* (2000) for his father, Ridley, *Twin Town* features some eye-catching cinematography that belies its £1.7 million budget (£500,000 of which was lottery money). Most notable are an ambitious dog's eye-view sequence, and the gorgeous helicopter footage of a male voice choir singing on Mumbles Pier that closes proceedings. Uncharacteristically for such a cocky film, things end in grim uncertainty, with the Lewis brothers, having taken violent revenge on Williams and bent cop Terry (Dougray Scott), contemplating sailing to Morocco in Williams' boat.

Elsewhere the soundtrack flits from classics such as Petula Clark's 'Downtown' to Welsh Britpop from Catatonia, Manic Street Preachers and the Super Furry Animals (of which Rhys Ifans was once the lead singer). There is also, naturally, a Keith Allen[4] cameo – one of Britpop cinema's best, in fact – which sees him naked and cuddling a sheep, having consumed a spiked hotdog. In *Shoot Out in Swansea: The Making of Twin Town* (Robertson, 1997), the actor complains that 'being on the busy end of a sheep's mouth, wearing no clothes, and looking like a complete moron', wasn't much fun. To his credit, he pulls it off with aplomb.

Like Renton's iconic assertion that, 'It's shite being Scottish,' *Twin Town* is happy to take pot-shots at national heroes like Dylan Thomas and deflate any big-city pretensions with parochial irreverence. 'This isn't fucking Miami, Terry, it's fucking Swansea, we're in the third division,' says Greyo (Dorien Thomas). Explains Allen:

> We killed a few Welsh babies, that's for sure. You know, the clichés of Welshness: a few of them were put to bed. It was, 'Fuck you, Wales isn't just about fucking sheep and Shirley Bassey and Max Boyce and rugby – fuck off!'

But despite its larky start, *Twin Town* soon develops into something far darker, with decapitated dogs and the death of patriarch Fatty Lewis (Huw Ceredig) in a caravan fire (a similar fate befalls the mother of Brad Pitt's character in *Snatch* [Ritchie, 2000]). Inspired by a documentary he had made on police corruption, Allen always intended the film to undergo this tonal about-turn:

> I knew I was committing a cardinal sin with its structure. It was a case of getting the audience all teed up with a bit of comedy and then hitting them across the head with my tale – I was trying to hang on to that awful reality of what I learned making that documentary, that it's really fucked-up and nihilistic out there, that was the risk.

Frankly, the switch does not completely come off, and the film is at its strongest when skewering the eccentricities of Swansea life, from a urine-soaked karaoke competition to pub toilet coke-taking, where even *Trainspotting*'s debatable glamour feels a universe away. 'Swansea was buzzing with counterculture,' says Allen. 'The energy we captured is very much reflected in the movie, and it forgives the flawed bits and pieces here and there.'

Despite, or perhaps because of, that aggressive PolyGram campaign, the film only made £700,000 (Parry 2007) at the box office, eventually finding favour on DVD. 'We all thought it would do better here than it did,' admits Macdonald. In fairness, it is a difficult sell, featuring, as the BBC's Neil Prior noted, '318 expletives in 99 action-packed minutes at an average of 1 every 19 seconds' meaning that it ranks 'alongside such films as *Nil by Mouth*, *Reservoir Dogs* and *Goodfellas* as one of the most expletive-packed films of all time' (2017). *Sight & Sound,* meanwhile, claimed, 'The most depressing thing about *Twin Town* is that it seems to mark the almost instant decay of a new and exciting cinematic language in British films,' as if Allen had singlehandedly killed off Britpop cinema. Liberal Democrat MP David Alton went even further, calling it, 'sordid and squalid, plunging new depths of depravity' (Macnab 1997) – a DVD quote, you imagine, which Allen might prefer to 'the Welsh *Trainspotting*'. Looking back, the director is, relatively, sanguine:

> It is what it is. That's what happened, I made the Welsh *Trainspotting*. In actual fact I made *Twin Town*, and I'm proud of it and a lot of people like it a lot. It is what it is. It sold 250,000 DVDs, even on the back of hugely misjudged theatrical campaign. That's a lot of DVDs. I never got a penny, but that was in the days when you had to consider yourself lucky to have your first feature.

While Allen was working on his second feature, *The Big Tease* (2000), 'Those massive *Twin Town* posters went up all around the UK, saying it, "Raises a fat index finger to Hollywood and invites it to spin." But it was fuck-all to do with me. The irony was: I was in Hollywood doing a satire about Hollywood.'

'If the British know how to do one thing,' muses Ian Smith, a suicidal film buff in the Irvine Welsh short story *Snuff*, 'it is how to make terrible films' (1995: 75). Though a lot of the UK's post-1997 output proved Smith's (or is it Welsh's?) point, Film4, tired of anointing new releases 'the next *Trainspotting*', went back to the source in search of the pure stuff. Whether Britannia, cool or otherwise, could handle it was another matter.

Published in 1994, between the novels *Trainspotting* and *Maribou Stork Nightmares*, Welsh's *The Acid House* is a collection of tales set in Edinburgh, London and beyond, the most striking of which expand on the author's familiar themes: drugs (*Stoke Newington Blues, A Smart Cunt*), domestic disharmony (*A Soft Touch*) and old scores darkly settled (*The House of John Deaf*). As ever, Welsh's prose roars with life, however unsavoury. What *The Acid House* lacks is a clear cinematic quality – although the same could have been said, pre-Boyle, Hodge and Macdonald, about *Trainspotting*. Recalls Welsh:

> *The Acid House* was basically an opportunistic film off the back of *Trainspotting*, to be blunt and honest about it. I was asked if I wanted to do some TV with Film4 and we adapted *The Granton Star Cause* as a TV show, then we decided to shoot another couple [*A Soft Touch* and *The Acid House*] to make it into a trilogy and give it a theatrical release. We didn't know if it was going to be three TV shows, or a feature, and I think there was a bit of internal wrangling between Channel 4 and Film4 as to who would progress with it. Film4 won, and it came out as a movie.
>
> (2016)

Director Paul McGuigan was making documentaries at the time:

> *Trainspotting* had just been out that year at Cannes. I guess there was a sense of, 'Let's get this out.' But Irvine didn't want to do another *Trainspotting*, he wanted to do something that was totally Scottish. When the posters came out, they said: '*The Acid House*, The Real Irvine Welsh' because it was the real voice of Scotland – it was even subtitled in England.
>
> (2016)

If *The Acid House* is the real voice of Scotland, it needs more than subtitles. Set in the unprettified Edinburgh schemes, without a Ewan McGregor or Kelly Macdonald in sight, it occupies the more harrowing end of the Britpop cinema spectrum, evincing lots of the style, but none of the hope.

Though rougher around the edges than Brian Tufano's work, Alasdair Walker's cinematography is impressively experimental, particularly in the opening tale, *The*

Granton Star Cause. This sees the hapless Boab (Stephen McCole) turned into a fly by a magnificently grumpy God (Maurice Roëves), and features lots of giddy aerial footage. Britpop's influence, meanwhile, is everywhere. Boab's girlfriend Evelyn (Jenny McCrindle) has Pulp and Menswear posters in her bedroom; Oasis's 'Wonderwall' provides newlyweds Johnny (Kevin McKidd, aka Tommy from *Trainspotting*) and Catriona (Michelle Gomez) with their doomed first dance; and the soundtrack features indie bands such as Primal Scream, The Verve and The Pastels.

McGuigan shares Danny Boyle's fondness for signs and onscreen signifiers, although here the graffiti warns us that, 'Cheryl's hole smells of fish,' instead of *Trainspotting*'s slightly more poetic 'hard times'. There are even a few postmodern feints. In the first scene, Irvine Welsh can be seen cleaning the men's changing rooms in a *Reservoir Dogs* T-shirt, and none other than Sean Connery himself was offered the role of God. Says McGuigan:

> I did ask Sean, and he called us in the office. I remember someone saying, 'There's Sean Connery on the phone for you!' and I was like, 'What the fuck?' It was Sean and he uttered these words, and this is the honest truth: 'Sorry Paul, I can't come and play God'. He's such a big Irvine fan, he had the rights for *Malibu Stork Nightmares* for quite a while. It was nice of him to call, but it would have been brilliant to hear him say the line: 'You're just like me, a lazy slovenly cunt.' That would have been amazing.

Beginning with a football match, and introducing its characters with their names written across the screen, *The Acid House* may share some of *Trainspotting*'s pop-art aesthetics, but it is much less restrained. One scene has Boab, in fly form, trailing dog faeces in Evelyn's leftover curry; another has his mum (Annie Louise Ross) pleasuring his dad (Alex Howden) with a dildo; while the final story sees the narcotically unhinged Coco (Ewen Bremner aka Spud) turned into a foul-mouthed animatronic baby. Says McGuigan:

> You know when you have an animatronic baby sucking on Jemma Redgrave's tits, you're like, it doesn't get any more surreal than that – and he's getting an erection at the same time! It was funny to go to work every day, because it was like, 'What are we going to do today? Oh, someone's being turned into a fly.' It was good because you had to really use your imagination because we were working on a low budget, so we just went for it. We had the word cunt the most in 30 minutes than anyone has in any movie ever, because in Scotland it can be a term of endearment you know, like, 'He's a nice wee cunt,' so we don't think anything of it. But in America, obviously, they're like, 'What the hell is this?'

Where *Trainspotting* is about escape, *The Acid House* is about being trapped: whether in the body of a fly (*The Granton Star Cause*) or a baby (*The Acid House*), or a loveless marriage (*A Soft Touch*). And while the film could never be accused of pulling its punches, we are never entirely sure what it is aiming at. Says Welsh:

> I think it's a great movie in a lot of ways. Very grungy, even darker and more on the nose than *Trainspotting*. *Trainspotting* is the guy in the pub who's been a bad boy, telling these stories to their mates; whereas *The Acid House* is like the nasty little brother who's actually in the young offenders' institute being an absolute terror, that's the way I saw them.

According to McGuigan:

> I didn't watch *Trainspotting* for a while when I was making the film. I watched it while I was editing, and then I was horrified by how close it was to what I was doing, some of it. But, of course, the communality was Irvine's work. I wasn't daunted by its success. It was, and still is, the film that everyone talks about, but that just helped us get seen. After it was released, I didn't think I'd ever work again, but it didn't matter. I didn't see myself as a drama director at that point, I always felt I could go back and do documentaries, that was fine. I had a sense of being brave, I didn't care about anyone.

Predictably, the public preferred Boyle's more streamlined vision, and Welsh is under no illusions why:

> The characters in *Trainspotting* look like actors playing bad guys and that's what you really want; but the characters in *The Acid House* look like bad guys, and a lot of them were. And that naturalism often doesn't work on the big screen because you go to the cinema to be entertained as well as everything else. Sometimes some things can be too real basically, even though in some ways it was more out there than *Trainspotting*. Obviously it was a hard film to live with at the time, on the back of *Trainspotting*, but I've got a lot of love for it, I still think it's pretty cool.

Says McGuigan:

> It didn't break the box office, but it did OK. It got its money back and more. Although I'm sure there were a few grannies who went by mistake and had a heart attack. I'm just proud of the fact Film4 didn't censor us. It's a very raw piece because that's the way I wanted it, and that's the way Irvine had written it, you know, so we went with it, full on, we went hard-core on it, and you always have to be proud of that. I think Film4 enjoyed the fact it was controversial and naughty, they went for that. I remember being at Cannes and Rosie Boycott[5] came to interview me and Irvine, she'd just watched the movie, and live on Radio Four she said, 'Can I just say that's the most disgusting movie I've ever seen?' Irvine grabbed the mike off her and said, 'You know what I find atrocious and upsetting? *Four Weddings and a Fucking Funeral*,' and walked away.

Although *The Acid House* was never a likely candidate for reappraisal, *Twin Town* has since become something of a cult favourite. And just as *Trainspotting* was grudgingly adopted as a Scottish icon, so too have local attitudes to *Twin Town* changed over the years. Says Allen:

> Weirdly enough, even though there was an element of outrage here as though I was making something for the fucking tourist board, they honoured me for services to film.

'People love that film,' says Macdonald, 'If I go to Wales and say I produced *Twin Town*, they go crazy.' In 2017, for its 20th anniversary, a 3,000-ticket screening was held at Swansea's Singleton Park, with Allen in attendance, as well as a mock-up of the Lewis twins' van, selling hotdogs, with one crucial difference: 'There'll be no magic mushrooms on these ones,' organizer Anna Redfern told the BBC (Prior 2017).

Allen has even written a sequel, something he refused to do in the 1990s, however much Film4 clamoured for one. He explains:

> I couldn't have made *Twin Town 2* in the Blair cappuccino years. It was just too cosy, people were making too much money. Everyone was having it off during the Blair years, there was no real struggle. Course we're now back to post-Blair, it's pretty grim and it's going to get grimmer.

Provisionally titled *Tin Town*, the new film will feature the Ifans brothers, Welsh icon Charlotte Church and William Thomas, who returns as Bryn Williams, having barely survived the original. The subject? 'It's about sheep shit and weed really.'

What Happened Next…

Kevin Allen… Became disillusioned with the British film industry, then the American one. 'I didn't have a second film written but I had what I thought was a great fucking idea, but what they wanted was just another *Twin Town*… that's all PolyGram wanted.' Instead he went to Hollywood, where he had an equally rough ride. Having turned down *Confessions of a Dangerous Mind* (eventually made by George Clooney, 2002) and *Elf* (Favreau, 2003), he hit the road in an Airstream caravan to write a 'crazy counterculture indie movie' called *RV*. Allen assembled a stellar cast including Randy Quaid, Scarlett Johansson and Rhys Ifans, but the funding fell through. 'It was heartbreaking,' he says now, 'I'd had enough, my back had been broken.' Having told Hollywood to, 'Shove it up your arse and see you later!' Allen used his £1 million payoff money to build a pig farm in Ireland. 'While everyone else was making hay, I was shovelling it,' he says, happily.

***Trainspotting*-alikes on film…** Proved, perhaps mercifully, thin on the ground. Based on the Martin Amis novel, *Dead Babies* (Marsh, 2000) was the nadir, a grubby tale of repulsive toffs (including *Gangster No. 1*'s Paul Bettany) taking drugs, having sex and popping pustules in a stately home. *The Guardian*'s reviewer Peter Bradshaw described it, rather charitably, as 'boring, embarrassing, nasty and stupid – and not in a good way' (2001). The DVD cover, meanwhile, positively screams 'Britpop cinema', with a splurge of splashy fluorescents. Quotes comparing the film to *Trainspotting* are, however, notable by their absence. The best they can muster is, 'A toxic cult comedy', from *Total Film*'s Simon Crook. Crook insists this was cribbed from a set visit report, not a review (2017).

Irvine Welsh adaptations… Have rarely found the directors they deserve. *Irvine Welsh's Ecstasy* (Heydon, 2011), about the criss-crossing social lives of Edinburgh pillheads, is, it is fair to assume, a film made by people who have seen *Trainspotting* more than once. An odd Canadian co-production, it represents a smoother watch than *The Acid House* – but then so does *The Blair Witch Project* (Sanchez and Myrick, 1999) – with flashy visuals that feel woefully behind the curve, like a (very) poor man's *Human Traffic* (Kerrigan, 1999). The well-received *Filth* (Baird, 2013) turns one of Welsh's best novels into a broad tragi-comedy about a bent copper (James McAvoy) going show-stoppingly crazy. Despite McAvoy's full-bore performance and a lovely cover of Radiohead's 'Creep' by Clint Mansell and Coco Sumner, it fails to elevate the material quite the way Danny Boyle did.

Notes

1 *Blur* (1997) by Blur nods to American lo-fi, grunge and the band's rumoured drug dalliances, featuring such downers as 'Death of a Party'. Pulp's *This Is Hardcore* (1998), meanwhile, begins with 'The Fear' and unravels from there.

2 In terms of Northern Irish films from the 1990s, only the darkly satirical *Divorcing Jack* (Caffrey, 1998) could make even the vaguest claim towards being Britpop cinema.

3 On the subject of *Spice World*, in which Allen plays an Italian director, he says: 'I think they just needed someone quick. I was up the road in Notting Hill and I just a call saying, "Kevin come down and play this fucking Italian guy." Oh god, my kids think it's fantastic, but I don't mind. There's all sorts of credits in there I've given up worrying about, and yet if a journalist ever saw them, then fucking hell!'

4 Of his older brother, Kevin Allen says, 'Keith was quite an iconic rogue around town in the halcyon days of Soho nightlife. I'm not sure he was really happy becoming an actor, I think he wanted to become a pop star. He was a bad boy. I'm not saying this because he's my brother, because he can be a complete cunt, but he was the best comedian of that generation, he blew them all away, and you can get other people to ratify that. He was dangerous, close to the bone, he either bombed or he was utterly brilliant, there was no in between'.

5 The former editor of *Esquire*, *The Independent* and *The Daily Express*, Boycott has spoken candidly of her alcohol addiction and heroin use.

Chapter 7

Caught by the Fuzz

Starring: *Lock, Stock and Two Smoking Barrels* (Ritchie, 1998), *Gangster No. 1* (McGuigan, 2000) and *Sexy Beast* (Glazer, 2001)

Chapter 7: Caught by the Fuzz

Crime and punishment in Britpop cinema

Hatchet Harry (P.H. Moriarty): You must be Eddie, JD's son.
Ed (Nick Moran): Yeah. You must be Harry. Sorry, didn't know your father.
Hatchet Harry: Never mind son, you just might meet him if you carry on like that.
Lock, Stock and Two Smoking Barrels

Bethnal Green Road, East London, 29 March 1995. All traffic stopped, the crowds standing six-deep. Some say Ray Winstone's in there, among the white-haired heavies and faithful old-timers; that Roger Daltrey, Barbara Windsor and Morrissey sent wreaths – a real best of British. When the hearse comes, it is pulled by six black horses, floral tributes proclaiming the deceased to be 'free at last'. Behind, his brother follows in a nondescript car, the third time he has tasted fresh air in 27 years, although he wears handcuffs over his suit. At the church, at least one of the men who carry the body is no stranger to carrying bodies. Afterwards, Frank Sinatra's 'My Way' sings the deceased to eternal rest under the inscription, 'Legend Ronald Kray. Never to be forgotten.'

As far back as anyone in the British film industry can remember, they always wanted to make gangster flicks. In the 1970s a particularly rich seam was struck, with *Performance* (Cammell and Roeg, 1970), *Get Carter* (Hodges, 1971) and *Villain* (Tuchner, 1971) balancing glamour and grit. But things tailed off after *The Long Good Friday* (Mackenzie, 1981), perhaps because, as in the film, the 1980s' biggest offenders were switching their attentions from armed robbery to real estate.

In truth, gangsters had always been fascinated by the power of show business, too. 'I believe that Ron and I were always destined to become known, either by fame or by infamy,' wrote Reggie Kray (1991: 165). The relationship was often reciprocal. James Fox, Richard Burton and Martin Kemp all visited the incarcerated Ronnie in preparation for playing criminals (Barra 2015) – indeed it might have been quicker to list the actors who declined. Combining East End community spirit with a weary sense of post-war deprivation and sudden, lip-splitting violence, *The Krays* (Medak, 1990) made the comparison explicit, by stunt-casting Kemp and his brother Gary, better known as two-fifths of the pop group Spandau Ballet, as Reggie and Ronnie. The Krays, apparently, did not approve – how dare the filmmakers depict their dear mum (played by Billie Whitelaw) swearing? (Leyfield 2015: n.pag.).

Thanks to Quentin Tarantino, the gangster genre enjoyed a resurgence in the mid-1990s, creating Britpop cinema exemplars such as *Lock, Stock and Two Smoking Barrels* and *Sexy Beast*, as well as tons of DVD landfill. *Hard Men* (Amalou, 1996), the first of these stack 'em high, sell 'em cheap efforts, is best summed up by its villain Pops Den, played by 'Mad' Frankie Fraser. 'Fucking amateurs!' he pronounces, though Fraser himself was anything but. A violent career criminal who spent 42 years behind bars, Fraser became something of a celebrity in the mid-1990s, appearing on TV comedy quiz *Shooting Stars* (1993–2001, UK: BBC), and in his own one-man-show *An Evening with 'Mad' Frankie Fraser*, a proposition criminals of a certain vintage would have once done time to avoid.

More sophisticated than its fightier, flightier brethren, Antonia Bird's *Face* (1997), is too down-to-earth to qualify as Britpop cinema, despite the presence of 1990s stalwarts Robert Carlyle, Ray Winstone, Phil Davis and Blur's Damon Albarn as armed robbers. '*Face* was one of my favourites,' says Davis now, 'I think it deserves a bigger reputation, that film, it sort of disappeared without trace' (2016). Also looking for a way out is Carlyle's conflicted hero 'Red' Ray, a socialist activist turned thief. Set in the strip-lit London gloaming and riven with regret, the film follows Ray and the gang through a series of disastrous if dynamically mounted raids. Recalls Davis:

> You got the impression that these guys who were robbing banks were kind of dinosaurs, you know, like no one's doing that anymore, they're into fraud. They're the last of an old breed of villains, and they're coming to the end of their tether.

Indeed, with an emotive soundtrack including the Longpigs' 'On & On', which mourns a love that will not end, let alone end well, *Face* can be seen as a farewell to old-style gangster films. Alternately tough and tender, it remains something of a one-off. Says Davis:

> This was an action-packed gangster movie. It was really unusual for a woman to get her hands on a gig like that, and Antonia[1] [who died in 2013] did it proud, you know, she was very, very good, a great loss.

Perhaps *Face* has been forgotten because it pilfered the plot of *Reservoir Dogs* (Tarantino, 1992)[2] rather than its postmodern spirit, though it was the altogether looser *Pulp Fiction* (Tarantino, 1994) that inspired the Britpop cinema gangster boom. According to *Lock, Stock* star Nick Moran:

> Everybody watched that film and thought, that's how you do it, That was what made cinema cool. Then Danny [Boyle] comes along and thinks, if you can make a bunch of

> bums doing smack in a series of vignettes cool, I'll do a whole film of bums doing smack and I'll make that cool! And he did. Then Guy [Ritchie] came along… but Tarantino was the guy who cut a swathe for us.
>
> (2016)

The boom would bring forth one out-and-out Britpop cinema masterpiece in the form of *Sexy Beast*; the compelling, if lopsided, psycho-thriller *Gangster No. 1*, which laced Britpop cinema visuals with something far darker; and *Lock, Stock*, one of the best-loved films of the era.

Shot for under £1 million[3] in London's yet-to-be gentrified East End, writer/director Guy Ritchie's cock-of-the-walk crime caper is a film built on clash and contrast: old vs new, real vs fake, experience vs exuberance. The central conflict sees Ed and his likely lad mates Soap (Dexter Fletcher), Bacon (Jason Statham) and Tom (Jason Flemyng) trying to outmanoeuvre gangster 'Hatchet' Harry and his old lags, after Ed racks up a £500,000 debt in a rigged card game. But we also watch Winston (Steven Mackintosh) and his posh weed-dealing pals face off against Dog (Frank Harper)[4] and his Cockney bother boys; 'Northern monkeys' Gary (Victor McGuire) and Dean (Jake Abraham) take on 'Southern shites' (almost everyone else); and, in terms of cameos, peace-loving singer Sting (as JD, Ed's dad) contrasted with nut-crunching footballer Vinnie Jones (as enforcer Big Chris). The heady cocktail of confidence and cynicism proved too much for some viewers, but even the doubters could not deny the allure of the film's studied cool.

With a washed-out look that would inspire numerous men's magazine photo shoots, *Lock, Stock* mixes familiar faces like Moriarty (from *The Long Good Friday*) with fresh ones such as Statham[5]; ingredients from classic films[6] with a very modern sense that we are always watching a movie. It is the cine equivalent of 'vintage', the fetishization of the old-new or the real-fake, just like the patinated wood and distressed paintwork that would become the default look for East End bars. One plot strand has Gary and Dean burgling a manor house for its antique guns – surely not a common criminal enterprise outside of Dickens? Upon inspecting the spoils, Tom says: 'They look nice, I agree, but lacking in criminal credibility, aren't they?' Critics levelled the same charges at Ritchie and his work, while the converted came back for more.

As with the best of Britpop cinema, *Lock, Stock* seemed to arrive fully formed, and the PR machine was keen to confer gangster status on its writer/director, however inaccurately. In fact, Ritchie was an upper middle-class Hertfordshire boy who, after being expelled from private school, worked his way through the ranks to become the director of a series of commercials and music videos, mostly: 'moody European rave techno shit' (Klein 1999). Having impressed with his debut short *The Hard Case* (1995), he and producer Matthew Vaughn started shopping the *Lock, Stock* script around their contacts, until it landed on the desk of Trudie Styler, Sting's wife. 'It wasn't an easy read,' she said. 'It was a long rambling screenplay with terrible typos' (Leyland 1998). But something in its infectious, kid-in-a-pie-and-mash-shop energy kept her hooked, and the film went into off-again/on-again pre-production with funding from HandMade Films (who pulled out), then private investors including French Connection UK's Stephen Marks. This period saw the budget slashed, and cast downgraded from the (relatively) starry – Jude Law[7] as a potential lead, Ray Winstone as Hatchet Harry – to the more speculative. In fact, each of these decisions would play to the film's strengths, because what would ultimately distinguish it was not polish but chutzpah. Says Moran:

> Guy wanted to make a big, sprawling British *Godfather*, but he ended up making something intense, colourful, good-humoured – if a little bit sick round the sides. Instead of a sprawling landscape, he made this detailed masterpiece rather than a great big fucking Pizarro the size of a room.

Pizarro or not, *Lock, Stock* would come to embody a certain strain of Britpop cinema so completely, it almost toppled the genre into self-parody. Exploding into life to the strains of 'Hundred Mile High City' by Ocean Colour Scene, an indie band whose music would become a byword for sun-drenched 1960s nostalgia, the opening chase is a belter. We find Bacon and Ed selling knock-off jewellery, although, as ever, it is confidence rather than contraband they're really peddling. 'Look at that one there,' says Bacon of a necklace. 'Handmade in Italy, hand-stolen in Stepney. It's as long as my arm. I wish it was as long as something else.' The police turn up, and the boys race through an empty Borough Market, with Bacon vaulting the barrier, then down a set of grotty stone steps familiar from *Naked* (Leigh, 1993) and *Gangster No. 1*. Here, time stretches into slow-mo, the chase suddenly a dance. The suitcase spins out of Bacon's hands, its contents flying towards Ed like an abundance of stolen riches spilling from the screen. Cue *Lock, Stock* logo, cue voiceover, cue movie.

It is a bracing start, and neither the pace nor Tim Maurice-Jones's limber camerawork let up. Like Ritchie and *Sexy Beast*'s Jonathan Glazer, Maurice-Jones cut his teeth on adverts and music videos (including Pulp's 'Common People'), so there is a fizz to his work that belies the budget, and backdrop. The scene where Ed takes on Harry in the card game, in particular, is a thing of woozy beauty, with the camera lazily circling the players as if spectating, then swooping into close-ups of towering gambling chips, as the stakes get, literally, higher. When Ed loses and leaves the table, the camera stays, swaying, on his face as if seasick with shock while Iggy Pop sings The Stooges' 1969 hit 'I Wanna Be Your Dog', a far cry from *Trainspotting*'s 'Lust for Life'.[8] Later, having ripped off Dog (who, in turn, has just ripped off Winston), the boys get riotously drunk, the frame rate speeding up and slowing down like an unreliable memory, and the camera flipping upside down, as if finally off the leash. The result is somewhere between a boyband video and a Bacardi advert, but if *Lock, Stock* is selling anything, it is membership of this Britpop cinema brotherhood.

Charismatic, but without distinctive characters – there is no reason Dexter Fletcher could not have played Jason Flemyng's role, for example, or vice versa, and the jokes about Tom being fat were left over from a previous cast/draft – the boys are cut from the same spivvy linen. Like seasoned actors in a gangster panto, they spout the same inverted-comma dialogue, and react with weary sarcasm to whatever the cartwheeling plot throws their way. Indeed, often their camaraderie appeals – and convinces – more than the situations they find themselves in.

Whether Samoan Joe's cocktail bar or Harry's porn emporium, the boys inhabit a cartoon London where everyone is a crook, and the walls echo with tall stories in subtitled Cockney. Bizarrely, it is almost completely devoid of women, as if some unmentioned apocalypse has silently stolen half the population. Ed's girlfriend, played by Laura Bailey, was cut from the finished film because, as Ritchie told the *Independent*, 'Wussy-wushy scenes just bore the hell out of me. I just want them to get on and start bashing people up' (Chibnall 2005: 284). This is a fair enough genre manifesto, but even the most regressive gangster films usually make time for the odd anguished moll, tart-with-a-heart or gyrating lap-dancer. Counting Tanya (Vera Day), the dealer at the card game, and Gloria (Suzy Ratner), the stoned girl who Plank (Steve Sweeney) sits on, inspiring the reductive exchange, 'What's that?'/'That's Gloria', the film contains two named female characters and one, as the academic Claire Monk[9] notes, is basically furniture (2005: 162).

Not that Ed and co seem to notice. Although the drinking scene reaches near-stratospheric levels of homoeroticism, with the friends splashing fluids over each other then falling asleep together, they're terrified of looking gay. 'Who wants their bank manager to know they tickle arse?' asks Tom after outlining a highly involved 'arse-intruding dildos' scam he must have been thinking about for ages. Another scene has Harry literally beating someone to death with a phallus, a fate apparently worse than getting car-doored by Big Chris. In comparison, *Gangster No. 1* and *Sexy Beast* are refreshingly frank about how men who exclusively keep the company of men might, perhaps, fancy men.

With no girls – or gays – allowed, but plenty of plot twists, pithy lines and people-bashing to grab waning attentions, the film becomes exactly the sort of post-pub DVD its characters might watch. Viewed through that prism, the stunt-casting makes perfect sense. Sting, for example, brings the same untouchable otherness as he did to *Quadrophenia* (Roddam, 1979). Says Moran:

> I always thought it was going to be Michael Caine, or Terence Stamp. Then I walked into the dressing room, there's Sting playing on a knockabout acoustic. He went, 'Alreet?' and I went, 'Alright mate, didn't know you played?' And he said, 'Oh, I play a bit actually,' and did this really complicated riff. I picked up the guitar, did the opening chords to 'Message in a Bottle', and he goes, 'Fucking funny, ha ha!' From that moment on he gave as good as he got. I mean, he's a supply teacher from the northeast so he's not going to take any shit.

Coming to the set straight from the police station with a conviction for ABH,[10] ex-footballer Vinnie Jones was also not a man to be trifled with. His first scene saw him smashing Dog's head (actually a block of wood) in a car door, which he attacked with enough gusto to give anyone who had seen his criminal record PTSD. Less well known, but no less dangerous, was Lenny Maclean who plays Barry the Baptist, a former bare-knuckle boxer and bouncer who had served time for GBH.

Though increasingly common throughout the era, this vein of real-fake violence is the film's most troubling aspect; cruel enough to curdle the comedy, but brushed off like a bad punchline by the characters. While Ed plays the fateful card game, Bacon, Soap and Tom watch a man, set on fire, stumbling from Samoan Joe's without commenting – or helping him. Later, they beat up a traffic warden (Rob Brydon) because he is in the way. And even though the protagonists are not killers, just chancers hoping to get rich quick, they barely raise an eyebrow at the corpse-strewn finale. At an early industry screening, recalls Moran:

> Someone put their hand and said something really idiotic about this being a violent film for violent people, and it was condoning violence. I said, well, so's *Popeye*. Everybody laughed and that was the end of that.

But the film's moral ambivalence comes at the expense of genuine engagement. From the opening scene, in which Ed explains the rules of three-card brag to the audience, before asking, 'So, you want to play?', to the cliffhanger ending, which sees Tom teetering off a bridge trying to reach the guns, everything is a game. Fortunes turn on the twist of a card, and nobody is in it for keeps. At the climax, when Big Chris tells the boys they are – finally – in the clear, he signs off with a deadpan, 'It's been emotional.'[11] But the real issue is that nobody feels anything at all.

If *Lock, Stock* turns, as academic Steve Chibnall put it, 'the honourable tradition of "realist" underworld films, exemplified by *Get Carter* and *The Long Good Friday*, into a semi-comedic travesty in which authenticity is replaced by pastiche' (2005: 282), *Gangster No. 1* attempts to elevate it to stylized tragedy. They may prowl the same Shoreditch backstreets, but *Gangster* is *Macbeth* to Ritchie's *Much Ado About Nothing*, rotten to the core and fully aware of the emptiness of criminal life.

Based on a play, then screenplay, by *Sexy Beast* writers Louis Mellis and David Scinto, then refashioned by Johnny Ferguson, the film stars Malcolm McDowell as London kingpin 'Gangster' in the modern day, with Paul Bettany as his younger 1960s self. At a boxing match booze-up full of ageing 'faces', Gangster (McDowell) hears that Freddie Mays (David Thewlis),[12] the 'Butcher of Bethnal Green', is being released from prison after 30 years. The film then dials back to show how Gangster (Bettany) came into Mays' orbit, first as his enforcer, then as a challenger to his throne.

Though McDowell circa 2000 projects mischief in place of Bettany's undiluted malevolence, it is an inspired piece of dual casting. 'Look at my fucking eyes,' is Gangster's constant entreaty, and when either actor fixes us with their intense, Alex DeLarge stares it is impossible to look elsewhere. Frankly it is hard to imagine the rather more placid Peter Bowles,[13] who played the part onstage, conjuring quite the same levels of intertextual menace. Says director Paul McGuigan:

> I wanted to use Malcolm because I was thinking of the era we were shooting in, which was 1969, and about who was relevant then. I wanted to go in with a preconceived idea of who this person was, because he didn't have a name, you don't know anything about him, so you have to use what you can. So I wanted to use Malcolm McDowell as Malcolm McDowell, because of how people perceive him. I wanted to put him in a great suit and make him brash and pathetic and harsh. So basically I jumped on a plane to LA, and he was kind enough to meet me for lunch, and he did the funniest thing ever. He went to the toilet, it was this really posh restaurant full of old ladies who lunch, and when he came out he kicked the door open and the old ladies looked round, and he went, 'What you looking at, you cunts!' Then he sat down and said, 'Right, do I have the job?'
>
> (2016)

McDowell summed up the appeal of the character perfectly on the DVD extras: 'Do I want to know this person? No! Do I want to play this person? Yes!' (2008) He also enjoys one of the era's greatest pieces of direct address. When Gangster stands at a urinal, we see a few drops of urine splashing into his champagne glass on the floor. He finishes up, tips the elderly attendant, then picks up the unfortunate cocktail. Just as he is about to drink, he turns to the camera, offers that Cheshire Cat grin familiar from decades of outlaw cinema, and asks us, 'What do you take me for, a cunt?'

With split-screens joining the two Gangsters across the years, and a looping chase down a spiral staircase, Peter Sova's inventive cinematography has style to spare. One scene shows Gangster dropping a taxi on one of Mays' debtors (Gary McCormack), a mechanic. It is shot from the driver's seat, so it feels like it is the camera, not the car, crushing the unfortunate cabbie. 'Very nice, creative,' says Mays as if congratulating Sova's work.

But these flourishes are never just for their own sake. Where *Lock, Stock* fetishizes the gangster lifestyle without question, *Gangster* fetishizes the stylings of the era – all Decca Records, shagpile and champagne – while underlining the danger of unchecked wanting; of valuing things ahead of people. Says McGuigan:

> I wanted to be in that world and I wanted to feel like sure, there's a coolness to it, because you've got the clothes and all that, but that's because the characters are fetishizing them, not because we were as filmmakers.

When Gangster performs his first act of violence for Mays, he is given £500 to get himself 'kitted out'. Later he describes himself as 'drunk on the smell of Italian leather, arseholed on the smell of success', violence and its spoils irreversibly intertwined, and exerting a narcotic influence. It soon becomes apparent that Gangster either wants to be Mays, to fuck him, or to destroy him, the three impulses mixing with murderous ambition. When he glances across the club at Mays dancing with wife-to-be Karen (Saffron Burrows), McDowell's voiceover slithers with sexual jealousy: 'And you Mr Freddie Mays, you had to go swimming in her eyes. Dancing in her hair. You had to slip into her mouth, slide over her tongue. Fall down her throat, deep down into her belly. Right into her blood. You had to fall asleep wrapped around her beautiful beating heart.' As *Sexy Beast* confirms, Mellis and Scinto have a wonderful ear for the poetry of violence.

It is about this point that *Gangster No. 1* and Britpop cinema irretrievably part company, despite the elastic flashback structure, calculating voiceover and stylized camerawork. Where the exaggerated characterizations of Begbie and Big Chris allow us to experience their actions at one remove, what we see through Gangster's eyes is, in McGuigan's words, 'a world full of hatred and malice and revenge and envy, all the stuff that we try to repress in our lives, and he's swimming in it.' Britpop cinema may encourage the illicit pleasures of the antihero, but it cannot cope with Gangster's levels of sadism. In one scene, which sees young Gangster driving with the doomed Roland (Razaaq Adoti), a scream splits Bettany's face, making him look like one of the melting Nazis in *Raiders of the Lost Ark* (Spielberg, 1981). One possible narrative explanation is that Gangster is mimicking the sound of the puncture that will force Roland to stop the car and meet his fate. But it feels more like a howl of direct address aimed at the audience. As if Gangster can no longer contain the violence inside him, instead letting it bleed through the screen to engulf the film.

It does not take long. When Mays and Karen are ambushed by rival Lennie Taylor (Jamie Foreman),[14] Gangster's revenge is as vicious as it is virtuoso. With McDowell's voiceover providing a running commentary of a scene he will, no doubt, relive forever, Bettany pulls up in the carpark under Taylor's flat armed with a machete, a Beretta and his favourite axe. 'Walking, door, corridor, lift,' goes the VO, 'I'm Superman, King fucking Kong, filling up, I'm filling up!' The lift doors close on another of Gangster's straight-to-camera screams. 'Fifth floor, stop, open, out, corridor, walking, machete, axe, gun, chisel, tools,' gasps McDowell, while Bettany stomps down a corridor tinted a queasy green. As distorted sound effects and the OCD VO echo and crescendo, he kicks in Taylor's door, shoots him in the leg, and the savagery begins. With Frankie Avalon singing, 'I'll never let you go. Why? Because I love you,' too loud, too sweet on the stylus, Gangster lays out his tools, strips off and folds his clothes so as not to get blood on them. He then unleashes a berserker rage of stabs, bites and blows on the defenceless Taylor, the camera blinking and blacking out in time with the victim. Recalls McGuigan:

> It was horrible to be in his head, a violent place to be. And that's why that scene where we're killing the guy has to feel like the most horrific thing you've ever seen. Because to me, growing up in Scotland, in Glasgow, and seeing a guy getting axed in the back of his head, the sound of it was just horrific. It's not the actual axing itself I remember, but the sound. I remember it to this day, and I vividly wanted to capture that violence.

In fact, he captures it so well, the film barely recovers. As Mays goes to prison for the murder, Gangster takes over London, and the terrifying Bettany turns into the tragic-comic McDowell, *Gangster No. 1* loses focus, as if this extraordinary expulsion of bile has damaged the fabric of the celluloid itself.

Perhaps it is useful here to view these two films in terms of Chibnall's polarized categories: 'gangster heavy' and 'gangster light' (2005: 282), the former leaning towards tragedy, the latter towards comedy. If *Lock, Stock* skews broad, and *Gangster* dark, the yin-yang appeal of criminal life is better summed up in *Sexy Beast*'s seesawing tone.

Though it is a far more serious proposition than *Lock, Stock*, *Sexy Beast* also gets its energy from jarring juxtapositions. The heat and dust of Spain, where safecracker Gal (Ray Winstone) has retired with his wife Deedee (Amanda Redman), is set against the dank, grey environs of London, where he risks it all for One Last Job, that fateful gangster cliché. Mellis and Scinto's mercilessly matter-of-fact dialogue is contrasted with Glazer's music-video-inspired bursts of surrealism. And the ever-erudite Ben Kingsley plays tough, as envoy Don Logan, while eterna-geezer Winstone shows his softer side. It is a film that appears to be 'gangster light', before segueing into 'gangster heavy' territory, then back again: the perfect Britpop cinema trajectory.

We begin amid blazing sunshine and swollen summer hues, with the portly Gal lying prone by his pool. 'It's like a sauna. Furnace. You could fry an egg on my stomach. Oooooohhhhh,' goes his orgiastic voiceover as we see him surrounded by the detritus of the *Loaded* dream: cold beer, B&H, tanning oil. 'Who wouldn't lap this up? It's ridiculous, tremendous, fantastic, fan-dabby-dozy.' As the lascivious bassline of 'Peaches' by The Stranglers strikes up, Gal struggles to a sit, then places a cool flannel on his Speedo's, a big man but in bad shape, to paraphrase the rather chillier *Get Carter*. 'My rehearsing was lying on a beach for two weeks, eating and drinking because I had to put on two stone,' recalled Winstone. 'Fantastic' (Goodall 2011: 156). At the bottom of the pool are two interlinked hearts, representing Gal and Deedee's love inked forever in concrete, untouchable beneath apparently calm waters. Gal gets to his feet and that oxymoronic, faintly mocking title fills the screen in fluorescent pink. The image says it all: life may be sweet, but it is far too good to last.

Immediately, the first of many bad omens crashes into view. A huge boulder comes unmoored from the cliff, tumbling past Gal, and cracking the bottom of that perfect pool. Later, as Gal, Deedee, Aitch (Cavan Kendall)[15] and Jackie (Julianne White) enjoy a barbeque, the flames shoot up towards Gal, another of paradise's hidden hazards. The next scene has Gal, Aitch and the pool boy (Alvaro Monje) hunting rabbits, their bullets failing and guns falling to pieces like some sun-soaked Freudian fever dream.

Over dinner at a local restaurant, the real horror first breaks the surface. As Gal and Deedee try to decide between calamari and the 'chicken thing', a strained-looking Aitch and Jackie join them, immediately ordering brandy. There has been a phonecall, from London, asking if Gal is 'definitely retired', even for a 'no-risk' job. He is, of course, definitely. 'You've asked me and I've said no,' he says, evenly. 'That's it. So why are we still talking?' Jackie's lips twitch twice before she answers, 'It was Don Logan.'

The camera takes a perceptible step back, Deedee mutters, 'Oh Christ!', and Gal grips the table. It is a wonderful moment, shot like a Mexican stand-off. Logan is coming over tomorrow, it transpires, a done deal, and Gal's thoughts turn from dinner to a distracted eulogy for his new life. He says how much he loves this restaurant, his wife, his pool. That it is everything he dreamed of when he was in prison. 'No risk?' he almost cracks. 'No fucking risk? Nine years of my fucking life, no fucking risk!' He looks to the menu as if for wisdom, but finds only calamari, his fate sealed.

While the plot displays the hallmarks of 'gangster heavy' tragedy, how it plays out is pure Britpop cinema. Once Logan appears – the snarling embodiment of Angry Small Man Syndrome[16] – his profanity-strewn, ever-expanding flashbacks have the effect of concertina-ing time, as in *Trainspotting* (Boyle, 1996). 'I know a bloke who knows a bloke who knows a bloke. Now, you know this bloke,' he begins. 'Do I?' asks Gal. 'This is a bloke you know.'

Logan then details how his boss, the London gangster Teddy Bass (Ian McShane), met the manager of a private bank (James Fox) at an orgy, and plans to rob his top-secret facility. But the story unfolds in tense back-and-forths taking place between different characters in at least three different time-zones, a flashback within a flashback within a flashback. It is an extraordinary piece of writing/editing and, set to a throbbing bass, creates tension where there should not be any, the events having already transpired. There is also an unsettling sense of inevitability; that what has happened, and what will happen, are set in stone.

So far, so gangster heavy, albeit with a rare lightness of touch, but Glazer has a flare for abstract imagery, as shown in his music videos[17] for the likes of Radiohead and Blur. A cobalt-blue, day-for-night dream sequence shows Gal dining alone in the desert as a monstrous rabbit rides up on horseback and threatens him with a machine gun. As with Don Logan's reappearance, the rabbit seems to represent the return of the repressed (no doubt inspired by that disastrous hunting trip), and will crop up at moments of existential tension throughout.[18]

Meanwhile, Ivan Bird's glorious camerawork helps even the more mundane material soar. As the boulder starts to gather momentum, we watch it rolling down the hill from its own POV. Later, when Bass leaves the bank having planted explosives in a safety-deposit box, the camera turns 360 degrees, apparently mounted to the revolving door. Once the robbery is underway we spin back to this moment, moving in tight on Bass's face, then seemingly through his skull, along the street, through the foyer of the bank and into the vault. Here the explosives will trigger a flood from the Turkish baths next door, so Gal and co can carry out a daring underwater raid. It is an exciting, elegant piece of cinema, and while much of the film emphasizes how Gal is trapped, sequences like this speak of freedom, opening up different Pandora's boxes of possibility. Says producer Jeremy Thomas, now: 'The film itself was so unusual, it could never be thought of as being TV, it could only be film, Jonathan made a very cinematic film' (2016).

These elements confirm the film's place in the Britpop cinema cannon, but like *Trainspotting*, *Shallow Grave* (Boyle, 1995) and *Billy Elliot* (Daldry, 2000), *Sexy Beast* is so much more than the sum of its parts. As Thomas notes, Mellis and Scinto's dialogue, all rat-a-tat repetition and poetic profanity, is 'so incredible, it takes the film out of the ordinary into the extraordinary'. Kingsley agreed: 'It is unique in structure, relying, like Beckett or Pinter, on the rhythm of the words' (Goodall 2011: 154). Indeed, few actors could make the line, 'You're the fucking problem you fucking Dr White honkin' jam-rag fucking spunk bubble!' sound like Shakespeare.

In a canny piece of counterintuitive casting we see Kingsley, better known for playing nobler roles, tormenting the peace-loving Winstone, perhaps the ultimate Britpop cinema bloke. As the latter put it: 'This can't be right – he's Gandhi' (Goodall 2011: 157). Explains Thomas:

> There's a special alchemy where the actors find you or you find the actors. Instead of Ray Winstone finding Don Logan, he found Gal, and instead of Ben Kingsley finding Gal, he found Don Logan. It was a very clever twisting around of casting to give the film a special flavour because Ben Kingsley brought something incredible to Don Logan and Ray brought something incredible to Gal, a sort of sweetness, which he has.

Glazer agreed: 'Even though Ray's character is a criminal, I wanted him to play against that type, to strip away his macho side and show the vulnerability of Gal' (Goodall 2011: 152). The results are mesmerizing, as if gangster heavy wants to show gangster light what real evil looks like.

By any reckoning, Kingsley's performance is one of the era's standouts.[19] With the sleek, perfectly shaved head of a man with no time for the frivolity of hair, and a short-sleeved shirt that speaks not of comfort, but efficiency, Logan inhabits his body with lock-jawed tension, moves like a heat-seeking missile and speaks by sublimating violence into words. 'Not this time, Gal. Not this time. Not this fucking time. No. No no no no no no no no no!' he rants, a human Bren gun. 'I liked his purity, his singularity' (Goodall 2011: 154), said Kingsley, who based the character on his maternal grandmother. 'She was an extremely violent and unpleasant woman,' he told IFC's *Escape from Hollywood*. 'She was racist, fascist and anti-Semitic. When I play great heroic Jews… I'm sticking two fingers up at her. When I played Don Logan, I was channelling her' (Anastasia and Macnow 2013).

Like Old Mother Kingsley, there is little to redeem Logan, a human so swaddled in hate, he degrades everything he touches, whether pissing on Gal's floor or accusing innocent airplane staff of touching his 'front bottom'. In the indolent Spanish sun, he is a thunderstorm made flesh; a man who brings only pain and, unable to stop himself, has learned to thrive off the discomfort he causes. Recalls Thomas:

> I remember his first day on set, the first scene we shot, the fantastic costume designer Louise Stjernsward and Jonathan got him this costume that made him look really powerful, that

> shirt with the short sleeves, those shoes, the way he walked through that airport. When it came to lunch break I went into the canteen and Ben Kingsley was sitting by himself at one end and the entire crew were pressed into a corner down the other. They were all completely terrified by him, he already put out that strength of character: don't mess.

In fact, it is not fear that differentiates the film from *Lock, Stock* and the softer Britpop cinema offerings, but love. For all his twistedness, Don has come to Spain to see Jackie, for whom he carries a torch (or perhaps it is for Gal). 'Don't say nothing, but I quite liked her,' he sniffs, shy in the face of sudden vulnerability, although this quickly becomes, 'I fucked her!' when challenged. Indeed, Don seems more obsessed with upsetting the foursome's equilibrium than actually getting Gal to do the job. 'I won't let you be happy, why should I?' he spits at one point, like a spurned suitor. But Gal has found something Logan cannot begin to comprehend, let alone compromise. When Don brings up 'dirty' Deedee's past as a porn star, Gal's rebuttal is touchingly direct: 'I love her with all my heart.'

Glazer finds some imaginative ways to visualize the intensity of these feelings: those interlinked hearts at the bottom of the pool, Deedee framed by a heart-shaped smoke ring; a swoony kiss that has them, briefly, swimming in the stars. 'Usually I get to punch the geezer, not kiss the girl,' said Winstone (Goodall 2011: 153). As if to prove the point, when Don finally attacks, it is Deedee and Aitch who kill him, although we don't learn exactly what has happened until the end of the film.

In London, the job goes without a hitch, even though Teddy Bass suspects foul play, and Gal escapes to enjoy a typically uncertain Britpop cinema coda. Gal, Deedee, Aitch and Jackie chat contentedly by the pool, paradise restored except for a nagging voice in Gal's head. 'You were right Don,' he says. 'Technically speaking you were right. But you're dead. So shut up!' As the improbably sunny 'Sway' by Dean Martin plays, recalling *Shallow Grave*'s use of 'Happy Heart', the camera burrows through those interlinked hearts on the bottom of the pool, into the bowels of the earth, where Don lies dead, buried and distinctly unimpressed. But he has finally met his match. Above him stands the rabbit, readying itself for violence, and with all eternity left to enact it.

Of the three films, *Lock, Stock* was by far the biggest success. Thanks to a typically aggressive PolyGram advertising campaign, it all but earned its budget back on its opening weekend, making almost £12 million at the UK box office (IMDB 2018c). Says Moran:

> It got to be No.1 simply because, and no one was willing to admit this, simply because it was really good. And that's all there is to it. There's no magical fucking spells involved. It's just really good. And if you make another really good film it will be a tremendous success, instead of something that does an impersonation of a really good film.

Both Film4 releases, and both critically praised, *Gangster No. 1* and *Sexy Beast* could not hope to keep up. While the former underwhelmed financially, making under £0.5 million worldwide (IMDB 2018b), the latter did respectable business at $10 million (IMDB 2018e), despite its hard-to-translate dialogue and innumerable swearwords. Said Glazer:

> The film took so long in post-production… you saw the British public growing progressively more and more bored of British gangster films. But we were always at least confident in that the film was a psychodrama which really could have taken place in the court of King Arthur if it had to. It's more of a character duel, really. It's a film for me that happens within the genre, rather than about the genre. That's the key.
>
> (Goodall 2011: 159)

Recalls McGuigan:

> I was really concerned about making a gangster movie because of all the fucking terrible ones that had been made previous to *Sexy Beast* and *Gangster No. 1*. You know, of that era, tonally we got it wrong in the 1990s. They forgot what was interesting about those movies from the 1960s and 1970s, they were very working class, very real, a real sense of people and the violence was very real, they weren't trying to be cool and cheeky-chappy-ish, they weren't trying to do a sort of 1990s-era Danny Boyle *Trainspotting* rip-off. They were looking at the movies around them rather than the movies that had gone past, you know, that we as filmmakers grew up watching.

Not that the British film industry was listening. Soon there would be a glut of gangster knock-offs, starring anyone with an equity card and a passable London accent. *You're Dead* (Hurst, 1999) featured the late, great John Hurt robbing banks with a dubiously Cockney Rhys Ifans; *Circus* (Walker, 2000) saw TV presenter Brian Conley battling comedian Eddie Izzard to be Brighton's top boy; *Love, Honour and Obey* (Anciano and Burdis, 2000) posited a London underworld where everyone was famous, but nobody convincing; *Honest* (Stewart, 2000), a universe in which All Saints could act. The offspring of Ritchie rather than Glazer, these films featured postmodern narration instead of actual performances, a cacophony of laddish anecdotes in place of a convincing story, and began to give Britpop cinema a bad name. In other words, they looked nice, even if they lacked in criminal credibility. And sometimes not even that.

What Happened Next…

Guy Ritchie and Matthew Vaughn… Made the similar but starrier *Snatch* (Ritchie, 2000) before parting company. Ritchie married Madonna and began a string of cinematic missteps, beginning with the rom-com *Swept Away* (2002), while Vaughn directed *Layer Cake* (2004), a gangster film so upmarket it nabbed lead Daniel Craig the job as the new 007. Today, both make anglicized blockbusters such as *Kingsman: The Secret Service* (Vaughn, 2015) and *Sherlock Holmes* (Ritchie, 2009).

Lock, Stock... Continued as a TV show produced by DJ Chris Evans' Ginger Productions (2000), and starring *Human Traffic*'s Shaun Parkes as Bacon. But the film's locker-room laddishness had given way to outright misogyny. 'She was well into it,' claims Jamie (Scott Maslen) of an unnamed conquest, 'and anyway, she dropped the charges'. The results were, to use the lingo, irretrievably pony.

Nick Moran... Came back to earth with a crash. 'We thought we were pop stars,' he says now, 'but we weren't even buskers.' He spent his own money touring the meta-textual head-scratcher *Christie Malry's Own Double-Entry* (Tickell, 2000), round the country, to confused reviews. 'I look at *Lock, Stock* and that tremendous success and the kismet, the balance for that, is *Christie Malry* and its lack of exposure,' he says. 'It would have been great to have done another bunch of successful films and be sat by a kidney-shaped swimming pool in LA, but I don't give a fuck what anyone says, people can take the piss and do whatever they want, I was the lead in *Lock, Stock* and you weren't. That's it. What are you gonna do about that? Fucking nothing. Jog on.'

The *Gangster* trilogy... Finished with Mellis and Scinto's *44 Inch Chest* (Venville, 2009), a strange, slightly stagey evisceration of East End masculinity starring Winstone, McShane and Hurt. McGuigan, meanwhile, went to Hollywood to make the smart, post-Tarantino thriller *Lucky Number Slevin* (2006), before returning to direct episodes of the BBC's exuberant *Sherlock* (2010–17, UK: BBC). Glazer confounded expectations with the controversial drama *Birth* (2004), and the unsettling sci-fi *Under the Skin* (2014), perhaps the furthest marker from Britpop cinema imaginable. Thomas continues to champion offbeat auteurs such as Jim Jarmusch and David Cronenberg.

PolyGram... Died a lonely death in 1999, when it was unceremoniously sold to Seagram, a drinks company. In just ten years, this plucky upstart had made an unparalleled success of *Four Weddings* (Newell, 1994), *Shallow Grave*, *Trainspotting*, *Spice World* (Spiers, 1997) and *Lock, Stock*, among others. Says Kuhn: 'We always aimed to have a door that you could knock on, in the UK, and get any reasonably sized film made with one "yes", and [ensure] that the people you did that deal with could actually take it and then market it for you. That was the dream.' Andrew Macdonald was just one beneficiary. 'It was like working with an American studio but they were British. They pushed the boat out and made you feel confident, and that's ultimately what we needed,' he says. 'It was a sad day, but you have to move on,' says Kuhn now, 'Who else had the chance to build up a studio?' The short answer is, nobody. Britpop cinema had lost its greatest sponsor.

Notes

1 Mixing film and long-form TV work, Bird made issue-based dramas for the BBC such as *Safe* (1993), about homeless Londoners, and *Priest* (1994), also starring Carlyle, about

homosexuality in the Catholic church. Her time in Hollywood produced the historical horror *Ravenous* (1999), starring Carlyle and Guy Pearce, with an experimental score by Damon Albarn and Michael Nyman. She died of thyroid cancer at the age of 62.

2 Itself 'borrowed' from Hong Kong action flick *City on Fire* (Lam, 1987).

3 This is an estimate. IMDB puts the budget at £960,000 (estimated); Wikipedia at £800,000 with no citation; *Your Face Here* suggests a neat £1 million. Anecdotal evidence from Nick Moran and Michael Kuhn suggests this figure is more-or-less accurate, but that costs incurred in post-production have muddied the waters.

4 After Keith Allen, Harper should probably be considered the poster boy of Britpop cinema, playing London geezers in *Tube Tales* (various, 1999), *Kevin & Perry Go Large* (Bye, 2000), *Goodbye Charlie Bright* (Love, 2001), *The Football Factory* (Love, 2004) and *This Is England* (Meadows, 2007), among others.

5 Statham was an Olympic diver turned model turned street vendor who Ritchie made a documentary about. 'Jason sold me two hundred pounds' worth of gold… [which went] from gold to stainless steel overnight,' he told Edward Champion of 24fps.com, 'Jason refused to return my money. But he did it so tactfully that I felt that this was the kind of character I'm interested in' (Catterall and Wells 2002: 263).

6 The ending, for example, is a straight lift from the (literal) cliff-hanger closing *The Italian Job* (Collinson, 1969).

7 In an interview with the author for *King Arthur: Legend of the Sword* (Ritchie, 2017), Law was asked about this rumour, replying: 'I wasn't going to be in it, I was approached. The first time I met Guy was in a cafe we had, rather suitably, a fry-up one morning and a pot of tea, very English, and he told me about *Lock, Stock*. I don't remember what happened. I think I was going off to do [*The Talented Mr*] *Ripley* that summer so I couldn't do it...'

8 Ritchie is, perhaps understandably, touchy about the influence of *Trainspotting* on his work, but provides a rather neat summary of Britpop cinema in the following repudiation. 'Danny Boyle I have no interest in whatsoever. However, I respect the fact that he turned what I saw were rather miserable English films that didn't deserve the cinema [into films that] suddenly deserved the cinema. And they did, they had an identity – most English films don't. And that became obvious. I hate films about things like heroin addicts. I just didn't fucking want to know. I want to know about funny things, I don't want to know about miserable fucking things' (White 1998).

9 Monk credits this astute observation to her student Claire Meeghan.

10 Jones was found guilty of causing actual bodily harm and criminal damage during an argument with his neighbour Timothy Gear over the removal of a stile. Mr Gear accused Jones of biting, punching and stamping on him (BBC 1998c).

11 Also the title of one of Jones' memoirs and a tattoo he has across his back, according to the aforementioned book (Jones 2013).

12 In *Macbeth* terms, Mays is the equivalent of King Duncan, a role Thewlis played in Justin Kurzel's harrowing 2015 adaptation.

13 Peter Bowles was the well-spoken star of TV's *To the Manor Born* (1979–81, UK: BBC). McGuigan suggests that Jonathan Glazer was originally in the frame to direct *Gangster* instead of *Sexy Beast*.

14 Foreman's father, Freddie Foreman, was an associate of the Krays, and served ten years for helping to dispose of the body of Jack 'The Hat' McVitie, whose murder was dramatized in *The Krays*.
15 Cavan Kendall died of cancer aged 57 before the film came out. The closing credits feature the dedication, 'Good-bye, sweet Cavan.'
16 Angry Small Man Syndrome afflicts the likes of Begbie and Napoleon and can prove fatal.
17 Notable efforts include Blur's 'The Universal' (1995), which warns of a coming dystopia and nods to *A Clockwork Orange*; and Radiohead's 'Street Spirit' (1995), a beautiful black-and-white ballet of stop-start imagery and slow/fast frame rates that matches the song's free-flowing finger-picking.
18 Interestingly, oversized animals representing warning figures/paranoid delusions were something of a millennial motif. Jake Gyllenhaal has visions of Frank, a man in a monstrous bunny costume, in *Donnie Darko* (Kelly, 2001). In *It's All Gone Pete Tong* (Dowse, 2004), meanwhile, DJ Paul Kaye is menaced by a nightmarish 'coke badger' in a tutu, which looks for all the world like Courtney Love in mustelid form.
19 Apparently Winstone showed the script to Gary Oldman, an intriguing, if more traditional, choice for the Don Logan role (Godfrey 2000).

Chapter 8

Chemical World

Starring: *Human Traffic* (Kerrigan, 1999)

Chapter 8: Chemical World

Drugs, *Human Traffic* and the Ecstasy generation

TV interviewer (Nicola Heywood-Thomas): Why do you come to these nights?
Lulu (Lorraine Pilkington): I'd like to answer that one if I may.
Nina (Nicola Reynolds): Sure.
Lulu: To get absolutely trashed!
TV interviewer: Do you take Ecstasy?
Lulu: No, no, well we used to, but now we just jack up heroin and float round the club.
TV interviewer: You take heroin to come to the club?
Lulu: Well we never used to, but then we saw *Trainspotting*...
Human Traffic

It was in 1999 that the Ecstasy generation's weekend finally landed. Besides stealthing on to *Top of the Pops* in the shape of The Shamen's 'Ebeneezer Goode' (1992), sample lyric: 'Eezer good, eezer good, 'e's Ebeneezer Goode', and Pulp's rave lament 'Sorted for E's and Whizz' (1995), there was little mainstream acknowledgement of artists' experiences in the (often literal) field. Step forward twentysomething film school graduate Justin Kerrigan, who set the record straight with one of Britpop cinema's most exuberant efforts...

The 1990s saw the counterculture becoming, simply, culture. Outsider indie bands who, in the 1980s, would have been happy filling the sticky-floored backrooms of Camden boozers were topping the charts; rave had been profitably co-opted by superclubs like Ministry of Sound; while works by the Young British Artists (YBAs), such as Damien Hirst's *The Physical Impossibility of Death in the Mind of Someone Living* (1991), aka the shark in formaldehyde – its title an exhortation, albeit a pretentious one, to choose life – were making them millions rather than laughing stocks.

A similar process of public – if not acceptance, then softening – happened to the perception of illegal drugs. In the 1980s, an estimated 15–20 per cent of young people admitted to having tried illegal substances; by 1995, that figure had swollen to nearly half (Benedictus 2011). But while Britpop's biggest names dabbled in heroin,[1] and Oasis's Noel Gallagher joked about cocaine with Tony Blair[2] at No.10 Downing Street, Ecstasy use among 16- to 24-year-olds peaked in 1996 (Travis 2012).

Not that you would know it from the media. In 1995 the Ecstasy-related death of 18-year-old schoolgirl Leah Betts caused a tabloid furore.[3] In 1997, meanwhile, East 17's Brian Harvey was sacked for saying he had taken twelve Ecstasy tablets in one night (Wynn Davies 1997), not a claim even the 'streetwise Take That' could feasibly get behind. When quizzed by BBC Radio on the issue, Gallagher sprang to Harvey's defence, offering the famous quote that: 'Drugs is like getting up and having a cup of tea in the morning' (*The Independent* 1997).

While cocaine claimed the capital, not to mention celebrity scalps as diverse as *Blue Peter*'s Richard Bacon and Shadow from *Gladiators*, and Ecstasy use spread, seemingly outwards from Manchester's Haçienda club, media ire turned to irony. As the pupils of TV's *Grange Hill* had tunelessly entreated back in 1986, mainstream comedians Hale and Pace advised school children to, 'Just say no!' or, if they were privately educated, 'Just say no, thank you.' Chris Morris's TV satire *Brass Eye* (1997–2001, UK: Channel 4) took things even further. Inventing Cake, a 'made-up drug' that affected an area of the brain known as 'Shatner's Bassoon', he persuaded luminaries such as Noel Edmonds and Bernard Manning to decry it from the safety of their TV soapboxes, while poor David Amess MP was sufficiently suckered to ask a question about Cake in parliament. But even amid such eccentric outbursts, the scene's primetime TV debut took an unlikely form.

Directed by Danny Boyle, the 1992 *Inspector Morse* episode 'Cherubim & Seraphim' concerned illegal raves, experimental drugs and suicides, although it stopped several miles shy of the cutting edge. The climax sees Morse (John Thaw) and Lewis (Kevin Whatley) infiltrating a rave in Morse's trademark red Jag. 'We can't go in there, we'd stand out a mile,' sputters Morse. 'We're not even wearing trainers!' Lewis, meanwhile, dons a cap and gives himself over to the rhythm. 'Really gets you doesn't it?' he decides, tapping his feet like *The Mary Whitehouse Experience*'s embarrassing dad.[4] Morse, predictably, is less than impressed. An earlier scene has him donning headphones to listen to house music. 'That's the *Hallelujah Chorus*!' he notes in disgust. 'Conducted by Sir Adrian Boult!' ITV, apparently, were equally nonplussed. Said Boyle:

> They were horrified! Nobody really understood. I remember setting up this rave in a country house and getting a party crowd in who were all off their faces. These ITV producers came along and were totally bemused. John Thaw himself was very amused.
>
> (Raphael 2013: 30)

If Boyle had more empathy for the pillheads than the police, the one-off BBC drama *Loved Up* (1995), directed by *The Full Monty*'s Peter Cattaneo, went one step further. Starring Lena Headey and Ian Hart as young Londoners beginning a chemically enhanced clubland romance, it was well-intentioned if unavoidably of its time, featuring a soundtrack by Leftfield, an atypically fresh-faced Danny Dyer as a pill salesman, and Jason Isaacs (who played a rather suaver dealer in 'Cherubim & Seraphim') in a Kangol hat and none-more-1990s goatee. Recalls Cattaneo:

> It was the early 1990s, I was a film school graduate, so I knew a bit about going out in London and what everyone got up to. It was a great opportunity to tell it like it is, to give an honest portrayal of that culture without overglamorizing it or getting self-indulgent. No one wants to watch a film that feels like you're at a party where you're not on the drug that everyone else is on.
>
> (2017)

Thanks to funding from BBC Schools, the programme won a Children's Bafta, and an edited version (no smoking, no swearing, no sex) was shown in classrooms. 'I was glad there was something quite authentic out there,' says the director now.

Certainly, had those same children watched *Blue Juice* (Prechezer, 1995) instead, they might have come away even more confused. One scene, showing the straight-laced Terry (Peter Gunn) enthusiastically licking a scone in a stately home, is perhaps the UK's first big-screen Ecstasy sequence. Recalls star Sean Pertwee:

> It was one of the funniest as well, where he chases cows, painted silver. Strangely enough he'd never tried it, I think he's the only person on the planet who never did a drug, or ever tried Ecstasy, so where that came from I don't know. Probably watching other people.
>
> (2016)

Human Traffic would require no such assistance. Based on writer/director Justin Kerrigan's own days (and nights) of dilated pupils and vibrating speakers, and produced by his former tutor, Allan Niblo, *Human Traffic* is a frank, funny, freewheeling spin through the Cardiff club scene, a Britpop cinema exemplar unashamed to trumpet the joys of being young and wasted. Said Danny Dyer, who made his film debut as part-time dealer Moff:

> *Trainspotting* had been out, and I remember being fascinated by just how raw it was… [But] *Human Traffic* was the other side: the partying, the joy and the Ecstasy, which was basically the world I was living in at the time… It's just about a group of people going out and getting fucked up. They've got shit jobs, they get off their nut, bit of a comedown, roll credits.
>
> (Mullinger and Sothcott 2013: 21)

It is a pithy summary. Over the course of a long, druggy weekend, the film follows (largely un-Welsh) twenty-somethings Jip (John Simm), his 'dropping partner' (and love interest)

Lulu, best friend Koop (Shaun Parkes) and his girlfriend, Nina, plus Moff, Nina's keen but green little brother Lee (Dean Davies), and various scenesters, hangers-on and wrong-uns (including Andrew Lincoln from *This Life*,[5] and Kerrigan himself) through some chemically enhanced ups and the attendant downs. The kicker? Nothing bad happens. A routine from US stand-up comic Bill Hicks playing in Jip's bedroom sums it up perfectly: 'I have taken drugs before and… I had a real good time. Sorry. Didn't murder anybody, didn't rape anybody, didn't rob anybody, didn't beat anybody, didn't lose – hmmm – one fucking job, laughed my ass off, and went about my day.' As *Guardian* critic Peter Bradshaw wrote, under a headline declaring him 'mad for it', 'this simple fact arguably makes this film more radical than *Trainspotting*' (1999).

Though the comparison still rankles with Kerrigan, *Human Traffic* seems to reference Boyle's film in its styling as well as its dialogue. Jip and the gang are introduced – like most characters of the Britpop cinema era – with title cards; freezeframes, slo-mo and visual ticks abound; and DJ Pete Tong's carefully curated soundtrack (featuring Underworld, Orbital, Fatboy Slim and Primal Scream) plus John Simm's conspiratorial voiceover, added during a troubled post-production, bring the disparate elements together. But in many ways it is more radical: a genuinely independent movie, a debut no less, made outside the system with private financing ('a handshake on a boat in Cannes' [Niblo 2016]), its maverick spirit intact. Meanwhile, where *Trainspotting* (Boyle, 1996) presents an ambivalent attitude to drugs – using the energy of MDMA to subvert the familiar heroin narrative – *Human Traffic* is positively effusive in its endorsement. According to Dyer:

> It's important to remember it was off the back of Leah Betts' tragic death, which the tabloids exploited, so it was very controversial. [But] *Human Traffic* was not condoning drugs, it was just stating the fact that millions of people take drugs, and they take drugs because they want to, and the majority of people have a good time.
>
> (Mullinger and Sothcott 2011: 22)

'It's a minor miracle we got the film made at all,' says Kerrigan now:

> If it were just down to the usual channels of the British film industry, it would never exist. We tried everywhere, we knocked on every door, and there were a few reasons: one was that I was very young and inexperienced, but the biggest was that there was no moral lesson to taking drugs. But what I was writing about was the truth, I'd spent years going to clubs and parties, meeting all different kinds of characters and getting into all kinds of states – both good and bad – but in all my experience I'd never seen anyone die or jump off a rooftop thinking they could fly or any of those PCP-style aspects of drug-taking. Basically I was just trying to write something that was truthful, and if I'd put someone dying in there at the end then it just wouldn't resonate with people.
>
> (2016)

Human Traffic did resonate with people, making its £2.2 million[6] budget back at the UK box office alone (IMDB 2018a) and gaining a US release from Miramax, albeit in a truncated 84-minute form (Ebert 2000). All the same, 'On set was chaos,' admits Kerrigan, who planned each scene meticulously only to watch those plans evaporate, forcing him to improvise at every turn. 'There was very little money to do anything, cameras went missing, actors went missing, things were cut without me knowing.' Explains producer Allan Niblo:

> It was a baptism of fire. It was way, way, way too ambitious for the money we had, so it was naivety on my behalf to believe that we could do it, plus a lack of experience all round: actually, it was a lot of people's first film. It was a battle every day to just keep afloat: we were thrown in the deep end – with waves – and told to swim, fast, to face every problem, just get through it.

Watching the no-holds-barred 'Making of' (Haynes, 1998), – at times a genuinely tense experience – offers some insight into the disorder on set. The production loses first assistant directors like Spinal Tap drummers; Richard Harrington's narration talks of 'mutinous' crews, 'fisticuffs' and 'heart attacks', with only the last one, apparently, figurative; and a clearly frazzled Kerrigan openly questions his own future in the business. 'Considering it's a bag of shite to work on, you'll probably have a good film,' offers one crew member helpfully. But while the chaos lends the film its improvised, anything-can-happen feel, so does another key factor. According to Dyer, at least: 'We were all off our fucking nut' (Mullinger and Sothcott 2013: 27).

Upon reading the script, Dyer felt it was 'basically a description of my life' (2011: 71). During the audition, he and Kerrigan chatted openly about drugs, a process more image-conscious actors did not put up with, or indeed, pass. When it came to the shoot, 'I had no problem going method at all – for the six-week shoot I was Moff, right on it 24 fucking seven…' recalled Dyer. 'It was a complete six weeks of debauchery and we managed to make a film in between. I hardly slept. I think I blinked twice.' His wages were £3,000, his bar bill £3,250 (2011: 76). Kerrigan is more diplomatic:

> I can't say who did what, but drugs were certainly used on set by certain actors in certain scenes… I don't have control over what anybody consumes and I certainly wasn't trying to make anybody take anything. What we were trying to do was make it as authentic as possible and I think the actors, in certain scenes, did indulge themselves in chemicals… it's difficult to say what scenes. But if you look at the film with that in mind it can be quite apparent.

Two contenders are Moff's free-associating cab monologue where, chewing and smoking, he regales the cabbie with a stream-of-consciousness invective on subjects ranging, rather speedily, from Martin Scorsese's *Taxi Driver* (1976) to Peter Andre's 'Jap's eye'. Says Cathy Smith, a 22-year veteran of the NHS's drug and alcohol treatment unit:

It's a very good depiction of stimulant use. Nowhere near Ewen Bremner's interview performance in *Trainspotting*, but the flights of fancy you go on were really well captured. Dyer wasn't quite sweaty enough, he wasn't agitated enough, but he does look bad, like he's been in airing cupboard. Another convincing scene is the bit in the club where the two girls get interviewed by the Kirsty Wark-type character. Their pupils looked like they would if they'd been on stimulants, or had contact lenses in.

(2016)

'The hard thing,' Dyer mused, 'was trying to time your E for when the camera started to roll… to be off your nut at the right time. But what other job are you going to be able to do that?' Not writer/director, that's for sure. Although Dyer claimed, 'Justin won't mind me saying this, but he'd turn up for work on half an E' (Mullinger and Sothcott 2011: 27–28), Kerrigan, it transpires, does mind:

Oh no, god no, there was no way. I remember because it was so intense on my first couple of night shoots, because of the exhaustion, it gets kind of trippy, you know, because you're so tired and trying to concentrate. And I remember thinking, 'Thank god I've been through some big comedowns so that I could get through this.' So no, I had to be sober, 100 per cent, I had to be clear. I couldn't even have a joint on set. That would be hell, I can't imagine anything worse.

Niblo dismisses Dyer's claims outright:

On a complex schedule – for a low-budget film there were 56 locations, lots of extras, we shot on 35mm, not digital, so we had two 35mm cameras, all these club scenes. The actors had to be at the top of their game, there was no room to be out of their minds or getting their lines wrong, they needed to be focused. The young actors recognized that it was a chance for them, and they gave it everything. I think people watch the film and they're so convincingly off their heads that people think they're on drugs, and it becomes apocryphal after that.

A notable exception was Howard Marks, the well-known marijuana advocate whose 1996 autobiography *Mr Nice* seemed to grace every student bedside of the era, and who has a brilliantly canny cameo. Amid the after-party fug, Marks appears like a grizzled fairy godfather to preach the intricate politics of spliff passing – something he knew a fair bit about as a convicted smuggler. Recalls Kerrigan:

We arranged to try and sneak in a little bit of rehearsal about an hour before the shoot, upstairs in the mansion where we filmed the party scene – and Howard was very stoned. We kept on running the lines and he kept on losing it and laughing. It was very funny but it had a real edge for me, because he was getting more and more stoned. There was

> great energy, the feeling was there, but I remember closing the door and just being very concerned about what we were about to shoot. But take one, we roll the cameras and Howard nailed it, then he nailed it again and again and again. He was incredibly professional without taking himself seriously in the build-up. And we had a line of students all rolling him joints because they had to be the same size on each different take. I think it was something like 18 joints – and they were all real – he wouldn't use a prop.

Besides appearances from comedian Jo Brand as the voice of Reality, and DJ Carl Cox as a fearsome club owner, *Human Traffic* fizzes with ideas: comedy see-what-they-really-think subtitles (borrowed from *Annie Hall* [Allen, 1977]); songs (including *That's Paranoia!* and alternative national anthem *Who Is the Queen?*); and skits, such as when *Brass Eye*-alike newsreader Jeremy Faxman (Mark Seaman) roams the club, asking, 'What's your name? What have you had?' before signing off, 'Reach for the lasers. Safe as fuck!' Not everything works – a breakdancing insert looks a little *Ali G* these days – but the film's enthusiasm is infectious, its characters people you actually want to hang out with, rather than, as in *Trainspotting*, hang on your wall.

For the most part, *Human Traffic* is about interaction rather than ingestion – we never even see anyone taking pills. 'Usually in films about drug culture you see the obligatory shot of the geezer with the E in his mouth putting it in his bird's mouth,' said Dyer. 'It's all bullshit that.' Clearly nobody told Sick Boy, who does exactly this in *Trainspotting*. Equally, a scene with Jipp and Koop pushing coke around a mirror, shot, ingeniously, from below, is predicated on them chatting so much they fail to snort it. 'It wasn't a real line,' clarified Dyer, 'or it might not have survived the retakes' (2011: 78).

Another tricky scene showed Moff being caught masturbating by his mother (Carol Harrison). According to Dyer, this was originally supposed to include a fantasy threesome sequence between Moff and two beautiful actresses, but budgetary restrictions meant the services of two Cardiff prostitutes were procured instead.

'The idea of it being a fantasy just didn't work because they were too fucking rough,' he said, 'I don't like blokes who dig women out over their looks but there comes a point when you have to call a minger a minger.' Instead he had to finish the scene off solo, pretending to masturbate with a prosthetic hard-on. 'I had about three or four hours of that… tugging one off for a whole afternoon while the crew stood about drinking coffee and scratching their arses,' he recalled (2011: 79–80). If the crew were unimpressed, his mother and grandmother, who he took to the premiere, were presumably even less so.

Dyer's blushes aside, the film does not judge anyone for the drugs they take, only the bullshit they spout. The old-timers complaining how things are not what they used to be when, as evidenced by a dancefloor flashback to the so-called Summer of Love 1991, they clearly are (albeit with fewer whistles). The record-store dupe taken in by Koop's vinyl-peddling patter: 'This was recorded by a posse of crackheads on Death Row,' he twinkles, 'they call themselves the Itchy Trigger Finger Niggas.' The dribbling 3am drug chat, such as when Moff and Andy (a young Richard Coyle from the *Pusher* remake [Prieto, 2012]) expound their alternative readings of *Star Wars* (Lucas, 1977): 'What about The Emperor, yeah, the king crackhead of the galaxy?' says Moff. 'He's got so much fucking hard cash from selling crack to space junkies he's only gone and built his own planet!' But even these scenes are fond ones, because Kerrigan, you know, has been there too.

At the start of the decade, free parties such as 1992's Castlemorton, which saw 20,000 people descend on the Malvern hills for a seven-day Ecstasy-fuelled rave (Lynskey 2011), started to be shut down in *Daily Mail*-ish panic. This culminated in 1994's much-mocked Criminal Justice and Public Order Act, which outlawed gatherings based around 'sounds wholly or predominantly characterized by the emission of a succession of repetitive beats.' In solidarity, *Human Traffic* opens with archive footage of policemen bashing heads, among other things, with wide-eyed ravers at the 1994 Criminal Justice and Public Order Act demos. It's a piece of legislation that still incenses Kerrigan:

> The CJA stipulated that no more than ten people can dance in a field to repetitive beats in this country, which is pure insanity. And the only reason is because the government wasn't making the money out of those people, other people were. But they were taking away people's freedom to dance and that's criminal.

For many, the rave scene was a direct rejection of such conservative values. Said Boyle, 'The spirit of it was incredible. It was clearly an antidote to Thatcherism. It was blindingly obvious: people were determined to share their experiences, find an alternative to right-wing individualism and competitiveness' (Raphael 2011: 30). Haçienda founder Tony Wilson, whose story is dealt with in *24 Hour Party People* (Winterbottom, 2002), saw it even more plainly: 'There were no moral questions: it was the politics of joy' (Harris 2003: 14).

As with much of Britpop cinema, *Human Traffic*'s politics are personal, its radicalism gentle, such as the comic back-and-forth between Jip and an imaginary doctor (Eilian Wyn) delineating the risks of taking Ecstasy (serotonin depletion, overheating, palpitations) versus the benefits (empathy, intimacy, honesty). 'Statistically, you're more likely to die from choking on a cabbage leaf or an argument in a pub than you are from dropping an E,' says Jip channelling Kerrigan (the latter proving especially true in one of *Trainspotting*'s pubs). 'Alcohol kills 30,000 people a year alone in Britain. But that's all right because that's a good taxable drug.' The doctor counters with: 'Your penis will shrivel up, and you won't be able to get an erection.' Jip, himself suffering 'from an extreme case of Mr Floppy', just looks sheepish.

Whether Jipp's sexual hang-ups are caused by drugs or, as is also implied, Oedipal discomfort with his mum (Helen Griffin) working as a prostitute, it is Ecstasy's confessional nature that enables him to open up to Lulu – not ostensibly the greatest of pulling tactics, but one that reaps dividends for them both. This is drugs not just normalized, like Noel Gallagher's cup of tea, but applauded. An acknowledgement that they might have a purpose; that they might fuck you up less than the things that caused you to take them in the first place. Says Jip in a long, pilled-up monologue:

> Warm rush of chemicals through us. We fluctuate. Is this brain damage? We forget all the pain and the hurt in life. We wanna go somewhere else. We're not threatened by people anymore. All our insecurities have evaporated. We're in the clouds now. We're wide open. We're spacemen orbiting the earth. The world looks beautiful from here, man… I wish this was real… Heh, yeah, hang on, what the fuck was I just talking about?

But even as it remains aware of its ridiculousness, *Human Traffic* respects the sanctity of chemical closeness. Unlike Renton et al, who are always seconds away from screwing each other over, Jip, Koop and the rest are genuine friends who care about one another, and want to see each other succeed. Explains Kerrigan:

> It's a love story essentially. Thats the theme of the film, it's about people who love each other and they take a love drug. At that time, I used to go out on my own, and I met a whole new group of friends going to raves, clubs and parties, most of whom are still good friends today. I think it [Ecstasy] did a lot of good. There were good and bad aspects of the scene to be sure, but at the time, for me, and what I was trying to capture by writing *Human Traffic*, was that there was a real feeling of togetherness.

This spirit of inclusivity envelops the characters, and the audience, like an MDMA embrace. In *Trainspotting*, poor Alison (Susan Vidler) is not even named until baby Dawn dies, about 45 minutes in; Lulu and Nina on the other hand are strong, sexually confident women, whose friendship more than passes the Bechdel Test.[7] Jip and Lulu, meanwhile, begin a relationship based as much on mutual affection as it is on rampaging body chemistry. Says the writer/director:

> The film is about people trying to enjoy life with all the shit that tries to drag you down. They just have this little window at the weekend where they're forgetting about their shit jobs or their problems with their families, their insecurities, their paranoias and frustrations and anxieties in life. They're just saying fuck it, let's go out and try and enjoy ourselves and not hurt anyone.

According to Smith:

> Maybe it's not even about choice, but the lack of choice for a certain echelon of society. If you haven't got a degree or any ambition in a country that has lost its primary industries you're going to be left with a service culture. If you are doing that all day, every day, then you probably are going to want to get off your tits every Friday/Saturday night… it's the contemporary equivalent of coming out of the pit and going to the pub isn't it?

In this way the film speaks for an entire generation, let down by their parents and prospects, and turning to tribal togetherness instead. As Kerrigan puts it:

> The message is a simple one: choose love. Before fear, before money, before corporations and lies and manipulated media and all the rest of the fucking shit you can burn. It's only love, that's what it's all about.

What Happened Next...

Drugs in Britpop cinema... Despite the success of *Trainspotting* and *Human Traffic*, drugs remained surprisingly scarce in Britpop cinema, although cocaine regularly pops up in gangster flicks such as *Layer Cake* (Vaughn, 2004) and *The Business* (Love, 2005). Gillies MacKinnon's socio-realist *Pure* (2003) explores the relationship between a heroin-addicted mother (Molly Parker) and her son (Harry Eden), and features an early role for Keira Knightley, but its primary concern is parenting rather than pharmaceuticals. In terms of Ecstasy, the eccentric, Soho-set thriller *Sorted* (Jovy, 2000) features Tim Curry as a Shakespeare-spouting villain and Australian soap star Jason Donovan as a chemically savvy transvestite, but the results are as far from convincing as they are from boring. The cheap-and-cheerful *Club Le Monde* (Rumley, 2002) affectionately lampoons the many indignities of the 1990s club scene. Ignore that atrocious title and *It's All Gone Pete Tong* (Dowse, 2004) is a sophisticated story of a coke-addled Ibiza DJ going deaf. Featuring a ferocious central performance by Paul Kaye (aka TV's Dennis Pennis) it is comfortably the best film about DJing ever made.

Howard Marks... Continued to campaign for the legalisation of cannabis, publishing books such as *The Howard Marks Book of Dope Stories* (2001); cameoing in films like *Dirty Sanchez* (Hickey, 2006); and collaborating with Welsh stoners the Super Furry Animals, among others. The film adaptation of *Mr Nice* (Rose, 2010) starred his good friend Rhys Ifans (*Twin Town*). Marks died of colon cancer on 10 April 2016.

Allan Niblo... Formed Vertigo Films, one of the most successful British production companies of the era, responsible for the films of Nick Love, *It's All Gone Pete Tong* and Gareth Edwards' gorgeous *Monsters* (2010) among others. In 2002, he released an alternative producer's cut on DVD, called *Human Traffic Remixed*, which caused a fall-out with Kerrigan. In May 2016, they spoke for the first time in over a decade.

Danny Dyer... Faced his own battles with drugs, not least experimenting with crack while appearing in Harold Pinter's *Celebration* on Broadway in 2000 (Dyer 2011: 118). After *Human Traffic*, his career took off with scene-stealing parts in *Greenfingers* (Hershman, 2000) and *Mean Machine* (Skolnick, 2001). But it would take another reformed addict, the writer/director Nick Love, to redeem him with roles in *Goodbye Charlie Bright* (Love, 2001) and *The Football Factory* (Love, 2004). On 16 May 2016, Dyer, now safely ensconced in *EastEnders*, tweeted: 'Moff. One of my favourite characters. That's all I'm saying on the matter.'

Justin Kerrigan… Like many of Britpop cinema's brightest lights, Justin Kerrigan was almost persuaded over to America by Miramax, but ended up becoming 'the Terrence Malick of South Wales' (Bevan 2013), spending years raising the funds for his follow-up film, the highly personal mental-health drama *I Know You Know* (2008). Despite starring *Trainspotting*'s Robert Carlyle, 'It made about £4.50 at the box office,' Kerrigan told Bevan. 'No one saw it.' In May 2016, one day before Danny Dyer's tweet, Kerrigan broke the news that *Human Traffic 2* was written and ready to go to this – very proud – author. The Ecstasy generation waits with baited breath.

Notes

1 As far back as 1993's 'So Young,' Suede had been romanticizing heroin, with lyrics like, 'So young / And so gone / Let's chase the dragon.' Beautifully sparse B-side 'The Living Dead' (1994) paints a more plaintive picture of a love lost to narcotics: 'Where's all the money gone? / I'm talking to you / All up the hole in your arm / Is the needle a much better screw? / But oh what will you do alone? / Because I have to go.' Singer Brett Anderson would later admit to crack and heroin usage (Duerden 2003). The words to Blur's 'Beetlebum' (1997), meanwhile, seem to point to their rumoured drug dalliances – 'chasing the beetle' is another term for smoking heroin.

2 At a No.10 Downing Street meet-and-greet, Gallagher asked the PM how he managed to stay up all night during New Labour's victorious 1997 election. 'Probably not by the same means as you did,' was Blair's knowing answer (Harris 2003: 343–44).

3 On 11 November 1995, Essex-born teenager Betts fell into a coma after taking Ecstasy, and drinking seven litres of water. She died on 16 November, and became a figurehead for anti-drug campaigners. One poster read: 'Sorted: Just one Ecstasy tablet took Leah Betts.' The pop group Chumbawamba responded with an anti-poster that read: 'Distorted: you are just as likely to die from eating a bay leaf as from an Ecstasy tablet' (Blackman 2004: 172).

4 *The Mary Whitehouse Experience* (1990–92, UK: BBC2) was a TV sketch show showcasing the work of David Baddiel, Hugh Dennis, Rob Newman and Steve Punt. Among other grotesques (including a spoof of Suede), it included Hugh Dennis's dancing dad and his catchphrase: 'What's this? It's got a good beat.'

5 Created by Amy Jenkins, who also wrote some of the dialogue for 'Cherubim & Seraphim', *This Life* (1996–97, UK: World Productions) was one of the best-loved TV dramas of the Britpop era, and featured songs by Blur, Pulp and Suede among others.

6 According to imdb.com, the film made just under £2.2 million in the United Kingdom, on a £2.2 million budget, not counting foreign territories and DVD sales (IMDB 2018a).

7 Named after American cartoonist Alison Bechdel, the Bechdel Test is a measure of movie sexism. To pass, a film has to feature two named female characters who talk to each other about something other than men. Only 57.7 per cent of the 7,513 films surveyed did. See http://bechdeltest.com/ for more.

Chapter 9

Anyone Can Play Guitar

Starring: *24 Hour Party People* (Winterbottom, 2002)

Chapter 9: Anyone Can Play Guitar

Music and musicians in Britpop cinema

Tony Wilson (Steve Coogan): 4 June, 1976. The Sex Pistols play Manchester for the very first time. There are only 42 people in the audience, but every single one of them is feeding on a power, an energy and a magic. Inspired, they will go out and perform wondrous deeds. For instance, Howard Devoto at the front, Pete Shelley at the back, they organized this gig. They're way ahead of everyone in Manchester. They're already the Buzzcocks. Howard later sleeps with my wife. Behind me are Stiff Kittens. Soon to become Warsaw, later to become Joy Division. Finally to become New Order. The gingernut? Mick Hucknall. That's John the Postman. He's, er, a postman.
24 Hour Party People

It is Lou Reed himself who starts the assault. Against a backdrop of chilly parks, rushing clouds and careful topiary, he tunelessly recalls that 'Perfect Day' long past. Next up: a neon Bono, a pirate Bowie, then the full gamut of inappropriate musical acts, each mangling a line of the song in their own distinctive styles, from opera to hip-hop via orgiastic oboe solo. As an advert it is great – no matter that the song's new-found fame is from *Trainspotting*'s overdose scene – as a cover version, terrible. Still they come, a gospel choir, M People and Tom Jones each putting the boot in, all irony and emotion obliterated in a screech of car-crash karaoke. When it finally finishes, the BBC thanks us for the music, as Reed holds his fingers to his lips to shush us, four minutes too late.

Until the 1990s, British music and film kept themselves broadly to themselves. There were notable scores, of course, such as the synthesized yearning of Vangelis's *Chariots of Fire* (Hudson, 1981) theme; effervescent musicals, from *Oliver!* (Reed, 1968) to *Absolute Beginners* (Temple, 1986); even the odd promo film such as *A Hard Day's Night* (Lester, 1964). Perhaps the closest fusion of the two were so-called 'rock operas' such as The Who's giddy, gaudy *Tommy* (Russell, 1975) and Pink Floyd's *The Wall* (Parker, 1982): essentially a 95-minute pop video of no little power, or indulgence. But for the most part, music and film were dancers at opposite ends of the same hall, only occasionally coming together, and rarely in step.

During the Britpop cinema era, thanks to Danny Boyle (not to mention Martin Scorsese and Quentin Tarantino), what had previously been an afterthought became an essential component and commodity. The songs of Lou Reed, Iggy Pop and Underworld, for example, elevated *Trainspotting* (Boyle, 1996) to such an extent that two separate soundtrack albums were released, comprising more than 150 minutes of music, from Bizet to Bowie. No matter that the film's runtime is just 93 minutes, or that some of the songs on the second album do not even feature. 'It was ventured that this was the kind of music *Trainspotting*'s cast of characters – and by extension the movie's audience – would be listening to,' wrote journalists Ali Catterall and Simon Wells of such opportunism (2002: 253), as if viewers might relish piling back to Renton's flat to peruse any un-pawned albums. The BBC certainly seemed to. In 1997 it released 'Perfect Day' as an ill-judged corporate video/Live Aid-style charity singalong.[1] True gluttons for punishment could also pick up soundtrack CDs for *Shooting Fish* (Schwartz, 1997), *Love, Honour and Obey* (Anciano and Burdis, 2000) and *Kevin & Perry Go Large* (Bye, 2000) to relive the fun in their own time.

A more entertaining offshoot of the 1990s' pop-cultural cross-bleed was the chance to watch the era's musicians continuing a long and dishonourable tradition[2] by attempting to act. With a cap pulled down over his eyes as if hiding from paparazzi, or just hungover, Blur's Damon Albarn appears as wannabe geezer Jason in *Face* (Bird, 1997): exactly the sort of try-hard toe-rag he had tired of singing about. Jason, we learn, was expelled from school for sleeping with a teacher ('I gave her one in the language lab,' he boasts, perhaps euphemistically) and has a constant drip-feed of dance music through his earphones. 'I suppose it's all just noise though, innit?' he reasons. 'So you don't have to think.' Co-star Phil Davis recalls the experience fondly:

> Damon was lovely, his band were at their peak then, hugely famous, but he was very humble. He's a very intelligent man, Damon, so he was watching very carefully what was going on, and stepping very carefully through the minefield of being an actor for the first time.
>
> (2016)

Which is not to say it was an entirely smooth process. 'I didn't turn up to the first day till really late because I tried to get out of the fact that I'd got involved in the film,' Albarn admitted on the DVD 'Making of'. 'But then my manager told me they'd probably sue me for lots of money so I turned up' (1997). To be fair, few debutants would relish going toe to toe with heavyweights such as Davis, Ray Winstone and Robert Carlyle – let alone all three – so it is hardly surprising Albarn was nervous. Says Davis:

> There were a couple of touchy moments. When he first joined us we did a bit of improvisation. He hadn't done that sort of thing before, and my character Julian bitterly resented him being there, this young kid. I was very hostile to him in this improvisation,

and poor Damon didn't like it, he wasn't used to people he was working with insulting him and treating him with utter disdain. We had to have a little chat afterwards, with me assuring him that this was Julian not liking his character, not Phil not liking Damon. It's an easy mistake to make!

Of the resulting film, Albarn declared himself 'not that embarrassed', then promptly resigned from acting forever. More excruciating for all concerned was *Honest* (Stewart, 2000), a 1960s-set gangster flick starring three-quarters of the girl group All Saints and directed/scored by ex-Eurythmic Dave Stewart, although it may as well have been Austin Powers. Sisters Nicole and Natalie Appleton and bandmate Melanie Blatt play East End siblings who dress up as men to commit a series of ineptly mounted robberies, failing to convince on just about every count. Indeed, the film's greatest achievements are (a) being arguably worse than *Spice World* (Spiers, 1997), and (b) making the 1960s look rubbish. When the Cannes premiere was halted by a teargas attack,[3] it was tempting to surmise that those evacuated were luckier than anyone who actually sat through it.

Just as musicians have always fancied themselves as actors; actors always want to play musicians, often with similarly calamitous results. A Britpop cinema film in all but nationality, the US/UK co-production *Velvet Goldmine* (Haynes, 1998) is a love letter to 1970s glam rock, scrawled in capitals, sealed with lipstick kisses and strewn with glitter. Inspired by the life of David Bowie, who refused permission to use his music (BBC 1998d), and borrowing the structure of *Citizen Kane* (Welles, 1941), who had no say in the matter, it tracks the rise and fall of metrosexual British rock-star Brian Slade (Jonathan Rhys Meyers channelling Bowie and Marc Bolan), aka Maxwell Demon,[4] and his American counterpart Curt Wild (Ewan McGregor, channelling Iggy Pop, Lou Reed and, accent-wise, Sean Connery) through the investigations of journalist Arthur Stuart (Christian Bale).

Amid the blur of quirk, pastiche and allusion – including music video make-believe, delirious sex scenes, and talking Barbie dolls[5] – the film's greatest trick goes all but unnoticed. Thanks to co-producer Michael Stipe of REM, it features contributions/cameos from a series of late 1990s Britpop/rock stars. Placebo appear as the Flaming Creatures singing T-Rex's '20th-Century Boy', while Slade's backing band, Venus in Furs, compromises guitarist Bernard Butler (formerly of Suede) plus Radiohead guitarist Jonny Greenwood and frontman Thom Yorke. McGregor does his own (awful) singing (and stripping, naturally), so one can only guess how bad Rhys Meyers' original vocals must have been to require Yorke's intervention. While nobody could fault Haynes for effort, the film is so extravagantly affected it remains a love-hate proposition. 'Although what you are about to see is a work of fiction, it should nevertheless be played at maximum volume,' entreats an opening intertitle. Or perhaps slightly quieter.

In such erratic company, *24 Hour Party People* stands out as a shining example of the subgenre, and Britpop cinema in general. A sprawling, spliffed-out history of the

Manchester music scene from mid-1970s punk to mid-1990s indie-dance, it takes the form of a breathless backstage tour narrated straight to camera by Tony Wilson (Coogan). Wilson (1950–2007) was a TV personality, Factory Records co-founder and the driving force behind the legendary Haçienda club, and the film presents him as a flawed egotist-come-folk hero, mining the difference between the two for affectionate laughs. More scuffed and shambling than *Trainspotting*, it is one of the most playfully postmodern efforts of the era, toying with notions of anarchy and authenticity in a way that, as one critic told producer Andrew Eaton, 'makes *This Is Spinal Tap* look like fiction' (2016).

Though he would likely resist the term, Winterbottom has proved the quiet maverick of the British film industry, flitting from genre to genre with, as journalist Simon Hattenstone put it, 'studied messiness' (2002) the only constant. Graduating from TV[6] around the same time as Danny Boyle, Winterbottom moved from twitchy lesbian serial-killer thriller *Butterfly Kiss* (1995), also written by *24 Hour Party People* scribe Frank Cottrell-Boyce, to the Robert Carlyle-starring multiple-sclerosis drama *Go Now* (1995), to the anti-heritage[7] *Jude* (1996), a period-set, but modern-seeming, adaptation of Thomas Hardy's pulverising *Jude the Obscure* starring Christopher Eccleston. In short succession, he then made the war film *Welcome to Sarajevo* (1997), the neo-noir *I Want You* (1998), the sex comedy *With or Without You* (1999) and the multi-faceted family drama *Wonderland* (1999). The latter, perhaps his best work of the 1990s, is a symphony of city life that beautifully captures the buzz – and the loneliness – of London.

Winterbottom and Eaton joined forces on *Go Now*, forming Revolution Films in 1994. But it was while scouting locations for *The Claim* (2000), an ambitious attempt to turn Hardy's *The Mayor of Casterbridge* into a snow-bound Western, that they hit upon the idea for *24 Hour Party People*. Recalls Winterbottom:

> We were in Canada, in an old mining town 400 miles north of Vancouver, and we were snowed in. We were this stuck in this godforsaken place, and we were in the bar with nothing to do, sitting round and it was just like, 'Why are we making this stupid bloody film about the gold rush?' It was 150 years ago, we don't know anything about it, it's nothing to do with us and it's really cold and unpleasant out there. Why don't we do something nice – and local – something that we know something about, something that can be indoors? That afternoon at the bar we thought, 'Why don't we do something about Tony Wilson and Factory Records, the Haçienda and Manchester?'
>
> (2016)

Says Eaton:

> With *The Claim*, we didn't want to make a straightforward Western, so with this we didn't want to make a straightforward traditional musical either. We liked the idea of having a story that had music in it rather than a film like *La La Land*, where people start singing.

The history of Factory Records is much documented – and disputed – but the basic facts are these. Inspired by the Sex Pistols, Wilson and right-hand man Alan Erasmus started an independent record label in 1978, with Martin Hannett producing and Peter Saville designing each release. Everything associated with Factory, from singles to lawsuits, was allocated a catalogue number, as if part of a gigantic art project. Its most notable act was Joy Division, who Wilson signed with a contract written in his own blood, on a napkin. The band's manager, Rob Gretton, was brought into the fray and, in 1982, Factory opened the Haçienda nightclub (FAC 51), a now-legendary Manchester money-pit effectively financed by New Order, the band Joy Division became after singer Ian Curtis killed himself in 1980.

Winterbottom, who was born in Blackburn, remembers watching Tony Wilson on Granada TV while growing up, and had approached him for money to finance *Delirious*, an early, abandoned project written by Cottrell-Boyce. 'At the time I foolishly thought he must have loads of money because he was running Factory Records,' says the director now. Fiscal responsibility, it transpires, was not Wilson's strongest suit. A ceaseless self-promoter with a whirlwind personality, what Wilson had was panache, a preacher's gift for converting the cynical and making things happen, however chaotically. In short, all the qualities required to be the narrator of his own shaggy-dog story. Explains Winterbottom:

> Tony Wilson is a storyteller and he told us a lot of the stories in the film, so it was quite easy to have him telling them in the film. And, of course, he's a TV presenter so as a character he's constantly editorialising. One of things about him is that he's always myth-building, having this grand vision of things that are quite mundane, and the gap between the grand vision of what he was trying to do and the absolute banal reality of what's going on, seemed to me to be one of the things that's funny about him. And that's why we thought of Steve even before Frank came in, because he's obviously brilliant at doing that as well.

Coogan's performance shines through many layers of meta. Best known for playing non-PC TV presenter Alan Partridge,[8] Coogan grew up just outside Manchester, and performed at the Haçienda as a young stand-up comic. On the DVD commentary, he recalls Wilson being 'slightly embarrassing to watch' (2003) – like Partridge – and he often seems to be acting in inverted commas as if acknowledging that we are watching Coogan playing Partridge playing Wilson. 'Having known Tony Wilson for a long time, I couldn't imagine him being in a film and not knowing he was in a film,' said Coogan. 'He's such a larger-than-life character… he can't resist the opportunity to talk about anything and relate it to himself' (2003).

Lots of the fun of *24 Hour Party People* is in watching Wilson trying and failing to stay in charge of a story that is forever cannonballing out of control. At one point he turns to the camera to apologize for not mentioning the existence of his children, before reasoning, 'But this is not a film about me. I am not Prince Hamlet, nor was meant to be. I'm a minor character in my own story. This is a film about the music, and the people who made the music.'

Not so, says screenwriter Frank Cottrell-Boyce:

> I figured out on the very first day that Tony was far, far more interesting, more idealistic and more rock'n'roll than most of the musicians in the story; that he talked a lot and talked brilliantly and that this would give me the perfect unreliable narrator, so it wouldn't matter what was true and what wasn't: it was Tony's version of events.
>
> (2017)

Though based on painstaking interviews with the people concerned, that version of events is highly subjective. As Wilson walks us through his own chequered history, the film uses cameos, real and fake concert footage, and fantasy sequences to flesh out its tall but true-ish stories. Says Winterbottom:

> It's a complicated process because once you say you want to make a film about New Order, then you need all the connecting characters, and they're also real. It would be weird to have a film about one band where the other bands were fake, so then you're in a situation which is quite tricky: you're making a film about people's lives who have no desire to be in a film and don't have any connection really with the main story, but in passing they're going to pop in, so obviously we wanted people to be as happy about that as they could.

This was easier said than done. According to Eaton, the filmmakers were sued three times: by the Sex Pistols' management and Haçienda designer Ben Kelly over copyright disputes, and Tony's ex-wife, Lindsay (played by Shirley Henderson), over a scene in which she has sex with Buzzcocks singer Howard Devoto (Martin Hancock) in the Haçienda toilets in retaliation for one of Tony's infidelities. 'I definitely don't remember this happening,' says an awkward-looking cleaner straight to camera – in fact, this is the real Howard Devoto. Winterbottom explains:

> We met Lindsay before, obviously, then sent her the script and she said, 'I didn't have sex with Howard Devoto in a toilet, I had sex with Howard Devoto in a hotel bedroom,' or wherever, I can't remember where it was. We said, 'OK, well it's better for us to be in the club, so what we'll do is we'll put a voiceover in saying this isn't true.' Then, when she saw it, she was like, '[the actor playing] Howard Devoto looks so ugly and stupid, I don't want people to think I had sex with him.' And then she also said, 'Anyway, it's not true.'

The scene ends with Coogan-as-Wilson explaining: 'He [Howard] and Lindsay insisted we made clear that this never happened. But I agree with John Ford. "When you have to choose between the truth and the legend, print the legend."' As Lindsay would later write, quoting Tony, *24 Hour Party People* was 'a collection of lies that manages to tell the truth' (Reade 2009: 281). 'You think we got off lightly?' laughs Eaton now. 'Probably we did.'

From its acid-etched credits to its unresolved ending, *24 Hour Party People* is Britpop cinema through and through. With two thumbs up from Irvine Welsh on the DVD sleeve, production design by Boyle regular Mark Tildesley, music supervision by Liz Gallagher (*The Full Monty, Gangster No. 1*) and supporting roles for John Simm (*Human Traffic*) and Shirley Henderson (*Trainspotting*), how could it not be? Sometimes branded *24HPP*, it takes its name from a song by the Happy Mondays, a drug-loving Madchester band who provided (and indeed often resembled) the missing link between 1980s indie-dance and Britpop bands such as Oasis,[9] at least by placing attitude ahead of ability. And like Wilson himself, however far off-map the film wanders, it is all about the music, which is brought lovingly (back) to life in a variety of imaginative manners.

The Sex Pistols' Free Trade Hall gig has been painstakingly pieced together from real concert footage[10] matched with (fake) shots of Wilson, Lindsay and Alan Erasmus (Lennie James) watching and dancing.[11] Joy Division's doomy ferocity is recreated magnificently by actors Sean Harris (as singer Ian Curtis), Simm (guitarist Bernard Sumner), Ralf Little[12] (bassist Peter Hook) and Tim Horrocks (drummer Stephen Morris), who learned to play for real, often using the band's actual instruments. The beginning of acid house, meanwhile, is reimagined in a sequence that shows Wilson walking through the Haçienda crowds as they writhe in ecstatic slo-mo. 'They're applauding the DJ, not the music, not the musician, not the creator, but the medium,' he tells us, a square peg among the sweating hordes. 'This is it, the birth of rave culture. The beatification of the beat. The dance age. This is the moment when even the white man starts dancing. Welcome to Madchester.' The real Tony Wilson was even more enthusiastic:

> It was, 'Here's the drugs, here's the dance, let's fucking go!' You could take any human being, of any sort, to the Haçienda from mid-1989 onwards and they would just love it. Human beings love fun and happiness and exuberance, and it was the epitome of that.
>
> (Harris 2003: 13)

This is a fine Britpop cinema mantra, and one the film – which is positively picaresque with possibility – repeatedly makes good on. As Eaton puts it: 'We had a very strong desire to replicate the Factory ethos in the film – in other words, anything can happen in the next half hour'. And it does. The film begins with Wilson hang-gliding across the Pennines for *Granada Reports*, and intercuts footage of Coogan-as-Wilson with Wilson himself. 'You could say the real Tony Wilson performed as my stuntman,' said Coogan (2003). Upon landing – with a bump – he turns to the camera and mansplains:

> You're gonna be seeing a lot more of that sort of thing in the film. All of that actually did happen. Obviously, it's symbolic. It works on both levels. I don't want to tell you too much, don't want to spoil the film. But I'll just say, 'Icarus.' OK? Doesn't matter if you don't understand. But you should probably read more.

To underline the Icarus theme, obscure avian references abound, most notably in a scene where Shaun (Danny Cunningham) and Paul Ryder (Paul Popplewell), later of the Happy Mondays, feed rat poison to some pigeons. As the music from *The Dam Busters* (Anderson, 1955) blusters in the background, the pigeons swoop past the camera and plummet to the ground, a mixture of (terrible) CG and (genuine) corpses donated by the council. Says Eaton:

> It was definitely one of the strangest days I've spent in my life. Somebody shopped us to the RSPCA. I mean, it didn't look great. We were chucking dead pigeons off the top of a building. Then we had Rolf Harris's *Pet Rescue* team turn up.

Elsewhere, one of Wilson's news reports features a duck that rounds up sheep ('Stick to what you're good at…' muses Wilson, 'unless you're a duck, and then you can branch out.'), and we glimpse the final scene of the desperate *Stroszek* (Herzog, 1977), which features a chicken 'dancing' in tortured circles, the last thing poor Ian Curtis watched before hanging himself.[13]

Icarus is not the only classical touchstone. At one point, Christopher Eccleston cameos as a beggar claiming to be the ancient philosopher Boethius. He tells Wilson:

> It's my belief that history is a wheel. 'Inconstancy is my very essence,' says the wheel. 'Rise up on my spokes if you like, but don't complain when you're cast back down into the depths. Good times pass away, but then so do the bad. Mutability is our tragedy, but it's also our hope. The worst of times, like the best, are always passing away.'

Later Wilson repeats the quote on *Wheel of Fortune* (1988–2001, UK: STV), the TV quiz he hosts. If the gallery director who instructs his team to cut this 'bullshit' seems familiar, that is because it is Tony Wilson himself – the real one, as if the film's hall of mirrors has collapsed in on itself.

This is not the only well-cued cameo – indeed it sometimes feels like the film is *all* cameo, with most of the British indie film firmament turning up and tuning up to play most of the Manchester indie music firmament. Harris and Simm are familiar faces from TV; Paddy Considine, who plays combative Joy Division manager Rob Gretton (1953–99) is a Shane Meadows regular, and Andy Serkis, who plays eccentric producer Martin Hannett (1948–91) is better known as Gollum from *The Lord of the Rings* (Jackson, 2001–03). The rest of the cast is rounded out by comics such as Peter Kay (*Phoenix Nights*), Simon Pegg (*Spaced*) and John Thomson (*The Fast Show*) as well as musicians from the Manchester scene. The Mondays' Paul Ryder plays a (rather convincing) gangster, while the band's backing singer Rowetta appears as herself, no matter that two decades have passed; Inspiral Carpets' Clint Boon is a train conductor; and Mark E. Smith of The Fall pops up in the Haçienda queue. In fact, any time you see someone looking especially leathery or shifty it is most likely a cameo-ing musician.

No wonder things got confusing. According to Eaton, Smith disappeared with his costume: 'It was just a pair of shitty trousers, I thought that was quite a weird thing to do.' Harris, meanwhile, known for the intensity of his performances, brought his own. Recalls the producer:

> When we were in pre-production I remember seeing Sean running up the stairs, probably going to see Michael. And I said to Natalie Ward, the costume designer who happened to be in my office, 'I really love Sean's costume.' She said, 'That's not his costume.' He was living the role of Ian Curtis long before we started filming.

Naturally for such a free-for-all, Keith Allen turns up at the end, as a music executive looking to buy Factory Records – a futile gesture, thanks to Wilson's idealistic insistence that the label does not own any of the rights to the music it puts out. Although uncharacteristically clothed/sober, Allen's character Roger Aames does at least bring that other Britpop cinema standby: the promise of millions. Says Eaton:

> We got a message via an intermediary from Keith Allen that said if we didn't put him in the film he was going to find us and kill us. He turned up the night before and all the actors were camped out at the Palace Hotel where we had a deal. We'd always go there, every night, to the bar and Keith came down. I remember leaving them and Keith was on the piano, a big grand piano, which he broke. Then the next day we were all on set, you know, eight o' clock in the morning, and there was no Keith. Where's Keith? No Keith. So they eventually had to break down the door of his hotel room. When they went in he was lying on the floor beside the bed, fully clothed.

If Allen was deliberately re-enacting *that* scene from *Shallow Grave* (Boyle, 1995) he prepared a little too well. 'The best thing was,' says Eaton, 'we finally got him on to set three hours later, and he wore shades through the whole scene.'

To distinguish itself from kitchen-sink dramas on one hand and outright fantasy on the other, Britpop cinema requires a fluid sense of the real and the fake, an area that has proved something of a sweet spot for Winterbottom, who shot the film on digital video:

> I like having actors and non-actors, or controlled bits of the frame and uncontrolled bits, so you feel like your story is taking place on a canvas that's not necessarily been created for your film. It's more like you're inserting your film or your character into reality, so you've got a real character interacting with someone who clearly doesn't know they're part of the film or isn't part of the film in the same way. I like all those different textures rubbing up against each other.

This particular canvas required the filmmakers to rebuild the Haçienda – which had been demolished just four weeks into pre-production – in a north Manchester warehouse. They then organized two club nights, with original Haçienda DJ Dave Haslam plus bands, invited a few thousand guests, and filmed the results, often on the fly. Explains the director:

> You want it to be as close to reality as possible, so I try to avoid having any lights. For *Wonderland*, which we shot in Soho, we were filming in real bars, and if you put camera lights up people freeze, if you put a microphone up, people freeze, but if you can't see any lights and you can't see any microphones then weirdly the camera doesn't worry them. I don't know why, but when people see a light they feel a little more exposed. So we filmed the Haçienda scenes like that, and the people in the bands, and the extras in the crowds, they're not particularly aware of where the shot is – there's no lights, there's no marks, there's no microphones, and we're not necessarily saying when we start filming. We're recreating a gig. The bands would come on and play then go off again, so if you make the atmosphere on set as close to watching a real band as possible then that's the best way of getting the reaction from the audience to feel real.

Says Eaton:

> I defy people to watch some of the montage sequences and tell me what they think is real and what they think is fake, especially with the Mondays stuff. I mean Chris Coghill who plays [Mondays dancer] Bez was such a good physical resemblance. There's a great story that, when the Mondays reformed, they did a tour of America and Bez wasn't allowed to go because he has a drugs record, so he couldn't get an American visa. So the manager rang up Chris Coghill and said, 'Will you go as Bez? The Americans will never know the difference!' But he didn't do it in the end.

Even the fake Mondays get into some appropriately close-to-the-edge hijinks. Recalls the producer:

> We were shooting a scene at Manchester Airport where the Mondays go through security and Shaun spills his Methadone on the floor, and they were kicking a ball around, and I had a really angry letter from this guy saying he was so distracted by it he missed his flight. He wanted compensation, but we said forget it. I think I personally got banned from Manchester Airport for life. Then I was banned from a service station on the M6 for life, because Danny and Paul who were playing Shaun and Paul ran into the reception area in their underpants and the women pressed the panic button. I remember the manager came to talk to me and I just couldn't stop laughing. Then I got banned from [Manchester City football ground] Maine Road for life. We were filming a scene where the Ryder brothers are running along getting chased by United fans and they get into a fight. I was sitting in the stadium trying to watch the game, but I kept getting phoned up by the location assistant saying, 'You know, it's all kicking off here.' Because the police said, 'Yes, you can film here, but you can't recreate a riot,' which is what Mike wanted, so we got banned from there too.

The real-fake fun continued when the (fake) Mondays came to the (real) Cannes Film Festival. According to Eaton:

> We did a stunt where we chucked stuffed pigeons around on the beach, at the Majestic hotel. We got into really bad trouble because they were completely pissed at the time, just a bunch of kids, a couple of them had never been out of England before. So they started lobbing them into the restaurant, which is on the beach, and the Coen brothers were having lunch there at the time, and they said to me later it was their most memorable experience ever in Cannes. But one of the birds landed on the table of the head of a French TV channel, who was having lunch there. The security guards came over and sprayed us all with Mace, then we jumped into a taxi and went straight to the airport and left the country, as I think we would have been arrested. Later, I had to write a letter to the TV head to apologize, then pay for his lunch. I had to write a lot of letters of apology.

Although the film is not without its frivolous moments, unlike Britpop cinema's more plastic proponents, its intentions are mostly honourable, paying tribute to a great British success story, of sorts – its old ghosts and ragged glories. At the Haçienda's closing night, Tony Wilson scans the crowds to catch glimpses of Ian Curtis and Martin Hannett, both long dead, among the dancing hordes. And Wilson was not the only one getting emotional. When filming was almost shut down over fire regulations at 10am on the day of shooting – thought to be a stitch-up by a rival club – Eaton recalls:

> I went to the corner and wept. But, of course, everybody rallied round and it was like a *Challenge Anneka* thing to build an asbestos safety tunnel, which was ridiculous. But if they'd stopped us filming we would have lost half a million quid. So what it meant was, by the time we started that night I was on a massive adrenaline high, and then the icing on the cake was to realize that we'd recreated something that was a really important part of people's lives. People were coming up to me in tears and hugging me and saying it's exactly the same as it was, and I've seen friends I haven't seen for ten years.

According to Winterbottom:

> Everyone wanted to come back to the Haçienda. They were queuing up to try and get in. At the end of it a lot of people were crying, they were in the DJ booth not wanting to stop the night.

Peter Hook, the Joy Division and New Order bassist, called this real-fake closing party:

> The strangest experience of my life… I walked up to Barney [Bernard Sumner] and said, 'Fucking hell, all that's missing is Rob Gretton.' He turned and went, 'Look.' There stood the actor Paddy Considine dressed as Rob. I wanted to get drunk. I wanted to cry.
>
> (2010: 311)

The real Tony Wilson could not bear to attend the closing party at all, so Eaton took the actors to him:

> There was a nice moment, behind all the comedy and everything else. Obviously you had the situation where three people had died relatively recently – one was Rob Gretton, who died a year before we started filming, and then you had Martin Hannett and Ian Curtis. I remember sitting in a bar in Manchester, close to where Tony's flat was, and he came in and we sat at a table: Michael, myself, Andy Serkis, Paddy Considine and Sean Harris. And it was very emotional for Tony, he was almost in tears because he's sitting opposite three guys who're playing three of his best friends who are now dead. Stuff like that was incredibly poignant.

The film, of course, ends more irreverently. Following the Haçienda closing party, Wilson, Erasmus, Gretton and Shaun Ryder share a spliff on the rooftop as a weak dawn washes across the skies. After a few drags, Wilson has a vision of a Monty Python-esque God made, naturally, in his own image, and offering this bizarre benediction: 'Tony, you did a good job. Basically you were right…' he says, before admonishing, 'It's a pity you didn't sign The Smiths, but you were right about Mick Hucknall. His music's rubbish, and he's a ginger.' When Wilson comes to, he tries to explain his outlandish vision to the other three, not for the first time. 'Top gear, man,' offers Gretton finally, the Factory dream gone up in smoke.

For a while *24 Hour Party People* seemed destined to do the same. With PolyGram sold, and uncertainty surrounding the future of Film4 after high-profile flops such as *Charlotte Gray* (Armstrong, 2002), Britpop cinema's post-millennial drop-off meant the film did not easily find its audience. Says Eaton:

> We'd had a deal with PolyGram since *Jude*, and *24 Hour Party People* would have been perfect for them, but they didn't exist at that point. When PolyGram went it was a massive hole. *24 Hour Party People* was a frustrating experience for me in some ways because I think it may be the best thing I've been involved in and I'm really proud of it, and when we first did screenings people thought it was going to be huge. With the Film Consortium selling it, and Pathé distributing it, we tested it in Birmingham and you could almost sense the enthusiasm for the film die because it didn't test well. But then if you're going to make a film about Manchester the last place you want to test it is fucking Birmingham!

After what Winterbottom calls a 'terrible, terrible' Cannes Film Festival screening, followed by 'a mad, chaotic, Haçienda-esque party', the film was nominated for the Palme d'Or, but only made $2.8 million (Box Office Mojo 2018a) worldwide on a budget of around £4 million. According to Eaton:

> [Former PolyGram head] Stewart Till met his wife at the Haçienda, and he said to me you should just have released it on two screens in Manchester and run it for a month and beaten every record and then you should have gone wide, like they did with *Trainspotting*, they just opened it in Scotland first and they built it, and then they went wide. With *Trainspotting*, it was, 'This is fucking great, let's get it out there.' But with *24 Hour Party People* they went, 'This is fucking great,' but then they lost faith. The number of people who came up to me, even to this day, who said, 'I didn't go see that film in the cinema because I didn't think you could replicate what it was like because I was there, but now it's my favourite film ever.' And you go, 'Well I wish you'd bought a fucking ticket at the time.'

The famously narky members of New Order were less impressed. 'I've seen *24 Hour Party People* three or four times,' wrote Peter Hook. 'It's bollocks, but it's enjoyable bollocks. You couldn't make a boring film about the Haçienda if you tried' (2010: 316). Hook's cameo did not make the finished film, but it did inspire one of Eaton's favourite *24 Hour Party People* moments:

> We were filming in the centre of Manchester, the scene where the Ryder brothers poison the pigeons, and Peter Hook agreed to do a small cameo as a guy going down the road when some pigeons fall on his car. It was his daughter's 16th birthday that day and she was bored, and I remember we were standing round chatting on the street and she said, 'Daddy, why would anyone want to make a film about you?'

Not only did her comment crystallize the need to make the film in the first place, it cut to the core of what Britpop cinema was all about. Says Eaton, echoing *Trainspotting* producer Andrew Macdonald: 'We suddenly found a moment. And the Americans and many other cultures have been doing this for years, but we suddenly realized we actually had some pretty good stories in the relatively recent past and we started to tell them.' Whether anyone believed them, of course, is another matter.

What Happened Next…

New Order… Were put through the biopic mill once more, when Joy Division photographer Anton Corbijn adapted Deborah Curtis' memoir about her husband, *Touching from a Distance: Ian Curtis & Joy Division* (1995), into the film *Control* (2007). Shot in hopeless black and white, and starring Sam Riley as Ian Curtis, the results were beautifully bleak, but about as far from Britpop cinema as you could imagine. In 2001, New Order played live together for the first time since 1998. Recalls Eaton: 'They had their first reunion gig in Liverpool when we were in post-production, and I remember going there, and seeing Lesley [Gretton] and her two kids. She said this great thing, "You've allowed my children to understand what a real hero their father was," and that's a fantastic privilege to feel that you're a part of that celebration.' At the band's 2002 Finsbury Park gig, Bernard Sumner invited his onscreen counterpart, actor John Simm, on stage for a joyful version of Joy Division's *Digital*. According to Eaton: 'John said it was the greatest moment of his life.'

Frank Cottrell-Boyce... Wrote the ambitious *Revengers Tragedy* (Cox, 2002), an adaptation of Thomas Middleton's 1607 play; the cheekily postmodern *A Cock and Bull Story* (Winterbottom, 2005); and the marvellous *Millions* (Boyle, 2004), which is essentially Britpop cinema for kids. Of the latter, which features Manchester, a cache of secret money, and visions of Catholic saints, he says, 'Danny Boyle was obviously the perfect director for it but he seemed such an unlikely person to say yes. Working with him was the greatest joy of my film career.' Together the pair envisaged making *Millions* as a musical with songs by Noel Gallagher. 'We can but dream,' says Cottrell-Boyce now.

Michael Winterbottom and Andrew Eaton... Continued to confound and delight, crafting intriguing indie films mixing fact and fiction. Meta musical efforts include *9 Songs* (2004), a (fictional) romance played out across a series of (real) gigs by the likes of Elbow, and (real) sex scenes;[14] while *On the Road* (2016) attempted something similar, if softer, against the backdrop of a Wolf Alice tour. With Coogan, the pair made *A Cock and Bull Story* and TV's faux travelogue *The Trip* (2010 UK: Revolution Films) plus sequels. 'With TV most of it is absolutely mainstream, straight-down-the-middle stuff, there's very little space, especially in fiction, to do anything interesting,' says Winterbottom now. 'But within that space there are still margins to make something offbeat, and it's the same in cinema. The mainstream is boring and then there are margins at the edge where you can do brilliant stuff.' If the Britpop era ever receives a *24 Hour Party People*-style chronicle, these are definitely the men for the job.

Tony Wilson... Played the role he was born to embody – himself – in *A Cock and Bull Story*, and persevered in his personal mission to become Mr Manchester. When he died of a heart attack in August 2007, his coffin was numbered FAC 501. As part of Manchester's urban regeneration, the Haçienda site was turned into flats, where, just opposite, you will find Tony Wilson Place. When it came to *24 Hour Party People* (FAC 401), Wilson seemed pleased as punch with the notoriety, if vexed by the details, at one point suggesting it should be renamed *Frank Cottrell-Boyce Is a Fucking Liar*. Says the writer: 'I loved Tony. I hope that's clear from the film. I can't watch it for crying. His funeral was almost unbearable. I sang my heart out for him.'

Notes

1 In November 1997, 'Perfect Day' was released as a single for Children in Need. It reached No.1, raised £2 million and has sold 1.5 million copies to date. It also inspired a scarcely less tuneful 1997 *Harry Enfield and Chums* (1994–98, UK: Tiger Aspect Productions) spoof, and a 1998 Sony compilation album, featuring the soothing sounds of the Lighthouse Family and Brand New Heavies (Wikipedia 2018).

2 British singers who've tried their hands at acting include Cliff Richard (most notably in *Summer Holiday* [Yates, 1963]), Mick Jagger (*Performance* [Cammell and Roeg, 1970]), Roger Daltrey (*McVicar* [Clegg, 1980]) and the ever-present Sting.

3 *Lock, Stock and Two Smoking Barrels* star Nick Moran recalls, 'We got gassed! I was sat with The Edge, Dave Stewart and Bootsy Collins and everyone thought it was a smoke effect, but I thought, "Fuck, I know that smell!" Then I heard "Crack", this very strange noise – a real gunshot – because it's got a dry clink to it, I thought, "Fuck that's a bullet!" So I grabbed hold of the guys – this way, this way – and dragged them out the front and we all went to the Majestic to have a drink. It turned out to be some Marseilles gangster who'd thrown a load of teargas in' (2016). This story is mentioned in Christopher Fowler's *Film Freak* (2013: 183), but further corroboration has proved frustrating.

4 Glam-rock references in the film include, but are not limited to, the title *Velvet Goldmine*, which comes from a Bowie B-side; the names Brian Slade and Maxwell Demon, the former a reference to 1970s glam rockers Slade, the latter named after a Brian Eno band; Venus in Furs, meanwhile, comes from a 1967 Velvet Underground song.

5 A nod to the director's short, *Superstar: The Karen Carpenter Story* (Haynes, 1988), which retells the story of the tragic 1970s singer with dolls. After a lawsuit from her brother Richard Carpenter, the film was withdrawn from circulation (Lodge, 2016).

6 Winterbottom's most notable TV credit is *Cracker* (1993–2006, UK: Granada), created by Jimmy McGovern and starring Robbie Coltrane as the deeply flawed criminal psychologist Fitz. Winterbottom directed series opener 'The Mad Woman in the Attic', which was broadcast on ITV on 27 September 1993.

7 Anti-heritage films are a subgenre of literary adaptations such as *The Wings of the Dove* (Softley, 1997) and historical dramas like *Elizabeth* (Kapur, 1998) that brought a modern, revisionist edge to the period pieces British cinema was renowned for. In the press notes for *Jude*, screenwriter Hossein Amini announced his intention to 'destroy the heritage film from within'. Kapur, meanwhile, wrote inside his *Elizabeth* screenplay that it should have 'the intrigue of *The Godfather* and the shooting style of *Trainspotting*' (Gibson 2005: 117, 122).

8 A painfully accurate spoof of banal but bizarrely self-important TV presenters, Alan Partridge was invented by Coogan and Armando Iannucci for *On the Hour*, a 1991 BBC Radio 4 comedy that became TV's *The Day Today* (1994, UK: BBC). Numerous spin-offs followed, most notably the behind-the-scenes sitcom *I'm Alan Partridge* (1997–2001, UK: BBC) and the film *Alan Partridge: Alpha Papa* (Lowney, 2013).

9 Indeed, Noel Gallagher was once the roadie for Inspiral Carpets, a more genial Madchester group.

10 The Sex Pistols footage had been used in the documentary *The Filth and the Fury* (Temple, 2000). 'Julien Temple chopped it all up in such a way it was very hard to know what went together with what,' says Eaton. 'But Dave [Bryan] was able to identify the correct footage, because he knew that the Sex Pistols had stolen Mott the Hoople's gear from the back of the Hammersmith Odeon, several weeks before that gig.'

11 The real Wilson was less than impressed with this scene. 'Twenty-five years on, Britain's top commercial/art filmmakers made a movie about this evening,' he wrote in his bizarre spin-off book *24 Hour Party People: What the Sleeve Notes Never Tell You*. 'To explain the impact

on the twentieth century of this seminal gig, they had people like Wilson and Erasmus pogoing towards the end. That's called filmmaking, and who gives a toss about truth? How do you explain that no one moved. No one budged' (2002: 23).

12 Ironically, Little appears in *The Royle Family* (1998–2012, UK: Granada), co-written by and co-starring Caroline Aherne, aka the former Mrs Hook. According to Eaton: 'Someone interviewed Caroline Aherne and asked, "What do you think of Ralf Little [her onscreen brother] playing your ex-husband in *24 Hour Party People*?" And she said, "Why, was Fred West not available?"'

13 Curtis has been depicted as the archetypal tragic artist, but bandmate Stephen Morris called him, 'an ordinary bloke just like you or me, liked a bit of a laugh, a bit of a joke', in a 1987 *Option* interview (Dawson 2016). Suffering from epilepsy and depression, and unable to choose between his band, his family and his mistress, he hanged himself on 18 May 1980 with a washing line cord. He'd been watching *Stroszek*, and listening to Iggy Pop's 1977 album, *The Idiot*. This contains the song 'Nightclubbing', which features prominently in *Trainspotting*.

14 *9 Songs*, or *A Cock and Balls Story* as wags have called it, might be the most sexually explicit 'mainstream' British movie ever released, featuring several non-simulated sex scenes between leads Margo Stilley and Kieran O'Brien (also in *24 Hour Party People* and *Cracker*).

Chapter 10

The Living Dead

Starring: *Shaun of the Dead* (Wright, 2004)

Chapter 10: The Living Dead

Apocalyptic visions in Britpop cinema

Shaun (Simon Pegg): Where's safe? Where's familiar?
Ed (Nick Frost): Where can I smoke?
Shaun: [Imagining the scenario] Take car. Go to Mum's. Kill Phil – 'Sorry!' – grab Liz, go to The Winchester, have a nice cold pint, and wait for all of this to blow over. How's that for a slice of fried gold?
Shaun of the Dead

It was the end of the world as we knew it, and, in point of fact, nothing was going to be just fine. As the year 2000 ticked closer, the millennium bug – or Y2K in that uneasy *X-Files*-speak – threatened to stop all the clocks and cut off the phones. Power stations would go into meltdown, planes would fall from the sky, civilisations would crumble. At a cost of $300 billion, the government got to work, vowing to save us from digital disaster with pamphlets and re-programming. But once the NYE fireworks had fizzled, the damage was minor: some misfiring cash machines here, a faulty ticket machine there. Humanity had lived to fight another 1,000 years. Then came 11 September, 2001, and we realised the battle had only just begun.

For Britpop cinema, the new millennium brought not hope but uncertainty. PolyGram was long gone, UK lottery funding had notched up nine hits to 121 misses (Fitzgerald 2010: 7),[1] and Film4 was about to overextend itself with the ambitious but unwieldy *Charlotte Gray* (Armstrong, 2002).[2] The result? Fewer risks taken, except at the grittier end of the spectrum, and a preponderance of fluff. Working Title had struck pay-dirt with the American-actress-plus-Hugh-Grant-in-London rom-com formula as typified by *Notting Hill* (Michell, 1999), and it was not about to stop now, especially with Universal replacing PolyGram as its international sponsor. The excellent *About a Boy* (Weitz brothers, 2002) was more acid than the rest, but drafting in the Australian Toni Collette instead of Andie/Gwyneth/Julia hardly qualified as a major change of MO.

In 2000, the sources of UK lottery funding – the BFI, British Film Commission, British Screen Finance and the Arts Council – were amalgamated into the UK Film Council. With hits such as *Bend It Like Beckham* (Chadha, 2002) on the way, it would secure a better track record than the three lottery franchises of the 1990s: Pathé Productions, The Film Consortium and DNA Films. But only a fool would have bet against the latter, run by producers Andrew Macdonald (*Trainspotting*) and Duncan Kenworthy (*Four Weddings and a Funeral*). Although early efforts such as *Beautiful Creatures* (Eagles, 2000) and the Steve Coogan vehicle *The Parole Officer* (Duigan, 2001) barely troubled the box office, Danny Boyle's *28 Days Later* (2002a) caught the mood of the times perfectly. In the wake of 9/11 it felt entirely possible that, 'the end,' to paraphrase a stray piece of graffiti in the film, was 'extremely fucking nigh'.

After *A Life Less Ordinary* (1997) and big-budget gap-year misfire *The Beach* (2000), based on the smash-hit Alex Garland novel, Boyle might have felt that way himself. The new millennium saw him go back to TV, with one-offs *Strumpet* (2001, UK: BBC), starring Christopher Eccleston, and *Vacuuming Completely Nude in Paradise* (2001, UK: BBC) with Mike Leigh regular Timothy Spall. But in reality he was refreshing the guerrilla spirit that had fired his first two films. His comeback was a characteristically nimble apocalyptic horror, sparsely scripted by Garland, and shot for £6 million on digital, which added a harsh, cinema verité quality. 'The general idea was to try and shoot as though we were survivors too,' he wrote in the production notes (2002b), perhaps acknowledging how close his own career had come to calamity.

The film begins at lightning speed with activists breaking into a medical research laboratory. Here, they find captive chimpanzees, strapped down and forced to watch violent images in a manner reminiscent of Boyle's beloved *A Clockwork Orange* (Kubrick, 1972). In fact, they are infected with a rage virus, and once free, they attack the interlopers. Cut to 28 days later, and bike courier Jim (Cillian Murphy) wakes from a coma in a deserted London hospital. He – and we – have missed the spread of the virus, which has turned most of humanity into murderous hordes of sprinting 'zombies' (though they are not actually dead). As dawn breaks, we follow him through the eerily empty central London streets; with toppled red double-deckers and scattered souvenir stands providing some of the most enduring images of the era.

Filmed largely on the fly, in cordoned off sections of the capital, this bravura sequence makes you wonder how on earth the filmmakers achieved it without CGI. But there is real pathos too, a wall of messages to the missing at Piccadilly Circus unavoidably recalling the lives lost at Ground Zero. In truth, the rest of the film – which sees Jim fleeing the infected with hard-nut survivor Selena (Naomie Harris), cabbie Frank (Brendan Gleeson) and his daughter Hannah (Megan Burns) – cannot hope to top it. Boyle keeps things moving at a clip, helped by John Murphy's surging score, but the film never misses an opportunity to pay lip service to its paymaster, The National Lottery, the logo of which gets more screen-time than most of the cast, and its upbeat moments ring hollow. One awkward scene sees the four merrily shopping to the strains of Grandaddy's 'A.M. 180'; and the tacked-on happy ending (of four that were shot)[3] jars badly with the darkness of the rest of the material. Despite being a film of two halves, it was a huge hit, making $83 million worldwide (Box Office Mojo 2018b) and occasioning a more internationalist sequel *28 Weeks Later* (Fresnadillo, 2007). As a straight-ahead horror, *28 Days* was miles from the Britpop cinema template Boyle had perfected. But it set things up nicely for *Shaun of the Dead*, which took the ball and knocked it out of the park – with a cricket bat, naturally.[4]

If *28 Days Later* positioned London as a city global enough to deserve its own disaster, *Shaun*'s focus was much more parochial. Set in the yawning London suburbs so often romanticized/ridiculed in the lyrics of Blur and Suede, it gets a lot of comedy mileage out of the extreme ordinariness of its characters and their issues. Shaun is a feckless late-twentysomething caught between his frustrated girlfriend Liz (Kate Ashfield), who wants more from life than endless evenings in The Winchester pub, and his frustrating best friend Ed, a sofa-surfing stoner who would enjoy nothing more. Like the TV series *Spaced* (1999–2001, UK: Big Talk) from which it evolved, *Shaun* has much in common with US slacker films of the mid-1990s.[5] The crucial difference? Zombies, although the characters are far too British to feel comfortable saying the word.

Precocious, to say the least,[6] Wright made his first feature film aged just 20. Shot for £21,000, stretched to 78 minutes and starring his school friends (plus a cameo from TV trickster Jeremy Beadle), *A Fistful of Fingers* (1995) is a Western spoof based on an even earlier short. 'When it came to picking a subject matter for a comedy film, a Western seemed doable,' Wright told *Empire*'s Nick De Semelyn, 'We could just go stand in a quarry with some toy guns. No sets required' (2015). The result was both inspired and over-stretched, gaining a one-star review from the aforementioned film magazine. It ran for two weeks at London's Prince Charles Cinema, where budding comedians Matt Lucas and David Walliams (later of *Little Britain* fame) were among the audience. They asked Wright to direct their sketch show *Mash and Peas* (1996–97, UK: Paramount) for the Paramount Comedy Channel (now Comedy Central), which lead on to *Asylum* (1996, UK: Paramount), another comic grab-bag, where Wright met Pegg and Jessica Hynes, the principal talents behind *Spaced*. Says Wright:

> When we were doing the first series of *Spaced*, there was an episode where Simon Pegg's character Tim has been up all night playing *Resident Evil 2* and starts hallucinating that there are real zombies in the flat. And one of the many things Simon and I bonded over was that we both loved George Romero's zombie trilogy, specifically *Dawn of the Dead*.
>
> (2017b)

Recalls Pegg:

> Those films were the reason Edgar and I became friends. When we did that zombie sequence in *Spaced* we got to the end of the shoot and it was like, 'We should try and make a film like this!'
>
> (2018)

Wright continues:

> That scene was the last of the set work, I remember that because we had to trash the place and cover it in blood, and afterwards I remember vividly thinking, 'This is our job, we get paid to do this zombie thing, this is incredible!' Then I remember sharing a car with Simon to the wrap party, and us saying we should do a whole film of it. So we started thinking about doing a horror comedy, but we had to find our own angle.

They did not have to look too far for inspiration. Says Wright:

> Around the same time, there was a weekend when the *Resident Evil 3* computer game came out, and my girlfriend was away, and I very irresponsibly stayed up for like 72 hours playing it, in Barnsbury Road, Islington, north London. I remember at one point walking across the street to get the papers and some milk and there being nobody on the street at all, and because I'd been playing a lot of this game, I started to think, 'Hmmm, wouldn't it be interesting if you did this Sunday walk and there were zombies? Or what if you were hungover and you didn't even notice?' I told Simon about it, and it sparked off this idea: what if there was a zombie outbreak and you're following insignificant characters? Almost like a *Rosencrantz and Guildenstern* version of *Dawn of the Dead*. We liked that idea of focusing on these rather insignificant players, who were just there to get through the day, they're not there to save the world.

The key was to transpose this most American of genres to England without doing a disservice to either the genre or the setting. Recalls Pegg:

> Write what you know was our mantra from the start. We didn't really want to write about zombies on Westminster Bridge and stuff like that. We had no desire to have a Routemaster bus in there, in fact we specifically had a single-decker bus instead, so it didn't look like some postcard London thing. We wanted to shoot the film where people lived in London, not where people visited. We were essentially writing about our own lives. The Winchester was based on a pub called The Shepherd's which was on the corner of Shepherd's Hill on Archway Road, and it sort of formed the social hub for myself and Nick Frost for a long time, at the expense of us ever wanting to go anywhere else.

Wright agrees:

> *Shaun* was a very concerted effort to show suburban London as it really is. To us it was much like going in the direction of a Mike Leigh film with zombies. In fact, when we first pitched it to Film4, we said it was like *Life Is Sweet* with zombies.

Shaun, then tentatively titled *Teatime of the Dead*, was offered to most of the UK's funding bodies, but it was Film4 that first showed faith. Unfortunately, when the company 'briefly collapsed', the script was put, grudgingly, into turnaround. According to Wright:

> So in 2002 we had this rather humbling experience of going around to the companies that we'd already chosen not to make the movie with and re-pitch it now that Film4 had gone down. That involved going to the Film Council, Miramax in the UK, Working Title, Pathé, but most of the places just passed on it. In fact, I remember we went to the Film Council and they were really dismissive of it. Their attitude was, 'We've seen it all before, why should we make this movie? It's nothing new.' And I was like, 'Well, we think it's something kind of fresh.' It was interesting that if people who hadn't seen *Spaced* or weren't aware of it, they didn't really know what the tone was going to be. Even just based on the title it could be what it is, or it could be like, *Carry On Columbus*. No disrespect to the *Carry On* films.

There were more bumps in the road when he got wind of *28 Days Later* while working on the script:

> I was like, 'No fucking way!' I was so mad, I couldn't believe it. Because our whole premise was that nobody had done a zombie movie for years. The last proper zombie movie had been *Return of the Living Dead III*. And we had this theory that zombies had been killed off partly by Michael Jackson's *Thriller* video, which had been such an enormous pop-cultural artefact it had made zombies much more comedic. You can even see that in *Return of the Living Dead II*. It has a Michael Jackson gag, which, for me, is the low point of the genre.

Then, on 11 September, 2001, al-Qaeda terrorists crashed four passenger planes into the World Trade Center, The Pentagon and a field near Shanksville, Pennsylvania, killing 2,996 people. In the aftermath, it felt like the Twin Towers would not be the only thing going down in flames. Says Wright:

> For a moment, there was that terrifying thing of not knowing what was going to happen, whether World War III was going to break out, whether there was going be another attack, or an attack on London, or another big city. There was that feeling that a lot of comedy writers and satirists had, 'Oh, we can never be funny ever again after this terrible thing has happened.' Simon and I thought, 'Oh it's dead, we can't make this movie now.' But then, if anything, 9/11 and its fallout only made *Shaun* feel more relevant. On the day, I remember walking through the streets of London to get on the Tube, and looking at people's faces, and seeing the other people who knew what had happened, and other people who either didn't know or didn't care. And that was a very profound image for

me, and something which kind of carries over into the movie. If there's an outbreak, not everybody gets the news at the same time.

In a twisted way, 9/11 inspired the filmmaker to go darker:

> Before *Shaun* and *28 Days Later*, was *Resident Evil*, the Paul W.S. Anderson movie [based on the Capcom games][7]. Why zombie movies[8] came back into favour was partly millennial angst – after Y2K and then especially after 11 September, there was a real anxiety about where the next threat would come from, then the idea that the next threat is essentially coming from within. I think it was that deep-seated fear of the unknown, that the next World War would happen on the streets.

Shot over eight weeks in the summer of 2003, and backed by Working Title, StudioCanal, Film4 and Big Talk, the company founded by super-producer Nira Park (*Spaced*, *Black Books*), *Shaun* benefits from its extended development, with a script stuffed with character and detail. Early on, a witty long shot follows Shaun, yawning, as he traipses to the corner shop like Wright before him. On the way, he passes a boy playing ball, a tramp begging for change, a man washing his car, a jogger: the inconsequential asides of everyday life. Later, when we – but not Shaun – know a bit more about the coming apocalypse, he retraces his steps to get a Coke and a Cornetto. The ball sits still; the tramp shuffles forward ominously, arms outstretched; the car is ruined; the jogger, running in terror. The joke? Shaun's too hungover to spot the difference.

Meanwhile, the dialogue subtly foreshadows the carnage in store. At work, Shaun takes a phonecall from Liz, and mimes blowing his brains out in boredom, a prospect that will become all too possible by the final reel. At The Winchester, after Liz has dumped him, Shaun and Ed argue over whether the eponymous rifle hanging over the bar actually works (spoilers: it does), and Ed consoles him that, 'It's not the end of the world' (spoilers: it is). When the pair get home, drunk, Shaun's long-suffering housemate Pete (Peter Serafinowicz) tells Ed to 'go live in the shed'. To which Ed grumbles, 'Next time I see him, he's dead.' No prizes for guessing how that particular plot strand works out, but the point is, zombies or no, Shaun is a convincing everyman, occupying his own fully realized existence. Says Wright:

> Shaun is wrapped up in his own little bubble of problems, mostly work and family and love life. They are insignificant in comparison to the zombie outbreak, but he still has to solve them. So his first thought is to get his nearest and dearest together and go to the place he always goes to, because he has such a limited imagination of what else he can do.

Aided by Pegg's empathetic performance, the deliberately paced first act carefully sets up Shaun's dysfunctional relationships with Liz and Ed, his exasperated devotion to his mother Barbara[9] (Penelope Wilton), his Freudian battles with straight-edge stepdad Philip (Bill Nighy) and his animosity towards Liz's yuppie friends Dianne (Lucy Davis) and David

(Dylan Moran). 'Comedy, if it doesn't have a good story and good characters that you're invested in, then it exists literally from joke to joke,' explains Pegg. 'The second one of those jokes doesn't land, the whole things falls apart.'

Indeed, you could remove or replace the zombies, and you would still have a decent Britcom about a guy who needs to get his act together. Says Nighy now: 'I love the fact that it's a sort of how to get your girlfriend back movie which happens to take place during a zombie apocalypse, which is such a witty idea' (2017). According to Wright:

> Really, it's about Shaun and his problems and the resolution of those problems, but the zombies are just another obstacle for Shaun to overcome. So you could rewrite the film and there be a powercut or a storm, and it would still work.

The casting helps enormously, with a talented ensemble of (mainly) TV actors familiar enough not to need too much introduction, yet fresh enough to seem ordinary. The financiers had other ideas, suggesting Kate Winslet for Kate Ashfield's role. 'She really loved the script but eventually pulled out of doing it, which I think was a good thing,' says Wright. 'Because she was so famous at that point she could have overshadowed the movie.' Jim Broadbent passed up the chance to play Philip, a decision he regretted enough to take a pivotal role in *Hot Fuzz* (Wright, 2007). Even Penelope Wilton, Wright and Pegg's first choice, had to wait for Helen Mirren to say no. 'Helen Mirren's response to the screenplay was hilarious,' recalls Wright. 'She said, "I won't play the part of Barbara, but I'd do the movie if I could play the part of Ed."' Unfortunately for her that one was already taken. 'Simon and I have been best friends for ten years and we were flatmates for seven.' Nick Frost told Big Fan Boy's Mark Walters, 'So I think I've always kind of been his "Ed" in a way' (2004).

Once assembled, the cast had a few weeks' rehearsal to get into the same groove – a rare luxury on a low-ish budget film. 'We'd rehearse with everyone so people would improvise around their lines,' producer Nira Park told *Collider*'s Steve Weintraub. 'But then all of that goes into the script. On the day, nothing changes' (2010). Recalls Nighy:

> I thought it was one of the best scripts I'd ever read. I remember the first couple of days I was there I remember saying to everybody: the script! And they were like, really? Because they'd written it. I don't think they'd ever written a script before. They'd written, obviously, *Spaced*, but I don't know whether they were kidding or not, but they said they bought a book on how to write a screenplay.

Said Frost:

> The only part I improvised was when I'm talking about the people in the pub. We're talking about the porn star and I call her a 'cock-a-cidal maniac', and that lady is actually Edgar's girlfriend's mum. Edgar wanted Simon to laugh quite naturally, so every now and

> again you'd go over and he'd whisper to do something different. So I came up with about fifteen different things, each more perverted than the last. Edgar's whispers are quite nice, because it usually means he will put someone's life in danger.
>
> (Walters 2004)

Another of Ed's seemingly throwaway offerings is far too fiendish to have been improvised. 'You know what we should do tomorrow?' he tells Shaun. 'Keep drinking. A Bloody Mary first thing, a bite at the King's Head, couple at the Little Princess, stagger back here and – bang – back at the bar for shots.'

The next day, when the full extent of the outbreak hits home, Shaun and Ed encounter a bloodied check-out girl zombie (nametag: Mary) in the garden; kill Philip (the King), who has already been infected (the bite); join forces with Liz (the Little Princess) and a couple (David and Dianne); stagger (while pretending to be zombies) back to The Winchester; and – bang – test out the aforementioned rifle (a great example of the 'Chekhov's gun' trope). The fact this sort of smart-arsery also passes as convincing character dialogue speaks volumes. The filmmakers knew (or at least hoped) that anyone who enjoyed their first taste of rom-zom-com would be back for more. Says Pegg:

> Unless you're watching the film specifically with the intention of decoding it, you won't see this stuff the first time. So you're able to play with people's subsequent watches. Things like the plan in the pub, people didn't get that for years, until it popped up on the Internet. That's playing the long game, that is.

Make no mistake, despite its modest backdrop, *Shaun of the Dead* is one of the most ambitious films of the Britpop cinema era. Though the £4 million budget was four times higher than *Shallow Grave* (Boyle, 1995) a decade earlier, the film features multiple crowd sequences, tricky driving scenes, zombie make-up, stunts, weapons and gore FX galore. Says Wright:

> To shoot for eight weeks on a low-budget movie is a bit of a luxury. But we had to make some major savings elsewhere. And one of the places we made enormous savings was on extras. We had a core of specialist zombies who were stunt people or dancers or mimes or sometimes amputees. But the bulk of the crowds were friends and fans of *Spaced*, who were paid £1 for their role in the movie. I know that it was a reasonably hellish experience, just the sheer waiting around for hours, but we couldn't have made the movie without them, so we really owe it to the fans of our TV show that we could even approach the film in the scope we did.

Total Film journalist Jamie Graham was among them. Arriving on set at 6am for a 10am start, he was turned into a zombie with 'a streak of grime, a splash of blood [and] a pair of opaque contact lenses', then had to wait till 4pm for the rain to stop. 'I tried telling myself that the distress of nine hours in scratchy lenses would feed into my character,' he wrote. 'But all I could think about was my bursting bladder' (2014). Seems waiting for it all 'to blow over' inside The Winchester was a bad idea after all. And Graham's was not the only dissenting voice. As a statement of intent, the complex Steadicam sequence that follows Shaun to the corner shop and back was the very first thing shot. Says Pegg:

> Edgar really wanted to start the shoot on those long shots to establish the tone and the ambition for the movie. We were first-time filmmakers working with a crew who initially really didn't know what they were working on. They were very accomplished, but they didn't know anything about us. They knew we'd come from television so there was a slight prejudice from some of the more belligerent areas of the crew about that fact. More than once we were told, 'This isn't video, you know?', but I think it soon because apparent that we were serious about filmmaking. Edgar put that straight fairly quickly.

Explains Wright:

> I'm a big believer in starting with something very complicated. It not only shows the film crew that this is not going to be like other films [but] if you start with a real 'wow' shot, diving in with something really complicated is just a good way to get everybody to pay attention. 'We're going to work hard on this movie. And it's going to be tough but it's going to be worth it.' So on the first day of the shoot we did both those Steadicam shots with Simon. We did the one with the zombies first, then the one where everything's fine after. What's funny is the director of photography, David Dunlap, I remember him saying to me, 'This shot's gonna get cut out,' and I said, 'Why do you say that?' He said, 'You're never going to use the whole of this shot, I'll put money on it being cut out of the movie.' And I said, 'No it won't.' It made me really annoyed.

This apparently insignificant episode says quite a lot about the aspiration gap between what Wright and Pegg were trying to achieve and the no-frills attitudes of UK film[10] – as if cinematic flair was something to be suspicious of, rather than celebrated. Not that it stopped them. In response, the director says he 'tripled the amount of detail in the shot' to ensure it could not be cut. Said Pegg:

> It's weird, because some of the older members of the crew are more cynical than the others, thinking, 'It's trashy being on a zombie film.' But as time went on, they realized how much we were dedicated to it, and they started to get the feeling that maybe we were making something that was going to be worthwhile. We did a really clever thing, about halfway through the shoot we showed about 18 minutes of finished footage to them. Got loads of wine out and some nibbles, and showed the crew what we'd done so far. And it really, really worked. Because everybody thought, 'Hey, this looks OK, and it might get released actually.'
> (Walters 2004)

Nighy remembers things differently:

> It was very well organized. Edgar had, as the cliché goes, the movie in his head, as did Simon and Nick. A large part of my job was to bleed to death from the neck in the back of a Jaguar, which means sitting in a pool of dried blood for hours. It was one of the hottest summers, no air conditioning, and I had a blood tube going up my leg, a blood sack round my ankle and warm sticky bloody dribbling down my neck and down my whole body. But Simon and Nick just used to make me laugh all the time. They used to do Al Pacino impersonations. They were very funny.

The film's Britpop cinema credentials are announced immediately, with a series of jaunty musical cues that comment on the action. The first is the theme from Romero's *Dawn of the Dead* (1978), followed by 'Ghost Town' by The Specials, which plays on the jukebox in The Winchester. Next, over images of bored checkout girls, bus queue drones and shuffling hoodies, is 'The Blue Wrath' by I Monster. It is not hard to spot the point Wright and Pegg are making here about the crushing uniformity of modern life, but it is stylishly done.

Later, as Shaun flicks through TV news reports of the outbreak, we see a snatch of Morrissey singing 'panic on the streets of London'. When Shaun and Ed run over a zombie in Pete's car, then watch him creak back to life, the next song on the stereo is Ash's 'Orpheus' – named after the ancient Greek musician who returned, albeit wifeless, from the underworld. By changing the soundtrack to hard rock, it is as if Shaun and Ed are acknowledging they are in a film and wresting control of it, turning a dangerous rescue mission into a feat of cinematic derring-do in which they are the stars. Song choice becomes even more integral during The Winchester finale, when Shaun, Ed and Liz attack a zombie to the strains of Queen's 'Don't Stop Me Now', their jabs hitting home in time with the music – something Wright would explore in more detail in *Baby Driver* (2017a), a heist flick choreographed almost entirely to diegetic tracks.

Throughout, the film is littered with in-jokes and postmodern asides. Shaun works at Foree Electric, a nod to *Dawn of the Dead* star Ken Foree; the takeaway next to the corner shop is Bub's Pizzas, after the domesticated zombie Sherman Howard played in *Day of the Dead* (Romero, 1985); and Fulci's restaurant refers to Italian horror director Lucio Fulci, who made genre favourites *Zombie Flesh Eaters* (1979),[11] an unofficial sequel to *Dawn*, and *The Beyond* (1981), a classic of the splatter genre. Such playful references give even the most innocuous scenes a bit of Britpop cinema cheek, and they combine to form a kind of direct address; a hat tip to in-the-know viewers. Wright explains:

> That came from having done *Spaced*. We were well aware we had a very intensive audience, not a huge audience when it was first on, but the people who did watch it knew it inside out, and that was always a very inspiring thing to us. It meant that people were paying attention. This has continued through my other films: you can't put any detail in there

> that's not going to be seen. It might fly over the heads of somebody who's a more casual movie-goer, but as long as the movie is entertaining in its own right it's fine, and then if you want to watch it again, and see things like Nick Frost laying out the whole film in dialogue, or the foreshadowing and all of the detail, that's the icing on the cake. The film has to be entertaining in its own right and then all of the other detail is for people who watch things more than once.

One of the film's best, and riskiest, jokes is when Shaun, Ed and co – another Britpop cinema gang looking to escape – are sneaking through the back gardens towards The Winchester. They encounter Shaun's mate Yvonne (Hynes from *Spaced*) and her group heading in the opposite direction, each of them an equally famous, similarly dressed doppelganger of the main characters. Everyman leads Pegg and Ashfield are mirrored by Hynes and Martin Freeman (from *The Office*); malcontent Moran and dappy Davies meet their match in Reece Shearsmith (from *The League of Gentlemen*) and Tamsin Greig (from *Black Books*); Wilton greets the equally haunted-looking mum Julia Deakin (also from *Spaced*); and Frost nods to eternal-sidekick Matt Lucas, both of whom are texting. In lesser hands, the scene could seem like an obnoxious luvvie-fest, but instead it serves an intriguing dual function: reminding us that we are watching a film, but that within this fictional context there are millions of stories, of which Shaun's is only one. Pegg recalls:

> The meta quality of it was secondary to the gag. The idea was that they'd just come across a group of people that are very much the same as them and in the same situation, a sort of bizarro version of their own group, just having made different decisions. We always liked the idea that there was another film, maybe even a slightly more successful group on the run somewhere else.

In Britpop cinema, of course, it is less about the tale than how you tell it; the flair that so distressed Wright's DOP making the ordinary extraordinary. Wright's hyperactive style might best be described as real life with the boring bits on fast-forward; so Shaun getting ready for work becomes a zippy montage of toilet, teeth-brushing and work badge, as if he is an action hero getting tooled up for war. Says Pegg:

> Edgar was very keen to make a film that was cinematic. He shot it in 2.35 [widescreen] because he wanted it to look like John Carpenter, if John Carpenter had come to Crouch End. We wanted it to look and feel as cinematic as possible even as we were shooting the most mundane everyday things. That's why Edgar shot all the transitions of Shaun cleaning his teeth and getting in the car as if they were action moments, you know?

When Shaun and Ed plot how to save Shaun's mum and Liz, we're whizzed into a piece of lightning-fast wish fulfilment, which ends with the gang at The Winchester, and Shaun winking to the audience as he raises a pint and asks, 'How's that for a slice of fried gold?' another nod to *Spaced*. This restlessness stems, Wright told *Empire*, from what he learned on *A Fistful of Fingers*:

> I remember having a meltdown during editing, because I suddenly realized the film wasn't that great… There just wasn't anything to cut to, to speed up the pace, because every shot is in there. I think I've overcompensated for it ever since with the amount of coverage I get. You shoot more stuff to make the film faster.
>
> (De Semelyn 2015)

The effect is that *Shaun* blurs by at a pace unseen in Britpop cinema since *Human Traffic* (Kerrigan, 1999) and *Trainspotting* (Boyle, 1996). But it also offers glimpses of genuine emotion, particularly in the climax, when the zombies close in and the group starts dropping like flies. Says the director:

> Dylan Moran getting ripped apart is always fun to watch, but the creepiest death is when Penelope Wilton comes back as a zombie – it made Simon really upset. Simon is a great actor, and he really reacts in that scene like his own mother has died. It was Penelope Wilton's last scene, so literally the very last shot we did with her was her coming back and snarling and being shot in the head, then she was off and we never saw her again until the wrap party. Penelope Wilton's as nice as you would imagine she is, and so to see her as a cadaver about to attack Simon was genuinely distressing. Also, I think for some people, it's something that marks the film out and makes it more distinctive, in that it has moments of gravity and grimness and it's not all a big lark. If it had just been a big old goof I don't think it would have had as much resonance.

Pegg agrees:

> We realised when we came to shoot that scene that we couldn't treat it flippantly, we couldn't do it as a gag, it had to be real and serious and awful. It was a tough shoot, I remember that day everyone was crying, it was really difficult. But it would have done the film a disservice if we'd taken the piss out of it.

Trapped in The Winchester's cellar, Shaun, Liz and Ed consider a suicide pact, but there are only two bullets left, and Ed – who has been bitten in the last skirmish – opts to stay behind. There follows a touching farewell between him and Shaun, which is, tellingly, more tenderly played than anything that transpires between Shaun and Liz. Shaun says sorry, to clear the air between them; Ed does too, but for quite the opposite reason. A charmer to the last, he has farted. 'I'll stop doing them when you stop laughing,' he offers. 'I'm not laughing,' says Shaun, choked in more ways than one. Now reconciled, Shaun and Liz mount the beer barrel lift to freedom/certain death, but are saved by Yvonne and the army at the last minute.

Unusually for Britpop cinema, especially after such a bloody finale, the film ends with everything mostly resolved. Back at Shaun's house, while the TV details how zombies have been assimilated into day-to-day life, rounding up supermarket trolleys and being traipsed out on trashy TV shows, he and Liz plot a Sunday of blissful loafing. 'I might pop into the garden for a bit,' he says. 'Go on then,' she replies indulgently, much less concerned with being marginalized since Shaun has shown his mettle. But there is a surprise in store. In the shed, the now-zombified Ed sits chained, playing a console. 'Player two has joined the game,' we hear, as Shaun settles in beside him. Then Queen's 'You're My Best Friend' strikes up, reminding us this is not so much the world's first rom-zom-com, as a brilliant brom-zom-com.

When *Shaun* was released in April 2004, it earned £6.4 million at the UK box office (IMDB 2018g) – £2.4 million more than it cost – and confirmed former Film4 head David Aukin's assertion that, 'We can make films for ourselves' (Murray 1993: 55). Like *Shallow Grave* before it, *Shaun* takes American influences and assimilates them without apology into a very British scenario. When Shaun and Ed ponder what to do about the zombies in the garden, 'Have a sit down?' is the first suggestion. Meanwhile, the newscasters warning people that, 'In extreme circumstances, the assailants can be stopped by removing the head or destroying the brain,' are sober (and genuine) British broadcasters such as Jeremy Thompson, Carol Barnes and Krishnan Guru-Murthy, rather than the excitable, prophet-of-doom DJs of American horror films. Says Wright:

> I'm very proud that we kept it very British and we made absolutely no concessions[12] to making it transatlantic, and that specifically became something that was part of the overall charm and humour of the movie.

Indeed, this is a crucial factor in Britpop cinema, where the films that travel best are the ones that stay truest to their heritage, from *Four Weddings* (Newell, 1994) to *The Full Monty* (Cattaneo, 1997). Says Pegg:

> There was a desire for us to keep it as authentic as possible and not feel like we were pandering to anybody. Often culture gets lost in an attempt to be broad and appealing and ends up appealing to nobody. In *Notting Hill* the opening shot ends on a stained-glass window of Beavis and Butt-Head, and that wasn't for us. It was put in there specifically because it was a cultural touchstone in America. We really tried hard not to do any of that.

All the same, Wright flew to Austin, Texas, to show *Shaun* to the critics at aintitcool.com pre-release. It received rave reviews, which were then used on the UK poster. The ensuing online buzz – still a new-ish phenomenon[13] – saved the film from going straight to DVD in the States. He recalls:

> We did a mammoth press tour in America, and did Comic Con for the first time, and it was just an extraordinary time, one of the most exciting times of my life, because the world was getting smaller, suddenly our cinematic heroes were seeing the movie and loving it. During the course of this tour, everyone had seen it, Stephen King, Sam Raimi, Robert Rodriguez, Guillermo del Toro – it was just extraordinary.

Despite its Anglo-centricities, and no doubt aided by the success of *28 Days Later*, a kind of refresher course for anyone too young to remember the genre's heyday, *Shaun* made an impressive $13.5 million in America (Box Office Mojo 2018h). 'We never thought it would become such a hit,' Park told *The Guardian*'s Jason Solomons and Liz Hoggard, 'I mean, Quentin Tarantino ringing up and saying it's his favourite film, that's mad' (2006). Not too shabby for what was, in Hollywood terms at least, a niche genre film made by nobodies, for next to nothing. But the greatest tribute came from an altogether more unassuming source. Says Wright:

> We asked if we could screen it for George Romero, because it's a tribute to him, and we wanted the blessing of the man himself. So he watched it in Florida where he was on holiday, and I remember this particular detail because it was really funny. A security guard from Universal watched the movie with him, and I thought, 'Well, of all the people who should be allowed to pirate *Shaun of the Dead* and make money off it, it should be George Romero!'

Pegg takes up the story:

> George called and he was so thrilled, it was such a delight to talk to him. I remember apologising to him that Philip had reanimated quite quickly because, obviously, in *Dawn of the Dead* Roger [Scott Reininger] takes maybe a few hours before he starts to reanimate, but because of the plot we had to bring him round quickly. I'll never forget, George said, 'You know what Simon? I didn't mind.'

Wright was just as ecstatic:

> If nothing else had happened after that, it still would have been good enough, because George Romero loved the movie. He's said in interviews since then that it's his favourite zombie movie apart from his own, which is the greatest review you could ever get.

How's that for a slice of fried gold?

What happened next…

Pegg, Wright and Frost… Completed the so-called Cornetto Trilogy with the similarly inventive *Hot Fuzz*, and *The World's End* (Wright, 2013). Each featured best-of-British casts, American genres transplanted to unexpected UK settings and, of course, Cornetto ice creams – blue for the former, a cop film spoof set in rural Wells, Wright's home town; and green for the latter, an alien invasion flick shot in Welwyn Garden City and Letchworth. In between, Wright made the graphic novel adaptation *Scott Pilgrim vs. the World* (2010) in America, and Pegg joined Hollywood blockbuster franchises *Mission: Impossible* (various, 1996–present) and *Star Trek* (various, 2009–present). Frost, meanwhile, flies the flag for Britpop cinema in *Cuban Fury* (Griffiths, 2014), among others. An unexpected side-effect of their success is a newfound international curiosity for a certain frozen snack. 'Ironically, one joke that doesn't travel to North America, is the Cornetto bit itself,' says Wright. 'The idea of having a Cornetto on a Sunday morning and how ridiculous that is, that's something that gets tumbleweed in the States, they've never had them. Funnily enough, people who are fans of the movies do come to the UK saying, "I want to try one of those Cornettos."' Presumably, just the one though.

Big Talk… Continues to produce quality films often made by or starring Pegg, Wright and Frost. Besides The Cornetto Trilogy, these include *Attack the Block* (Cornish, 2012), a not-entirely-successful, Wright-alike attempt to bring Hollywood sci-fi to South London, and the endearingly dark *Sightseers* (Wheatley, 2012). Its inventive TV output includes *Rev.* (2010–14, UK: Big Talk), a sitcom charting the travails of Tom Hollander's gentle vicar in less-than-gentle Hackney. The latter was directed by *The Full Monty*'s Peter Cattaneo.

Alex Garland… Has emerged as one of the UK's most exciting filmmakers, writing the glorious *Sunshine* (Boyle, 2007) and the decent *Dredd* (Travis, 2012), before making his directorial debut with *Ex Machina* (2014), produced by DNA. Eagle-eyed viewers may spot a joke at his expense at the end of *Shaun*, where the idea that the zombie outbreak was caused by rage-infected monkeys is quickly dismissed. Says Wright: 'Alex Garland got in touch and he said, "I'm a big fan of yours and I'm going to assume that the *28 Days Later* joke is affectionate, if it isn't I'll feel really bad." We've been pals ever since.' Besides, he allows, '*28 Days Later* coming out and being a hit teed up our movie. If it hadn't come out, I'm not sure that *Shaun* would've been as big a hit, because it really felt like we were subverting something that people had seen quite recently.'

Zombie films… Became the genre that would not die. In *Shaun*'s wake, the UK produced such horror-comedy misfires as the brilliantly titled *Boy Eats Girl* (Bradley, 2005) starring pop-star Samantha Mumba; the wincingly sexist *Doghouse* (West, 2009), which pits stags Stephen Graham, Danny Dyer and Neil Maskell against a village full of female zombies; and *Stalled* (James, 2013), which takes place entirely in a toilet, and is by some distance the most inventive of the three. Thanks, in part, to the success of *28 Days Later*, Zach Snyder's excellent *Dawn of the Dead* remake (2004) and *Shaun*, George Romero was finally able to make the George W. Bush-baiting *Land of the Dead* (2005). Look closely at the bar-room sequence and you will glimpse two of the world's happiest extras: Pegg and Wright, in roles they were born to play.

Notes

1 Regarding the lottery franchises, Mike Southworth, the former head of Film4 Distribution, is supposed to have said, 'You might as just well take £100 million and set fire to the fucking lot' (Fitzgerald 2010: 7).
2 In 2002, thanks to huge budgetary and staffing cuts, Film4 was reintegrated with Channel 4. David Thompson, head of BBC Films, told the BBC it was 'a very sad day' for the industry (2002). Its new remit was to concentrate on lower-budget British films such as *This Is England* (Meadows, 2007), rather than trying to compete with Hollywood.
3 Two of the alternate endings show Jim dying in hospital, his story coming from full circle. Another shows Selena and Hannah living happily ever after, sans Jim.
4 In *28 Days Later*, Jim uses a baseball bat. Eagle-eyed *Shaun* viewers will notice that, as the film progresses, Shaun and Ed upgrade their weapons (from records to the cricket bat/spade to The Winchester's rifle) like the video game they play at the beginning and end.
5 As typified by *Clerks* (Smith, 1994), slacker films were cheaply made dramas of everyday life designed to mimic the boredom/dislocation felt by Generation Y.
6 In 1991 the sixteen-year-old Wright appeared on kids' TV show *Going Live!* (1987–93, UK: BBC) with an animated film he had made for Comic Relief called, appropriately enough, *I Want to Get Into the Movies*.
7 Against the odds, Paul W.S. Anderson's *Resident Evil* franchise, based on the popular computer games, would stretch to six films, making an estimated $1.23 billion (Box Office Mojo 2018g).
8 Zack Snyder's thrilling *Dawn of the Dead* remake was being made at the same time. Says Wright: 'Because *Shaun* was a Working Title movie [and thus released by Universal in America], whenever it came up at the Universal corporate meeting people would always laugh and say, "What the hell is that?" Eventually our movie opened two weeks away from *Dawn*, which at the time we were terrified about. Then, amazingly, *Shaun* outgrossed *Dawn* in the UK.'
9 Ed's line, 'We're coming to get you, Barbara,' is a quote from Romero's seminal *Night of the Living Dead* (1968).
10 Although Dunlap is in fact American, and a veteran of the industry since *Christmas Evil* (Jackson, 1980).
11 *Zombie Flesh Eaters* features one of the genre's most outrageous scenes, in which a (fake) zombie takes on a (real) shark.
12 Indeed, the only tweaks were minor. In another neat piece of foreshadowing, Shaun has a leaking pen in his shirt pocket, and is repeatedly told, 'You've got red on you,' rather than the originally scripted 'Biro', which fewer people outside of the UK would understand. Equally, a line describing the check-out girl zombie as 'pissed' was changed to 'drunk'. Pegg says this was because, 'If, in the event it would ever get seen in America, then the few people that did see it would get the joke. That's how much we cared about the comedy.'
13 And one that the filmmakers made clever use of during the shoot, sharing photos, stills and rushes day to day online.

Chapter 11

Three Lions

Starring: *The Football Factory* (Love, 2004)

Chapter 11: Three Lions

The not-so-beautiful game in Britpop cinema

Tommy Johnson (Danny Dyer): What else are you gonna do on a Saturday? Sit in your fuckin' armchair wankin' off to *Pop Idols*? Then try and avoid your wife's gaze as you struggle to come to terms with your sexless marriage? Then go and spunk your wages on kebabs, fruit machines and brasses? Fuck that for a laugh! I know what I'd rather do. Tottenham away, love it!
The Football Factory

Selhurst Park football ground, 25 January 1995, Manchester United v Crystal Palace, nearly 50 minutes gone. After lashing out at an overzealous marker, United's short-fused star player Eric Cantona is sent off. Collar upturned, he peacocks off to the dugout in disgust. From the stands, Crystal Palace fan Matthew Simmons casts aspersions on the virtue of Cantona's mother – on balance, a mistake. Before anyone can stop him, the footballer launches himself at Simmons with an explosive, if inexpert, kung-fu kick; 200 pounds of livid Frenchman landing hard, then punching harder. It is the most famous common assault in English legal history. Not that it affects the game's premier thug-philosopher, though, who walks off the pitch and on to the silver screen.

In the 1990s, football fandom became a growth industry. Once a large – largely working-class – subculture, it boomed with the economy and the rise of the New Lad. The 1990 World Cup saw two extraordinary occurrences: a semi-final place for England, who – rather less extraordinarily – lost to West Germany on penalties,[1] and a half-decent football song in the form of 1990's 'World in Motion' by New Order, co-written with the ever-present Keith Allen. In 1992 came the Premier League, and with it millions of pounds in sponsorship and satellite TV rights, not to mention Nick Hornby's memoir *Fever Pitch* (1992), an ode to obsessive supporters.[2] As Britpop chronicler John Harris put it, 'In Hornby's wake it was no longer sufficient in public life simply to enjoy football as a sport; a tribalism had also to be adopted, or feigned, if one wished to hold one's own in polite society' (2003: 75).

When Oasis, no strangers to tribalism, released *Definitely Maybe* in 1994, it was advertised in soccer magazines such as *Shoot*; when it debuted at No.1 in the charts, the nearest competition was *The Three Tenors in Concert 1994*, featuring 'Nessun Dorma', the BBC's 1990 World Cup theme. Indeed, by the time England hosted Euro '96, it felt like an extension of Britpop's patriotic exuberance. The nation held its breath as England reached the semi-finals again, losing to Germany on penalties again, and occasioning another notable football song[3]: 'Three Lions' by comedians Baddiel & Skinner[4] with The Lightning Seeds, which looked back to the national side's last significant win: at the 1966 World Cup.

British cinema was just as slow to celebrate. *When Saturday Comes* (Giese, 1996) starred Sean Bean as a suspiciously long-in-the-tooth Sheffield United hopeful who must choose between the boozer and the big time, but its *Roy of the Rovers*-style[5] wish fulfilment already seemed decades out of date. The turn of the millennium brought knockabout mockumentary *Mike Bassett: England Manager* (Barron, 2001), and *Mean Machine* (Skolnick, 2001). The latter was a Guy Ritchie-fied remake of the Burt Reynolds flick *The Longest Yard* (Aldrich, 1974), which saw jailed England captain Vinnie Jones out-acted by a prison full of Britpop cinema recidivists such as Jason Flemyng and Danny Dyer.

More successful was *Bend It Like Beckham* (Chadha, 2002), a culture-clash comedy-drama about an Indian girl (Parminder Nagra) with a forbidden passion for football. 'I realized no one in Britain would be interested in a worthy film based on a race element. So I thought of doing *Bend It Like Beckham*,' Chadha told *Sight & Sound*'s Edward Lawrenson, 'People said that football films didn't work, and in any case where were we going to find an Indian girl to play football convincingly? I was furious. Does Harrison Ford jump out of helicopters?' (2004: 36). Despite an appearance from the Golden Boy himself, the results are surer-footed off the pitch than on.[6]

Historically, Britain has proved better at making films about football violence than football itself. Although hooliganism was forced underground during the 1980s, it still made for incendiary viewing, with Alan Clarke's TV film *The Firm* (1989a) emerging as the genre's undisputed top boy. Starring Gary Oldman as 'Bex' Bissell, leader of West Ham's Inter City Firm (ICF) hooligan group, it depicts him as an upwardly mobile family man, hooked on 'the buzz' of violence. Oldman's ferocious performance, along with Clarke's searching Steadicam and some still-confronting scenes of Stanley knife violence, keep things from the kitchen sink.

'Wonderful film isn't it?' says actor Phil Davis, who plays rival firm leader 'Yeti' with an icy blonde hairdo that makes him look like a malevolent Mr Whippy. 'It was a good shoot, quite tough. There were moments when sparks flew just a bit on set, but it turned out beautifully, I thought' (2016). It may be hard to credit, but the original cut was even more violent. Davis recalls:

> The last fight, where Oldman beats me up, was far worse, because there was some buttock slashing that didn't make it in. It was really unpleasant. When I was lying on the floor, he leaned over me with a Stanley knife and slashed my bottom open! That was the measure of Clarke. Luckily Gary was very good at the action, so I never felt in any real danger. My buttocks were safe.

All the same, *The Firm* packs one hell of a punch, resonating with filmmakers to this day. Just a few years later, Davis directed his debut feature *I.D.* (1995), from a script by former undercover cop James Bannon and screenwriter Vincent O'Connell. Based on Operation Fulltime, an attempt to infiltrate the hooligan gangs of West Ham and Millwall, it follows policeman Reece Dinsdale and his colleagues into deep cover among the troublemakers of the fictional Shadwell Town FC. According to Davis:

> One of the lessons we learned from *The Firm* was that it wasn't about disenfranchised, bitter, twisted, unemployed youngsters hitting back at society, they were doing it for fun, that's the truth of it, they were doing it for the buzz. It was like a drug, and it was a drug that affected the undercover police officers as well as the people they were investigating.

Effective, if indelicate, the film features some remarkable crowd scenes inside actual football grounds, our heroes lost – both literally and figuratively – among a sea of hostile fans. For the most part, the filmmakers shot in nearly empty stadiums, trying to make 500 extras look like 5,000. Co-star Sean Pertwee recalls playing up to a stand full of Leyton supporters. 'They came along and we gave them some rubber bricks with nails in them to weigh them down, and they took all the nails out and threw the nails at us,' he says now. 'There was us giving it the large one, and them, the real deal, throwing nails at us. It was terrifying' (2016). Says Davis: 'None of the other football hooligan films have done what we did, which is go into the grounds – perhaps they wouldn't be allowed to now – so it was a thrill.'

'It was mind-blowing,' says Nick Love, writer/director of *The Football Factory,* when he read Bannon's original treatment. Why? 'It was all people I knew' (2016).

A South London football fan with a Millwall tattoo on his lip, the young Love was: 'A peripheral football thug, a wannabe, not a genuine football thug. I got involved with people that were genuine football thugs, and I realized I was very far from one.' The difference?

> Being scared, being a coward. Well, you know if you have a bit of contact with another firm, and bump into each other on the back streets of Bermondsey on a Tuesday night or whatever it is, and there's a load of Birmingham Zulus coming down the road at you, you test your mettle then, do you know what I mean? And I remember feeling, 'You're a fucking fake mate, you don't want to be doing this.'

Ironically, given the debates surrounding its depictions of violence, *The Firm* would prove a turning point for the director:

> That was the one that got me to make movies in the first place. I was 18, just out of rehab, and I watched *The Firm* and said to my girlfriend, 'I'm gonna make movies,' and she said, 'Fuck off!' Three weeks later I was working as a runner, so that movie completely changed my life.

Though it may surprise those more used to the brute force of *The Football Factory*, Love's debut was a deceptively sweet coming-of-age movie starring future *EastEnders* heartthrob Paul Nicholls. Displaying all the best qualities of Britpop cinema, *Goodbye Charlie Bright* (2001) begins with a – naked – chase through a primary-hued council estate, features appearances by 1990s stalwarts Danny Dyer, David Thewlis (*Naked*), Frank Harper (*Lock, Stock and Two Smoking Barrels*), Jamie Foreman (*Gangster No. 1*) and Phil Daniels (*Quadrophenia*), and boasts lovely, limber camerawork. Says John King, author of *The Football Factory*:

> I thought it was brilliant and I still feel that way. It is positive and colourful, a celebration of life, but with an underlying seriousness and sadness. Both Nick and I had the belief that books and films that dealt with our culture should be dynamic and unapologetic, written from the inside rather than the outside, and *Goodbye Charlie Bright* does that. It's a classic of working-class English cinema.
>
> (2016)

Classic or not, according to Love:

> *Charlie Bright* completely tanked. And I was basically never going to make another movie again. Before the call came to make *The Football Factory*, I was selling Christmas trees, I had no money and I was fucking desperate. If I'm really honest now I thought my career was going right down the pan, I felt wounded, I felt ashamed, so there was a lot at play to make it work.

Published in 1997, *The Football Factory* is a savage, state-of-the-nation novel with the beautiful game representing the battleground for the soul of working-class Britain. Like the film, it follows Tommy Johnson, a proud member of the Chelsea Headhunters, who spends match days with his mates fighting rival firms. 'You can't change human nature,' he muses. 'Men are always going to kick fuck out of each other then go off and shaft some bird. That's life' (King 1997: 2). Says King, '*The Football Factory* isn't about football or football-related violence as such, but England and Britain and the wider society.' Certainly it works hard to place us in the heads of characters who feel perpetually left out in the cold. Of mid-level thug Billy Bright (played by Frank Harper in the film), King writes, 'He was white, Anglo-Saxon, heterosexual and fed up with being told that he was shit' (1997: 116).

Both directly and obliquely, the book references Antony Burgess's novel *A Clockwork Orange* (1962),[7] perhaps the ultimate exploration of youth violence, and it deserves to share shelf-space with the work of Irvine Welsh, King's contemporary. Says King:

> Writers such as Irvine and I were teenagers in the 1970s and young men in the 1980s, which was a much more chaotic and fertile period than the 1990s and 2000s, so our

writing is more lawless I suppose, and comes from a poorer, more political time. Both *Trainspotting* and *The Football Factory* are political novels in my view, but the films much less so. Our books were rooted in previous decades, even though they were released in the 1990s, which was more squeaky-clean, and that conformity increased as the new century progressed. So there is that difference in generations and timescale, which influences things. We grew up listening to Bowie and punk rather than Blur and Oasis.

Like Welsh's writing, *The Football Factory* features exhilarating sections of turbo-charged, stream-of-consciousness action and, as in *Trainspotting*, the way loosely connected stories build into a matrix seems to render it all but unfilmable.

So it proved on the first attempt. Vertigo Films, the company founded by producers Allan Niblo (*Human Traffic*) and James Richardson, started shooting an adaptation with an untested TV director, who needs no naming here, and stars Sean Bean and Dougray Scott. A week into filming, according to Love, Niblo phoned him and said:

> 'Listen, we've just collapsed the movie because the rushes are so bad, and there was a revolt against the director.' They wanted me to stop selling trees the next day and stand in, and I said, 'No, I won't do that. I can make this film, but I'm not going to shoot someone else's movie.' They called me back later that day and said, 'What if we were to bin all the rushes, sack all the cast, have you write a new script and start pre-production straight away?' I said, 'Yes I'll do it,' because I had no other choice.

Another *Charlie Bright* talent fallen on hard times was Danny Dyer. According to Love:

> He'd been in *Human Traffic*, and he was a drunk. I'd watched him fuck up his career already in those days. I remember meeting him in the Groucho[8] and giving him the script, and saying, 'Listen, you have one fucking opportunity, Dyer, do not fuck it up.'

Dyer remembered things slightly differently, recalling that Love – 'a man who calls a cunt a fucking cunt, if you see what I mean' – slammed *The Football Factory* screenplay down and said: 'Look at that will you? I wrote that fucking script for you, as the lead, but because you are fucking running around acting like a cunt, I can't offer you the part.' Suitably chastened, he auditioned, beating Tom Hardy to the role of Tommy Johnson. The director's first note was appropriate, if pointed. 'You fucking dare turn up late once, or pissed, and I will punch you in the mouth' (Dyer 2011: 97, 139, 143).

The need to prove yourself, particularly in battle, runs deep in Love's work. Written over a weekend, and suitably pacy, his *Football Factory* script asks an open question – is the violence worth it? – then shows how, to Tommy and his mates at least, the answer is a resounding yes. Like John Hodge with his *Trainspotting* (Boyle, 1996) script, Love streamlines the source material, softening the edges[9] without selling the book short. The result may lack subtlety, but as a portrait of a misreported subculture it is as persuasive as *Human Traffic* (Kerrigan, 1999).

To illustrate its point, the film introduces four contrasting pairs of friends/rivals: Tommy and his best mate Rod (Neil Maskell); firm bosses Harris (Tony Denham) and Billy Bright; young guns Zeberdee (Roland Manookian) and Raff (Calum MacNab), both 'thieving little cunts'; and OAPs Bill Farrell (Dudley Sutton), Tommy's granddad, and his pal Albert (John Junkin), two World War II veterans planning to live out their days in Australia. Each pair is looking for an escape in – or in Bill and Albert's case from – violence. 'There's nothing different about me,' protests Tommy, a classic conflicted Britpop cinema hero, 'I'm just another bored male, approaching 30, in a dead-end job, who lives for the weekend. Casual sex, watered-down lager, heavily cut drugs. And occasionally kicking fuck out of someone.'

When it comes to the latter, Love throws us straight in at the deep end, sending Tommy and co into battle with a rival firm outside a London pub. But even in their downtime, the pull between war and peace is a strong one. When Tommy and Rod spend the night with two girls, Tommy wakes to death threats from their Millwall-connected brother, who gets a cricket bat to the head from Rod. Billy Bright, meanwhile, has an almost Begbie-esque penchant for casual violence – at one point launching an empty pint glass over his shoulder – but makes his living selling flowers.

Regarding the film's Britpop cinema inspirations, Love is refreshingly frank: 'Yeah, I ripped off *Trainspotting*,' he admits. As well as a proudly parochial soundtrack by The Streets, The Libertines and Primal Scream, among others, the film borrows Boyle-isms such as introductory intertitles, freeze-frames and a constant, cajoling VO. Says Love:

> I remember one of the lads' mags saying it was *Trainspotting* with Burberry caps, and I thought, that'll do. Danny Boyle gave me some help in the edit. He was a big fan of *Charlie Bright*, and he let me know that, and I was really touched because *Trainspotting* was amazing, so *The Football Factory* was unashamedly a nod to it.

Other moments half-inched from iconic films include the coach driving off without Zeberdee and Raff, inspired by *The Deer Hunter* (Cimino, 1978); a replay of Joe Pesci's 'funny guy' routine from *Goodfellas* (Scorsese, 1990); and a savage head-in-the-car-door beating courtesy of *Lock, Stock and Two Smoking Barrels* (Ritchie, 1998). Mostly, Love plays these greatest hits with a looseness that belies the material. 'It's got to be fast and fun and quick and elevating – adrenaline-fuelled and dynamic,' Love recalls Boyle saying. 'Don't start pondering on the politics. If you want to deliver something that becomes a memorable experience, you've got to hit them with it.'

The film achieves this with digitally treated shots of the London skyline that make it look exotic rather than ordinary, and glitchy CCTV close-ups that add immediacy to the action. Says Love:

> My emotional and social influences came from Alan Clarke, but stylistically they came from American movies; so I always thought, like Guy [Ritchie] did basically, that we should make English movies feel American. As much as I love Ken Loach, I didn't want to make movies that felt like his, I wanted them to feel warm: a bit of attitude, a bit of swagger. I grew up in the 1980s when everything was a heightened colour, especially football stuff. I had a lemon-yellow tracksuit at eleven years old! Also, the estates that I used to walk about when I was a kid, they felt very colourful, because you're young – even though they were just breezeblocks, your memories were colourful.

The scenes in which Tommy ponders his future amid premonitions of death are the least successful, a clumsy attempt to mimic *Trainspotting*'s 'black-magic realism'. Indeed, sports writer Richard Williams decided that, 'As a piece of cinematic art, *The Football Factory* makes *Lock, Stock and Two Smoking Barrels* look like *Wild Strawberries*' (2004).[10] But the film, like the best of Britpop cinema, crackles with energy and character. 'Look at it now and you can absolutely see the flaws all over it,' says producer Allan Niblo, 'But one thing it did have, was it had a voice in it, and that voice was new and distinct' (2016).

Unlike *Lock, Stock*, *The Football Factory* always feels authentic. For the fight scenes, Love brought in an old friend who used to run the Bushwhackers, the Millwall firm, as the 'technical advisor'. He explains:

> All the extras in that movie are mates of mine from Millwall and Chelsea, a hodge-podge of football thugs – B category, not A category thugs – good-time boys, who like a bit of quiver [cocaine] and ironing someone out. They're not orchestrators but they're all active.

As Tommy and his mob storm the streets, before forcing the Tottenham fans out of a pub with a smoke grenade, you can feel the adrenaline surge. Recalls Love:

> It was very highly charged on set. That was the first bit of contact that we filmed, and the first thing is, are your actors gonna be OK? The second thing is, you've got to avoid proper contact because these are football thugs, and they're not afraid to chin each other. Then the third thing is, it's got to look authentic, you've got to make it look good, and you've only got 400 grand so you've got no time. It was pretty nuts, but everyone got into it. There was definitely a few pep talks where my technical advisor would go round all the people in the scene, ask what team they support, then say, 'Right we're all here making a film, anyone fucking steps out of line, they're gonna get my right hand, do you know what I mean?'

According to Niblo:

> For me it was terrifying – you just want to get through the day without someone getting hurt. There's an edgy atmosphere on set with the kind of characters we were dealing with.

> In fact, the truth was they were there early, stood all day, then brushed each other down afterwards – 'You alright mate?' you know – even though they go out and fight each other at weekends. It was brilliant but very nerve-wracking as you just didn't know. Anything could've kicked off at any moment.

It almost did, when the West Ham firm called to say they were on their way down to the set. 'There was a real solidarity, a sense that if they turn up we'll fucking have it with them,' says Love. 'They didn't, but I remember thinking, "I wonder if they're all as scared as me?"'

Another cast member whose presence adds real-world weight is Tamer Hassan, who makes a big impression as villain Millwall Fred. As Dyer noted, Hassan, a former boxer and club owner turned actor, 'plays a right hard bastard from south London, so he didn't have to go very method on it, being a right hard bastard from south London himself' (2011: 150). Says Hassan now:

> I was never actually a football hooligan, but owning nightclubs and restaurants, I was friends with them. I used to run with the pack, but never actually get involved. It wasn't my thing, but I experienced a lot of football violence as a bystander. You'd be outside the ground, something would happen, the riot police on horseback would charge in, and you'd see little scuffles all over the place. If it excites you, you get involved in it, but I wasn't prepared to be arrested for stupidity.
>
> (2017)

Central to Tommy's arc is a climactic showdown between Chelsea and Millwall that ends with him getting badly beaten by Fred and his friends beneath the railway arches. Recalls Hassan:

> Some of the lads had had a few beers, and I said, 'Listen, when we come through that tunnel you got Chelsea the other side, this ain't a film.' And it just drove them: when they came out of that tunnel you could just see they wanted to kill everyone. You've got police over there, Chelsea over there, and they just lost it, they just absolutely went in, hence why that scene was so tough and so real. Tell you what, I wish we'd been sponsored by Nurofen because, oh my god, you've got to remember that a director's favourite words are, 'That was phenomenal. Can you do it again?' That was probably the hardest day's work I've ever had to do.

Perhaps inevitably, something a little stronger than Nurofen was required. Says Hassan:

> It went a little bit pear-shaped when the energy was up. You can actually see in the scene, there's a kid who's holding his arm against the fence and you see the policeman seeing if

> he's alright. He broke his arm. But we did say to our guys, 'Any of you been hit by a baton before?' I have, and it fucking hurts. And we said, 'Look, the police are ready to go, if you attack they're going to retaliate, it's as simple as that.' Hence why the scene was so fucking brilliant.

Even Dyer ended up taking one for the team, according to his co-star:

> There's a funny thing with me and Danny, when I hit him with the brick, we couldn't get it right. You know in film, you never get hit, you position the camera and you try and sell it so it looks real. So when I crash him in the face, it was actually a really tough polystyrene brick. [By accident] I just smashed him across the face and the brick broke on his head. He went, 'Oh mate, I knew you were going to do that,' and I went, 'Sorry mate, I didn't think it was going to be that bad.'

Scenes like this add fuel to the already fiery debate surrounding screen violence. 'There's nothing glamorous about it,' countered Dyer. 'I basically get battered in a tunnel for most of it' (2011: 152). Says Hassan:

> I saw it as a deterrent rather than a glamorization because my whole perception was: look, what my character did to Danny Dyer's character is actually going to happen to you, and if you're prepared to take that kind of punishment whether that's being injured, being hurt – and it could be worse, people have died – just know that that is the end game and it's not a good place to be.

A few key moments back this reading up: a woman with a pram calling Tommy and co 'fucking animals'; Billy and Fred trading blows at a children's football match (the only game we actually see in detail); and two rival firms screaming impotently at each other in the back of a (tiny) police van. Mostly the violence is galvanizing rather than glamorous – it always looks like it hurts – and if the clashes seem exciting, it is because they are. Says Love:

> I've grown up with mates who it's very clear-cut with. They like fighting, and it isn't because they come from shoebox flats on big estates. Yes they do, but you can't put it down to that. They just love fighting.

As Renton self-justified, 'After all, we're not fucking stupid. At least, we're not *that* fucking stupid.' Niblo agrees:

> It is fun for certain people. But the film also says the great majority of the time nobody gets hurt, it's just running around shouting at each other and feeling like you belong in a tribe. Then occasionally – and horrifically so – some people get very hurt and the film says that as well.

After the beating, and a spell in hospital, Tommy comes back to the fray, answering his own, 'Is it worth it?' question, with a cheery, 'Course it fucking is!' Says King:

> We discussed the line where Tommy asks, 'Is it worth it?', and at one point Nick wanted to leave it open, but I was keen on keeping it as it is in the novel. Tommy needed to be defiant. And in that defiance there is also a sadness.

As Tommy celebrates with his friends, we follow Zeberdee into the toilets, where he is shot dead by a dealer he robbed earlier in the film. It is a shocking ending, borrowed from King's sequel *Headhunters* (1998), but as in *Trainspotting*, the take-home message is mixed: the contact high of the violence hitting harder than the comedown, as it does for the characters. 'I think I do understand what causes the hooliganism,' mused Dyer. 'It's about territory and about the feeling that you belong to something' (2011: 152). King agrees:

> The appeal links to identity, friendships, excitement, youth cultures. People get involved because it is fun. The violence isn't really the point, it's everything else… the bonds of friendship, the use of language, and above all the humour – those are essential.

Perhaps *The Football Factory* works because it makes the audience feel part of the gang. The characters may be amoral, but they are unrepentant in their quest to enjoy themselves, and they spend far more time bonding than battering people. Says Love:

> *The Football Factory* is about four male marriages, about how the guys treat each other. Where I grew up was tough, but there were real moments of tenderness. I remember feeling in this hard, grey environment, moments of beauty with each other. Not quite *Brokeback*[11] but almost in that way. In all my movies there's a homoerotic frisson between guys where it could all burst into sex. I think a couple of my movies I probably tempered them in the edit, because they wouldn't reach a wider audience if they were more homoerotic. Not getting off with each other – Dyer sucking off fucking Neil Maskell! – but really what *The Football Factory* is about is male love. When you talk to people about it later, particularly now, weirdly, a lot of young public school boys who love it, they think it's the violence they like but it's not. On a certain level it's that, but what keeps them going back and learning the lines is something much more visceral, it's about the way the characters treat each other, the unspoken love for each other and the loyalty for each other.

In other words, those choosing Love are also, whether they intend it or not, choosing love.

Like *Trainspotting* and *Human Traffic* before it, *The Football Factory* had a ready-made audience among the subculture it depicted. Unlike those films, it had to contend with a new phenomenon, no doubt perpetuated by one of the Billy Brights of the world. Says Niblo:

> At this point we'd never heard of pirate DVDs. It had never happened to a British film. It was 2002, I was in The Junction Tavern [a pub next to Vertigo's Camden offices], and a man came in, opened his suitcase up and said, 'Five films.' I said, 'That's our film, *The Football Factory*!' And sure enough, it was the assembly cut of our movie. My best guess is that it was put in to get copied for our investors, someone pressed a button, thought, 'Oh this looks good,' took a copy, showed his mate, who showed his mate and it spread like wildfire and someone started pirating it. I was offered it three times in that pub!

The alternative version features songs by Danny Boyle regulars Leftfield[12] and Oasis, unfolds at a looser pace and retains more of the book's polemic. Tommy's opening monologue talks of 'trying to make ends meet in a country sinking into strikes and wars' and asks, 'Are you going to stand up and be counted, make a difference and feel the rush? Just for once say, fuck it?' By contrast, the finished version espouses football violence as entertainment rather than protest, and keeps its politics personal and therefore, perhaps, more palatable to the casual viewer – of which there were many, with an estimated 800,000 pirate copies in circulation before the film hit cinemas. 'It killed us at the box office,' admits Niblo. 'Had there not been a pirate DVD and we'd built our campaign up to fever pitch, I think we could've done £5 million to £6 million in the cinema.' Instead, when the film was released in May 2004, it made just under £625,000 (IMDB 2018h). Says Love:

> The whole piracy thing felt like it fucked us really badly. Of course, what it really told you was what an appetite there was for a film about football culture – because *I.D.* is not about football culture, it's about police – and what people wanted was a nihilistic, amoral film about men doing drugs and having it off and fighting, that's what they really want.

Not everyone was quite so keen. As well as some predictable press outrage, Love recalls getting death threats on the Internet:

> Because at the beginning of the film Tottenham get blitzed in that boozer, the Tottenham firm were like, 'Fucking cunt, I'll kill him.' I remember reading that and thinking, 'Jesus Christ, I thought I was making a movie!' I guess the point is it's a very fiery subculture, where a lot of the people involved are far from stupid, they're not Neanderthals outside boozers, these are small gangs of very well-organized boys, so when they start threatening you, you've got to take it seriously.[13]

Love, thankfully, survived and so did the film. 'I presumed the pirate would kill the DVD,' he says now, 'But all it did was stoke the flames.' Spruced up with enough extras to persuade people who owned the pirated version to buy it again, the DVD sold 'unheard of numbers in those days: two million copies. For a movie that cost 400 grand that's crazy.' According to Niblo:

> In a way it was perfect timing. That year, *The Football Factory* was the No.1 film in *Loaded* magazine, *Grand Theft Auto* was the No.1 game and Mike Skinner [aka The Streets] the No.1 artist; and *The Football Factory* had all three: it was part-financed by Rockstar Games [who created *GTA*] and Mike Skinner did some tracks for us, so it was a real lad culture moment.

Says Love:

> It felt like it was going to be a disaster but it was a great moment in a way. It was the rise of DVD, the lads' mags, I mean it was a wonderful explosion of all these things coming together at the same time, the kismet was great. In every lads' mag it was the favourite movie of the year. The truth was it did feel like a vindication. You had the left-wing media saying it's a fucking abhorrent piece of shit, but people like Will Self came to see it and said, 'You know what? This is a really important film, don't overlook it.'

It was also the start of a new, often regrettable, phase in British cinema. Launched in 1998, and peaking in 2005 (for rental) and 2008 (for retail), the popularity of the DVD meant an increasing number of films were made for the home market (Follows 2013). Says Niblo:

> *The Football Factory* went absolutely gangbusters. It was just at the time that DVD was coming out, and where home cinemas systems were just starting to come through. It really started the DVD market for young males with disposable income which is still very strong today. It's a business in its own right. It's not very good stuff in my opinion, but there's a whole ton of them, literally hundreds of films made in that vein. We did it first: *The Football Factory* is the first lads' culture DVD aimed at a mass audience, you know. It started an industry.

Ironically, that industry would revolve around cheap genre flicks of a certain stripe, often starring Dyer and/or Hassan.[14] It also suggested that the future of low-budget British film might no longer be in the cinema.

What Happened Next…

Hooligan films… As a subgenre continue to crowd the market, with the likes of *Rise of the Footsoldier* (Gilbey, 2007), *Cass* (Baird, 2008) and *Awaydays* (Holden, 2008). First out of the blocks was the laughably inauthentic *Green Street* (Alexander, 2005), which stars Elijah Wood as a wimpy Harvard dropout who, on a trip to London, becomes the world's least likely football thug. 'In my humble opinion,' wrote Dyer, 'it was a pile of shit' (2011: 154). While the original plays fast and loose with the geography of the capital, the belated sequel *Green Street 2: Stand Your Ground* (Johnson, 2009) is set, inexplicably, in a Californian jail.

ID2: Shadwell Army (Novoa, 2016) fared better, at least keeping the action to the same continent.

John King… Completed his *Football Factory* trilogy with *Headhunters* and *England Away* (1999). His other novels include *Human Punk* (2000), which tracks the movement from the 1970s to the 1990s, and *The Liberal Politics of Adolf Hitler* (2016), which imagines a nightmarish European superstate of the future. In 2007 he started London Books, an independent publisher of 'marginalized fiction'. Regarding Nick Love's film, he says, 'I was relieved. And then I was pleased. Today I feel quietly proud.'

Tamer Hassan… Kept up his brutal bromance with Danny Dyer in Nick Love's *The Business* (2005), a suitably garish, 1980s–fetishizing gangster flick set on Spain's Costa Del Crime, and remains the go-to guy for charismatic London heavies. 'You're lucky to have one cult movie,' he says now. 'I've had *Layer Cake* (Vaughn, 2004), *The Football Factory*, *The Business*, *Dead Man Running* (De Rakoff, 2008), *Bonded by Blood* (Bennett, 2010). But a lot of the British films I've done, people say they're just not making them like that anymore, they're just throwing them out: 100 grand, 200 grand, no production values, no premieres. They're pre-selling them, doubling their money then moving on.'

Nick Love… Did *The Business*, *The Football Factory*'s spiritual sequel, followed by hard-edged vigilante thriller *Outlaw* (2007). Much more characteristic were his remakes of *The Firm* (2009) and *The Sweeney* (2012). The former was an update of Alan Clarke's vision stencilled in bright, *Boogie Nights* (Anderson, 1997) neon, and as concerned with the clobber as the clobbering. 'It's a bold move to take on a great master's work – but I see my film as a companion piece more than a reboot,' Love explains. 'Anyway, Clarke was god, and I'm just an imitator at the altar paying my respects.' The film was the best reviewed of his career, causing *The Guardian*'s Peter Bradshaw to ponder: 'If some of the praise unhesitatingly lavished on Shane Meadows over the years might perhaps rightfully belong to Love' (2009: n.pag.).

Notes

1 West Germany won 4-3 on penalties on 4 July 1990. When Paul 'Gazza' Gascoigne was booked, meaning he would not play in the final even if England got through, the talented but temperamental player burst into iconic tears.
2 *Fever Pitch* was turned into a rom-com (Evans, 1997) starring unlikely everyman/Arsenal super-fan Colin Firth.
3 Another 1990s football song worth a listen is Del Amitri's 'Don't Come Home Too Soon', a string-laden acknowledgement that Scotland did not stand a chance at the 1998 World Cup, but 'even long shots make it'. Scotland went out in the first round.
4 Baddiel and Skinner were the hosts of laddish TV show *Fantasy Football League* (1994–2004, UK: Avalon), which ran on BBC2 then ITV from 1994 to 2004.

5 *Roy of the Rovers* was a boy's own comic published in various forms from 1954 to 2001. Its hero, Roy Race, was the star striker, then player-manager, of the fictional Melchester Rovers. His playing career ended in 1993, when he lost his left foot in a helicopter accident.

6 Against the odds, *Bend It Like Beckham* was made into a successful West End show that ran from May 2015 to March 2016, starring Natalie Dew and Tony Jayawardena.

7 Ironically, given the eventual fate of Love's film, the characters watch a pirate video of Kubrick's classic, and a snuff film of a gang-rape set to music by 'some dead German cunt' (King 1997: 6) – the latter scene recalling Alex DeLarge's fondness for a bit of 'Ludvig van'.

8 The Groucho Club is a long-standing Soho members' club, and the site of much 1990s/2000s Britpop naughtiness.

9 An example of the differences between the two is the way the novel tackles issues such as racism and knife crime, while the film steers clear to retain its Britpop cinema credentials.

10 *Wild Strawberries* (Bergman, 1957) is a melancholic meditation on life and death, and in that sense much closer to Ritchie's later, more spiritual, works, such as *Revolver* (2005).

11 As in *Brokeback Mountain* (Lee, 2005), a deeply moving adaptation of Annie Proulx's 1997 short story, starring Heath Ledger and Jake Gyllenhaal as sheep herders who fall helplessly in love in repressed 1960s Wyoming.

12 Leftfield's *Phat Planet*, from their 1999 album *Rhythm and Stealth*, is best known for its use in the award-winning Guinness advert *Surfer*, directed by *Sexy Beast*'s Jonathan Glazer.

13 In fairness, Love and Dyer made death threats of their own – not least to *Guardian* critic Peter Bradshaw on the DVD commentary to *Outlaw*.

14 Besides Nick Love's *The Business*, Dyer and Hassan appeared together in *City Rats* (Kelly, 2009); *Dead Man Running*, *The Last Seven* (Naqvi, 2010), *Freerunner* (Silverstein, 2011) and spoof film *The Hooligan Factory* (Nevern, 2014), very few of which received cinema releases.

Chapter 12

Everything Must Go

Starring: *This Is England* (Meadows, 2007)

Chapter 12: Everything Must Go

Exciting new voices, and the end of Britpop cinema

Combo (Stephen Graham): That's a proud man. That's what we need, man. That's what this nation has been built on, proud men. Proud fucking warriors! Two thousand years this little tiny fucking island has been raped and pillaged, by people who have come here and wanted a piece of it – two fucking World Wars! Men have laid down their lives for this. For this! And for what? So people can stick their fucking flag in the ground and say, 'Yeah! This is England. And this is England, and this is England.'
This Is England

Madstock, Finsbury Park, London, Saturday 8 August, 1992. As 75,000 ageing ska fans await the newly reunited Madness, support act Morrissey, that icon of ascetic 1980s indie, takes the stage. Among the shaven heads and fading, full-face tattoos, he seems an odd choice, and his photographic backdrop – two sullen skinhead girls – is ill-advised, possibly suicidal. The crowd are unimpressed. Somehow, his song 'The National Front Disco' fails to quiet the unrest. During 'You're the One for Me, Fatty' he drapes himself in a Union Jack flag, and is pelted offstage with bottles of piss. His reputation for having – at best – a naive grasp of multicultural politics never fades. Fast-forward four years to Maine Road, Manchester, Saturday 27 April, 1996. When Oasis's Noel Gallagher appears holding an Epiphone Sheraton guitar hand-sprayed that divisive red, white and blue, there is no misunderstanding. The flag that once stood for triumphant nationalism, now just stands for triumph. Or maybe it no longer stands for anything at all.

By the mid-noughties, the Britpop cinema bloom had withered. New Labour, led by a stony Gordon Brown rather than a shiny Tony Blair, was on its way out, and the 1990s economic boom was striding blithely towards the cliff edge of recession. The cinematic landscape had changed too. Those populist Friday-night films pioneered by Boyle and co were few and far between; and the British film industry had polarized into three reductive, if lucrative, strands.

One was made up of huge international co-productions such as *Casino Royale* (Campbell, 2006) and the *Harry Potter* franchise (various, 2001–11). Though based on homegrown source material, these were essentially studio blockbusters with British accents. Another was a resurgence in highbrow heritage films such as *Pride & Prejudice* (Wright, 2005) and *Atonement* (Wright, 2007) – beautifully made safe bets that continued the Merchant Ivory tradition. But the most striking were under-the-radar kitchen-sink thrillers such as *Red Road* (Arnold, 2006) and *London to Brighton* (Williams, 2006), which owed as big a debt to Alan Clarke as his 1990s admirers. No matter how fine these films were, the world would never embrace them the way it had Britpop cinema: they were too dark, too downbeat, looking to the gutter not to the stars. Meanwhile, young British directors with commercial nous such as Christopher Nolan and Sam Mendes went straight to Hollywood never to return. And who could blame them? The median budget for UK features in 2006 was £1.5 million, half of what it had been in 2003 (UK Film Council 2006), and – in practical terms – less than *Shallow Grave* had been made for all those years before.

For the most part, Shane Meadows' Midlands-based, semi-improvised films are not Britpop cinema any more than the works of Richard Curtis, but they share something of its can-do spirit. As writer Kate Ogborn puts it:

> The interesting aspect to Meadows' progression and development as a filmmaker is that he paid no attention to the kinds of films he was supposed to make, and didn't waste time trying to second guess the successful formula for getting funding. Instead he concentrated on the resources that were available to him on his doorstep, and on telling the stories he and his friends wanted to hear.
>
> (2005: 65)

Which is not to say he was without help. Scrappy early short *Where's the Money, Ronnie?* (1996) was nudged into the limelight by seasoned producer Stephen Woolley (*The Crying Game*), who recalls:

> That was great, I had 29 shorts to watch for a TCM prize, which is a lot of shorts. And I saw *Where's the Money, Ronnie?* last thing before I went to sleep. I woke up in the morning and thought, 'God, I had a drink last night, was that really good?' So I watched it again, and I thought, 'This is great!' So I rang the other jurors, who will remain nameless, and said to them, 'Look, you probably won't see all these films because there's so many of them, but I have and this one is a bit of a find. What I suggest you do is give zero to all the other films and give all your points to this one.' So I basically nobbled the jury and Shane won the prize. Then I discovered he'd made all these other movies – he had this cottage industry up in the Midlands on his own, not getting any money and beg, steal or borrowing his equipment, and that's why we made *TwentyFourSeven*. I just fell in love with Shane, I thought he was a genius.
>
> (2016)

Whichever way you cut it, *TwentyFourSeven* (Meadows, 1997) is one hell of a mission statement. The story of Alan Darcy (Bob Hoskins), a boxing coach bringing a brief glimmer of hope to the dispossessed teens of a grim Midlands town, it was inspired by Meadows' own experiences, and co-written with regular contributor Paul Fraser. Despite the talismanic presence of Frank Harper (*Lock, Stock and Two Smoking Barrels*, *The Football Factory*), it is too bleak to count as Britpop cinema, but it has ambitions way beyond its station: in the handsome black-and-white cinematography, the heavyweight casting of Hoskins, the indie soundtrack that somehow manages to afford both The Charlatans and Paul Weller, and the (broken) promise of escape. At times, Meadows picks out moments of real beauty on his forgotten estates, even as he knows they cannot last. 'It doesn't matter how much or how little you have,' says Darcy in voiceover. 'If you've never had anything to believe in you'll always be poor.'

His fellow filmmakers were impressed. Recalls Gillies MacKinnon, director of *Small Faces* (1996) and *Pure* (2003):

> I was on a jury at Dinard Film Festival. I stood on a chair and made an impassioned speech in favour of *TwentyFourSeven* because I could see they were going to vote for the wrong film. The other film was about a boy coming out, and the argument I made was, if this film was released 15 years ago it would be radical, but right now you're all just trying to make yourself feel better by voting for it, it's just a little TV film. Shane Meadows' film is cinema. It's pure cinema.
>
> (2016)

Follow-up *A Room for Romeo Brass* (1999) is less assured, the ambling tale of schoolboys Romeo (Andrew Shim) and Gavin (Ben Marshall) who fall into the toxic orbit of local oddball Morell (Paddy Considine). Though something of a placeholder film for Meadows, it introduces key members of his ensemble (Harper, Shim, Considine and Vicky McClure), and crystallizes some recurrent motifs: absent/inadequate father figures, the dynamics of male friendship and the steady simmer of bored background violence. As Meadows told *Sight & Sound*'s Nick James, 'I seem to have cornered the market where kids are hanging out with psychopaths' (2007: 41).

In truth, his only real misstep was thinking about the market at all. Though closer to the populism of Britpop cinema, *Once Upon a Time in the Midlands* (2002) was exactly the sort of knockabout working-class dramedy he seemed to stand against. Kevin Allen, director of *Twin Town* (1997), is predictably vocal on the subject:

> I remember watching *Once Upon a Time in the Midlands*, and thinking, 'Oh, you poor bastard, how did you get roped into this? You must have got put through the mangle at Film4 and it must have fucking killed you.' Because it's got that Film4 jigsaw shite: right, we'll have Kathy Burke from *Nil by Mouth*, Rhys Ifans from *Twin Town*, Whatsisname Carlyle, and it's just awful. That's the problem with the British fucking film industry, a horrible little clique, no originality: we'll get one of them and one of them and one of them, and we'll just shaft Shane Meadows up the arse, do you know what I mean? Any original filmmaker just has it thrashed out of them.
>
> (2017)

Broadly speaking, Meadows was in agreement, vowing: 'I'm never again going to be involved in something where someone gives me a bunch of money to make a film I don't care about' (James 2007: 41). After seeing his authorial signature smudged, if not altogether erased, his next two efforts would be so intimate you could practically feel them ache. Working with Warp Films, a branch of the experimental Warp Records label, he asked producer Mark Herbert how cheaply he would have to make his next film to operate with complete autonomy. One million pounds was the Dr Evil-like response. Says Herbert of what would become *Dead Man's Shoes* (2004):

> It was a small, guerrilla unit. We put them in a minibus and said: you can only have one camera, everything has to be shot on location with natural light and you've got to shoot it in three weeks. It was like a school project really. We were all in the van together.
>
> (2016)

Suffused with small-town claustrophobia, *Dead Man's Shoes* combines Meadows' pally, conversational style with the ever-tightening narrative of a revenge thriller, like a soulful, kitchen-sink *Get Carter* (Hodges, 1971). Co-writer Paddy Considine stars as Richard, a soldier returning home to investigate the abuse of his brother, Anthony (Toby Kebbell), who has learning difficulties, by local dealer Sonny (Gary Stretch) and his gang. Inspired by the suicide of one of Meadows' friends and dedicated to the memory of Considine's late father, it is *all* personal. And due to a clever structure that intercuts the past and the present, there is no distance between the heinous acts committed against Anthony and their horrible consequences, as perpetrated by Richard.

Although there are moments of levity, mostly provided by the gang's less-than-glamorous pastimes (snorting parmesan, squeezing into a Citröen 2CV), the bleakness quickly assumes biblical proportions. 'God will forgive them,' begins Richard's voiceover. 'He'll forgive them and allow them into heaven. I can't live with that.' This desolate confessional plays out over images of Richard and Anthony trudging the Midlands countryside to a soundtrack of forlorn folk and Americana.[1] Even the ending, an ambitious helicopter shot that suggests a spirit sweeping skywards, offers precious little mercy. Richard may have had his vengeance, but any god who would turn a blind eye to such suffering is hardly the kind you would want to meet.

A critical and commercial success, *Dead Man's Shoes* is Meadows' masterpiece, bringing him (and Warp) greater autonomy and bigger budgets. More mature and more playful, his follow-up, *This Is England*, contrasts the emotional rawness of kitchen-sink drama with flashes of Britpop cinema brio.

When it came to putting skinheads on screen, Alan Clarke, as usual, got there first. His TV film *Made in Britain* (1982) featured a young Tim Roth as Trevor, an unrepentantly racist teen sociopath with malevolence in his eyes and a swastika tattoo between. 'You can lock me in here,' he snarls, while in care, 'but you can't take away the hate inside my head.' As the film follows Trevor's self-defeating logic to its depressing conclusion – jail – it moves from incendiary character study to painful-to-watch polemic. Though you never doubt that Clarke knows exactly what he is talking about, Meadows actually lived it, telling journalist Ali Catterall:

> I got into the skinheads through my sister going out with one. He got me into reggae and took me out hunting in big gangs. Then a split happened. Whereas with the first skinhead it was all parties and fun, this other guy was the one who had been to prison and came in with a much darker, political idea… When you're 13 and you've got long, straggly hair and people are taking the piss out of your trousers, and you see this charismatic group of guys in smart Ben Shermans walking down the street, you want to be like them.
>
> (*The Guardian* 2007)

It was only when Meadows witnessed an act of violence he 'almost prompted' (Fuller 2007) that he realized the error of his ways:

> I wanted to see a real fight and I got taken and shown one for my own benefit and it was the most horrific thing I'd ever seen in my life. That was when I moved onto a different path.
>
> (Solomons 2007)

Set in 1983, the film recasts Meadows' story as a traumatic coming-of-age tale. Young Shaun Fields (a regular Meadows pseudonym), played by Thomas Turgoose, is a lonely boy who has lost his father in the Falklands War. Bullied at school for his out-of-date clothes, he meets Woody (Joe Gilgun),[2] the kind, charismatic leader of a gang of skins including his girlfriend Lol (McClure), British Jamaican Milky (Shim) and the put-upon Gadget (Andrew Ellis). 'Uttoxeter wasn't big enough to have a really cool gang of skinheads,' said Meadows, 'it had a fat one, a thin one, a long one, a small one' (Solomons 2007).

As Woody brings Shaun into the fold, buying him a Ben Sherman shirt and getting Lol to shave his head, the film is all sunshine and ska tunes. Then Combo, an older skinhead, is released from prison, and the gang splits between its two 'fathers': the gentle Woody and the violent Combo. Looking for something to blame for his dad's death, Shaun is swayed by Combo's racist rhetoric, and goes with him to a National Front rally headed by Lenny (Frank Harper, naturally). Soon Shaun and co are terrorizing the local immigrant community, and the increasingly unstable Combo, rejected by Lol, turns on poor Milky, beating him into bloody unconsciousness. The film leaves Shaun, like its writer/director, older, sadder and wiser, having recognized and rejected the violence in himself.

As in all Meadows' work, even the slightly too-slick *Once Upon a Time in the Midlands*, unorthodox casting is part of what gives the film its spark. Says producer Mark Herbert:

> Shane always starts off with a place called the Central Junior Television Workshop in Nottingham. We cast *Romeo Brass* there, we got Toby [Kebbell] from *Dead Man's Shoes*,

> and he always goes from there and works with the youngsters to get the gang, if you like. Getting the little boy to play Shaun, we knew we had to look in unconventional and hidden corners. The instinct with Shane was that it wouldn't be someone coming out of drama school, so he and casting director Des Hamilton went around the east coast near Grimsby, looking in amusement arcades and youth clubs trying to find some kids who looked right, felt right.

The thirteen-year-old Turgoose, some distance from drama school material, impressed the director by demanding a fiver during his audition. According to Herbert:

> Little Tommo came along and was cheeky and naughty and he had everything. But once we found him, the hard thing was keeping him in tow for the duration: someone who'd been excluded from school and not got a lot of structure in his life, having to get up at 6am and do a 12-hour day on camera, that was the next challenge.

Meadows regular Andrew Shim went through a similar process for *A Room for Romeo Brass*. He recalls:

> At the audition were 30 kids doing voice exercises and being dead professional. I turned up late with a bacon sandwich in one hand and a motorbike magazine in the other. Shane always looks for someone who's a bit rough around the edges, who isn't very finely polished. Luckily, that landed me the role.
>
> (2016)

Once the actors were assembled, says Herbert:

> Shane gets them to behave like a gang. Before they're even on set we're sending them out with a fiver to go and have a day out together. It's about building the gang so that, whenever they do something on set, it's real.

Shim has fond memories of the period:

> We did a lot of bonding, that was basically how Shane did it. It wasn't like fresh faces that you had to pretend to know. People like me and Woody and Tommo got on like a house on fire. Shane got us to go to Alton Towers and Laser Quest, stuff like that. It was wicked.

The fact he still refers to Joe Gilgun by his character name speaks volumes. But there were more quirks in Meadows' methods to come. Explains Herbert:

> Shane likes to shoot chronologically. Normally on a film you might have an actor only for three weeks, so you shoot all their scenes together, or if you're filming in a location

> you shoot everything in that location, out of sequence. But on *This Is England*, because we were dealing with some non-actors, we had to shoot chronologically. So for Tommo it wasn't thinking, 'What's my emotional state in this scene?' But, 'What did I do yesterday?' It becomes a little bit more of a challenge for production – you might be in Shaun's house in week one then not again until week six, so you just have to keep the sets dressed, which is not easy – but it allows things to be more truthful and honest.

To this end, Meadows sets out with just a loose blueprint of the film in mind, getting the cast to improvise the rest. Says Shim:

> Literally on *This Is England* and everything I've ever done with Shane, everything we do, we improvise, so everything is our own words, you're not just an actor, you're kind of a writer as well. Nothing's ever done with a script. I suppose it adds a slightly more real element, because it's real reactions, emotions, not something you're having to work towards.

Meadows is characteristically self-deprecating on the subject:

> I did improvisation to begin with because I couldn't write. As a director my ambition is to get to that natural, beautiful place where people are just responding to each other and punching you in the mush as they're doing it.
>
> (Harvey 2015)

Onscreen, autobiographical details entwine with fiction. For example, Stephen Graham has a Jamaican grandfather, so when he spouts racial abuse as Combo, you can see the self-loathing bubbling through. McClure and Shim were a real-life couple, adding another layer of unspoken backstory. 'Obviously she was going out with Woody in the film, but because me and Woody were such good friends anyway it was absolutely fine,' says Shim. 'It would have been a little bit more difficult if I hated him!' Meanwhile, Turgoose was estranged from his father and his mother died of cancer shortly after the shoot,[3] so Shaun's howling loneliness could not have been too far from the truth.

In the early stages of the film, these methods add a sense of scuffed Britpop cinema spontaneity. Once Combo's agenda becomes clear, however, they bring a real sense of danger. Says Herbert:

> My wife's half-Indian, so I've got mixed-race kids. They were in a scene cut out of the film, where Combo is shouting abuse at them across a park. But what Stephen did is amazing. He came round the night before, the kids wanted to be in it, and he said, 'Look, I'm going to shout some stuff tomorrow, it's just acting, I don't mean it. It's a horrible man. We're trying to show that it's not nice.' And he did the same thing with Tommo, tenfold, where

> he would go, 'Look this is what it is, you need to react and it is repulsive, but this is what the character would do.' Once Shane yelled cut it was different, but what Stephen was great at was making Tommo feel alright about it, all the way through.

The climactic scene, where Combo attacks Milky after an afternoon smoke – and apparent rapprochement – is particularly hard to watch. Recalls Shim:

> A lot of the prep for that scene came from Stephen. We shot it in Nottingham, where I live, and I was brought up by my grandma, because my mum passed away when I was young, so I had an old-fashioned Caribbean upbringing, like my uncles would have had. Stephen asked a couple of days before we started shooting the scene, if me, him and Shane could go round to my grandma's house and have dinner. They came round and my grandma and my uncle cooked rice and peas, curried chicken, a bit of mutton, salad and whatnot, and some Guinness punch, and we all sat round and had a frigging awesome night drinking white rum. Stephen asked if he could see some old pictures of my grandma when she was growing up and came to England. It was just a really, really nice night. And it set the emotion for the scene, it made a huge difference. So in the scene when I'm saying [to Combo], 'You should come round to my house have rice and peas, they'll always be a good handful of cousins there.' I was talking about my actual life and just changing it a little bit. And Stephen didn't have all of that in his own life growing up – what I had is what he probably would have liked to have had, you know – and he used that to drive this scene forward, the emotion and the anger and the jealousy. He did a great job.

Graham is, indeed, extraordinary here: lulling Milky into a false sense of security with stoned smiles, then needling him about his childhood, all the while getting angrier and angrier, until his self-loathing overflows into violence. Having beaten Milky half to death, he lashes out at his own right-hand men Banjo (George Newton) and Meggy (Perry Benson), then is instantly remorseful, admonishing himself under his breath as if reliving a past trauma. Says Shim:

> It's misplaced anger. He's striking out at Milky when it's not really Milky that he hates. He hates himself. He hates the fact he doesn't have what Milky has. That's what I took from it.

For Herbert:

> That scene was unbelievable. It took three days to film, we were in this little flat that was real so it's actually quite claustrophobic.[4] You're trying to get little Tommo to not be tired and have the energy, and you're trying to create this incredible tense atmosphere. So it was something that had to be really crafted, but weirdly enough, when it explodes, it had to feel fresh, authentic and real. It had to have energy, so it's a fine line. And of course [once Combo loses control], Shane doesn't know how the other actor's going to react. He

> knows roughly what's going to happen, but you just sit there hoping. It was exhausting for the whole team.

According to Shim:

> It was the hardest thing we've ever shot. It lasted for a good three days, and it was so difficult, because we're improvising the whole thing, so some of the takes were lasting like 20 minutes, it was just so emotionally draining. Everyone was in tears. But it was physically demanding as well because in order to make it seem as real as possible, the actual fighting side of it, you have to be physical with each other. So Stephen's not punching full force or anything, but hits still get through. I remember once, he turned the bed over that I was on and I was lying on the floor and he was kicking me. It would have looked like he was kicking my head, but he was kicking the wall, and one of the times his steel toe-capped boot caught me right on the top of my forehead – little things like that. No matter what you're doing, you always want to make it as real as possible, so if you can actually hit the person and you're not going to hospitalize them or anything then you will.

Says Herbert:

> At the end of it, once Shane knew he'd got the scene in the can, it was like a religious experience: some people were elated, some were in tears, some were in shock. It was like the end of a marathon, I think everyone just slept for a week.

Shim agrees:

> When we finally finished, it was just the biggest weight off your shoulders because you knew you'd bagged something that's going to stick around for good. You've just shot something that will forever be remembered. So I was happy to give it my all.

It is not just Shaun's soul that Woody and Combo, the good father and the bad, are battling for. The clash between dark and light, which splits the film in two, could be characterized as Britpop cinema optimism pitted against kitchen-sink grittiness: a tussle between Danny Boyle and Mike Leigh.

The first act is – relatively – happy-go-lucky. Shaun, who lives in a council house with his mum (Jo Hartley), certainly inhabits a recognizably drab milieu, but the arrival of Woody and the gang brings a dash of Britpop cinema spirit into his life. In one scene they put on fancy dress to go 'hunting'; that is, smashing up derelict houses. It may sound grim, but seen through Shaun's eyes it is heart-warming, with very little narrative function other than to demonstrate the gang's (albeit destructive) joie de vivre. At one point, as if to underline the switch from Leigh to Boyle, they actually hammer a (kitchen?) sink to pieces. Shaun ends the day on Woody's shoulders, the summer stretching before them, and the warm reggae of 'Morning Sun' by Al Barry & The Cimarons on the soundtrack. Says Herbert:

> We have a great location manager who does all of Shane's stuff called Richard Knight, and we asked him, 'Where would you go if you were having the day that they're trying to have: anarchic, dressing up, just going completely fucking mental.' And he said, 'Right, well, there's an old army base,[5] but it's been empty for a while.' So we went and thought, 'Well, that's exactly where they would go.' The houses were about to be demolished so we had one take, we couldn't reset, we just went, 'Let's do it, go on!' Shane allowed them to have a riot, and the camera followed them like you would in a documentary.

Says Shim:

> Yeah that was awesome. That was a good day. It's the sort of thing people like me and Woody would have done as kids, if we could've, so it was just amazing to be able to do it legally.

Not to mention safely. Explains the producer:

> If you notice, the actors are wearing goggles. You don't question it. One of them might just end up going a little bit crazier than you intended, so you keep rolling but you say, 'Look, don't go nuts. This is dangerous here, don't do this, try not to do that, don't throw anything at him.' You give them guidelines to try and make it as a safe as possible but you can never be sure of anything.

When Combo arrives, leading the gang – and the film – into darker territory, the Britpop cinema optimism evaporates. The turning point itself is a classic Meadows moment: that sinking feeling when innocent fun becomes suddenly sinister. Shaun, Woody and co are at a house party, where Shaun has his first (slightly improbable) kiss with the much older Smell (Rosamund Hanson). Combo and Banjo gatecrash, wielding a machete, and Combo proceeds to talk about his experiences in prison, trying to protect his food from 'this fucking wog'. Some of the boys laugh, Combo makes a sorry-not-sorry apology to Milky, but something has changed forever. Woody's face falls, Combo holds the floor, and Ludovico Einaudi's[6] mournful piano, which lends Combo's scenes their tragic edge, laments the end of an era.

Despite the misery that ensues, there is a strong case for *This Is England*'s inclusion in the Britpop cinema canon, at least as an outlier. As critic Jon Savage puts it, 'Although it inhabits classic social-realist territory, the film is amplified by lustrous colour and excellent editing into fantasy and, on occasion, arresting beauty' (2007). On the DVD cover, meanwhile, *The Times* acknowledges the link, comparing it to *Trainspotting* (Boyle, 1996).

Like Boyle's pioneering picture, *This Is England* centres on a group of (mostly) young men looking to escape/enliven their surroundings, even if they are not really sure how. Music, drugs and violence all play a part, but, unlike *Human Traffic* (Kerrigan, 1999) or *The Football Factory* (Love, 2004), none of them are offered as much of an answer. Equally, in the film's early stages there is the sense that, within broadly realist boundaries, anything could happen; the improvisation adding a sense of busy unpredictability. Indeed, Meadows goes one step further than Nick Love or Justin Kerrigan. *This Is England* is not just about a gang, it was made by one. We do not need to see their names scrawled across the screen à la Guy Ritchie, because each of the actors has already given themselves to their roles.

As in *Trainspotting*, the film is distrustful of group dynamics, acknowledging that the friends that hug you one minute might hurt you the next; just as Woody and co kick downwards at Gadget. 'I feel like I've gone down in the ranks,' Gadget complains when Shaun joins the gang. 'What ranks?' asks Woody, who can afford to deny the pecking order because he is at the top of it. But Meadows knows better. Having seen gang violence first-hand, he is aware how often mob rule degrades everyone involved, and was keen to put some distance between his film and the competition. 'If I'd wanted to make money, I could have tapped into that whole *Football Factory*/*Quadrophenia* teen gang film,' he complained in *The Guardian* when the film received a heavy-handed 18 certificate. 'But I chose not to do that' (2007). Ironically, the younger members of the cast were particularly excited to meet Harper *because* he had appeared in *The Football Factory*.

Named after a 1985 protest song by The Clash,[7] which confronts many of the same issues (unemployment, nationalism, the Falklands, the Thatcher government), *This Is England* puts music front and centre. The first half pulses to an exuberant soundtrack of reggae and ska tracks such as 'Louie Louie' by Toots & the Maytals, which represent the inclusive beginnings of the skinhead movement, before the racial divides set in. Explains Herbert:

> I knew how important that classic reggae was, so I actually cut a deal with Sanctuary Records. We asked, 'Can you do us X amount of tracks for X amount of money and you'll get a profit in the soundtrack?' So we actually got back catalogue access before the film was even shot.

Later tracks are more reflective, most notably Einaudi's trickling piano score and a heart-sick cover of The Smiths' 'Please Please Please Let Me Get What I Want' by Meadows regular Gavin Clark, recording as Clayhill.[8]

The most consciously stylized moments take place during the 'Louie Louie' montage, which sees the gang playing football, mucking about at the swimming pool, and striding straight-to-camera in slow-motion. Shaun calls this 'the best day of my life', but it feels like a whole summer shrunk into one afternoon. That iconic walk-to-camera is pure Britpop cinema, a little too perfect to belong to the film's mundane universe. Recalls Shim:

> Yeah we did feel pretty slick that day. Apart from Gadget because he always gets the shittest clothes. You never quite know exactly how it's going to turn out until you see it, but once they put the backing track on it, do a slow-mo, it makes a huge difference. When you saw it in the cinema for the first time you knew it was going to be pretty epic.

This montage is intercut with flashes of graffiti, a subtle form of direct address. Some of it comes from the world of the story – 'Lol 4 Woody', say – but some appears to be an extra-diegetic comment on the action. 'The Maytals' is the band that the audience, but not the characters, can hear on the soundtrack, while 'Kes83' name-checks the 1969 Ken Loach film, the epitome of gritty realism.

The gang's slow-motion walk is mirrored in a later sequence that shows Combo, Shaun, Banjo and Meggy stalking threateningly towards us to the haunting strains of Einaudi's score.[9] Whereas the early shot is realistic but heightened, as if the colourful cinematography is expressing Shaun's excitement at finally belonging, this second sequence is more clearly manufactured. The group are striding away from a brick wall, like models in a fashion shoot, with no narrative explanation for the spatial confusion. Without a sense of what is behind them – a sharp corner, say – it looks (and indeed, is) staged, a moment drawn only from the movies, as if Meadows is highlighting the falseness of their bond. Later they threaten a group of Indian children and steal their ball. In the background is more diegetic graffiti – 'Milky woz ere too' – and some that seems to address the audience, albeit subtly. Higher up the wall, we see the word 'Shane' written upside down, as if Meadows is signing his own work, but still ashamed for what happened all those years ago.

The final link between *This Is England* and its Britpop cinema brethren is the way that, like *Trainspotting*, it looks back at 1980s politics, while slyly commenting on its own era. As Meadows said of Clark's gorgeous Smiths cover, 'It's something to say it [the film] is about then and about now' (2008). Margaret Thatcher only appears in passing: in the news montages bookending the film, on the radio at Shaun's house and on graffiti that reads, simply, 'Maggie is a twat.' But she is still the puppet-master of the piece, the deprivations of Conservative rule giving dispossessed men like Combo an excuse for violent protest. Said Meadows:

> I suppose if you look at massively important movements, especially in music – things like punk, against a backdrop of there being no electricity and no TV – you don't know whether to slap Thatcher or thank her for the sense of oppression that was going on. She was such an iconic baddie – she was almost like a Victorian baddie from a melodrama. In 1983, you had unemployment going through the ceiling, and the skinhead movement regenerated from being quite cool and listening to reggae to being fucking angry and looking like SS soldiers.
>
> (Channel 4 2015)

Those montages also contain sobering images from the Falklands War: shivering British soldiers swigging booze to celebrate a hollow victory, body bags on lumbering tanks, a lonely Union Jack flag fluttering in the wind. 'We shouldn't have been there, she lied to us,' Combo tells Shaun, before making his own self-serving call to arms in the iconic 'This is England' speech quoted at the start of the chapter. As heard in 2007, it is hard not to link these words to Tony Blair's backing of the 2003 Iraq invasion on dubious grounds. But Meadows is mourning something else here too:

> You don't see people on the streets anymore, whereas back in the 1980s it seems like everyone – women, the miners, the riots in Birmingham, Handsworth[10] – you know, everybody seemed to be out saying what they thought. It was a completely different place back then. Everyone's now sat in front of the old Sky Plus – including me – watching *Britain's Got Talent.*
>
> (Channel 4 2015)

As if to illustrate his point, the opening montage moves from images of Maggie in a JCB and police clashing with skinheads, to 1980s children's TV favourites such as Roland Rat[11] and *Knight Rider;*[12] popular popular protest smothered by pop culture; Boyle besting Leigh.

But the film never completely comes down on one side, remaining a hybrid of regretful realism and Britpop cinema exuberance. A moving coda sees Shaun, dressed in anonymous denims and carrying a holdall more suited to the world of work, wandering down to the shore. To the resigned strum of 'Please Please Please Let Me Get What I Want,' he revisits the beached rowing boat he sat in earlier, still adrift, still going nowhere. Walking across the desolate sands, he takes out the St George's Cross flag gifted him by Combo, and hurls it into the water.

The penultimate image – that flag sinking in slate-grey seas – stands as a eulogy for his childhood, and for Britpop cinema itself. We finish on Shaun's face, his eyes downcast as the song sighs to a close. Then, like Renton before him, he looks straight through the camera, at the audience, to the future, as if to say, 'I'm gonna be just like you.'

What Happened Next...

This Is England... Was edited down from a three-hour rough cut to a sleek 102 minutes that honed in on Shaun's story. It was named Best Film at the 2006 British Independent Film Awards, where Turgoose picked up Most Promising Newcomer. At the 2008 Baftas it won the Alexander Korda Award for Best British Film. It was not nominated for Best Film where, in a strong category including *There Will Be Blood* (Anderson, 2007) and *No Country for Old Men* (Coen brothers, 2007), the winner was *Atonement*.

Warp Films... Has gone from strength to strength, winning plaudits for surreal comedies such as *Submarine* (Ayoade, 2010), and high-wire satire *Four Lions* (Morris, 2010), supporting first-time filmmakers, and gravitating to darker material such as *Kill List* (Wheatley, 2011). Says Herbert: 'You never know how something's going to turn out. You never know until it's finished, you really don't. You've just got to go, "Oh this director's brilliant, so we'll support them, we trust them, we trust their judgement, we trust the script." Even if you don't have a script.'

Shane Meadows… Remains one of Britain's most celebrated – if elusive – directors. He followed *This Is England* with *Somers Town* (2008), a modest, London-set drama shot in black and white and starring Turgoose. Next was *Le Donk & Scor-zay-zee* (2009), a slight music mockumentary with Paddy Considine made for just £48,000. His last cinema release was *The Stone Roses: Made of Stone* (2013), a celebration of the band's reunion concerts, but he is yet to make another film to match *This Is England* or *Dead Man's Shoes*. Cinema's loss, however, has been TV's gain. In 2010 Meadows co-wrote (with Jack Thorne) and directed (with Tom Harper) *This Is England '86* for Channel 4, the first of three series continuing the narrative on the small screen. Meadows explained: 'Not only did I want to take the story of the gang broader and deeper, I also saw in the experiences of the young in 1986 many resonances to now – recession, a lack of jobs, the sense of the world at a turning point' (Holmwood 2009). The results were exceptional, particularly a scene where Combo gets his comeuppance from Milky – or does he? 'Who knows what's happened to him?' says Shim now. 'I genuinely don't. Until Shane decides we're going to do another series, if we do another one, that's when we'll all find out. Probably Shane doesn't even know himself.'

Notes

1 Founded in Sheffield in 1989, Warp specializes in avant-garde electronica, from Aphex Twin to Autechre. For *Dead Man's Shoes*, Herbert says, 'We went to Steve Beckett, who's the founder of Warp Records, my business partner in Warp Films, and said, "We have to find really good singer-songwriters who are about to be signed, or going to be good. It's the people who are about to explode but haven't exploded yet."' The resulting soundtrack, which combines British up-and-comers such as Adem with old-timers from the American indie scene such as Calexico, is one of the most evocative of the era.

2 Presumably based on Pecker, Meadows' sister's boyfriend. Characters called Woody, Gadget and Meggy also appear in *TwentyFourSeven*, played by different actors.

3 The closing dedication reads 'In memory of Sharon Turgoose, 1964–2005'. She only lived long enough to see a small fragment of the finished film.

4 One idea jettisoned during the shoot was a more expansive fight at the finale. 'We had in mind this big filmic ending, a big battle, and as it's Shane you go that way, you work it with the actors, but it didn't feel right, it needed to be more intimate,' says Herbert. 'That's what Shane does. If he doesn't believe it, he won't go there.'

5 This is appropriate given the film's condemnation of the Falklands War, Combo's 'proud fucking warriors' speech and the way he self-styles as a general leading his 'troops'. The

numbers that appear on the film's credits are, according to Meadows' audio commentary, meant to symbolize Falklands dog-tags (2008).

6 Since *This Is England*, Italian pianist Ludovico Einaudi has had his compositions used in everything from French comedy-drama *The Intouchables* (Nakache and Toledano, 2011) to Clint Eastwood's *J. Edgar* (2012) and Ricky Gervais' small-screen simper-com *Derek* (2012–14, UK: Derek Productions).

7 The final single by The Clash (1976–86), 'This Is England' was taken from their poorly received album, *Cut the Crap* (1985). Lyrics such as 'The British boots go kick them / Got' em in the head / Police ain't watchin' / The newspapers been read,' were a broadside against the injustices of the Thatcher government and the apathy of the times. Singer Joe Strummer was said to have called it the 'last great Clash song'.

8 Clark died on 16 February 2015, aged 46, of breathing complications brought on by alcoholism. The end credits of TV's *This Is England '90* bear a by-now typical tribute. His haunted folk songs can be heard throughout Meadows' films, from 'Monkey Dead' (by his band Sunhouse) in *TwentyFourSeven* to 'Afterlight' (by his band Clayhill) in *Dead Man's Shoes*. When Meadows, who was in a group with Paddy Considine, first heard Clark play, he thought, 'Fuck me, I'm not a musician, I have to find something else to do,' he told *The Independent*. 'That was the best thing that ever happened to me' (Montgomery 2015).

9 It's a coincidence, but an intriguing one, that Ludovico Einaudi shares a name with the Ludovico Technique, as featured in Britpop cinema inspiration *A Clockwork Orange* (Kubrick, 1972). Appropriately enough, seeing as Einaudi's score adds an emotional element to Combo's more violent outbursts, the technique is a form of aversion therapy used to forcibly 'cure' juvenile delinquents of their darkest urges.

10 The Handsworth riots lasted for three days from 10–12 July 1981. This previously integrated, peaceable area of Birmingham experienced street violence in the wake of the Brixton riots due to rumours of a National Front march.

11 A Brummie children's puppet operated by David Claridge, Roland Rat was brought in to change the fortunes of the ailing *TV-am* in 1983, which he did, described by one wag as 'the only rat to join a sinking ship'. He transferred to the BBC in 1985, then Channel 5 in 1990.

12 *Knight Rider* (1982–86, USA: Glen A. Larson Productions) was an American TV series about one man (David Hasselhoff) and his talking car. Hasselhoff credits his song 'Looking for Freedom' with helping to unify Germany after the Berlin wall came down in 1989. His most famous cultural offering, *Baywatch* (1989–99, USA: NBC), was less known for its political commentary.

Epilogue: Don’t Look Back into the Sun

Epilogue: Don't Look Back into the Sun

Oliver Tate (Craig Roberts): I took a photo of us, mid-embrace. When I am old and alone I will remember that I once held something truly beautiful.
Submarine (Ayoade, 2010)

Film genres never die, they just date – and the shelf life of a subgenre is often brutally short. After the exuberance of the 1990s and early 2000s, the Britpop cinema flame flickered and faded. New Labour had become old hat, Cool Britannia optimism calcified into cynicism, and the public soon wearied of second-rate Danny Boyle knock-offs. Says producer Andrew Macdonald:

> You see all these other movies and they try and repeat it. I mean how many Irvine Welsh films were there – *The Acid House* and other films after *Trainspotting*? How many Ewan McGregor films were there? How many films were trying to play off the success of *Trainspotting* and they didn't work? Not bad movies, the effort was good, but they fell into the normal humdrum British film production line and that's the problem. It's not easy: while those [original] films could pay for another ten of the same, the chances are that nine out of ten of those [new] films aren't going to repeat that success.
>
> (2016)

Another major factor was the folding of PolyGram in 2000. Says producer Andrew Eaton:

> I think the significance of PolyGram was their chutzpah and their belief that, they always said this, 'We're not the talent, you're the talent. We're going to give you the money to do the best job.' Honestly, we [at Revolution Films] have been doing this for a long time, and it hasn't been as a good as that since.
>
> (2016)

Of the production companies that remained in the United Kingdom, flashes of Britpop cinema brilliance can be seen in Working Title's *Hot Fuzz* (Wright, 2007), Film4's *Sightseers* (Wheatley, 2012) and Warp's *Submarine*, but these are the exceptions rather than the rule. It didn't help that the UK Film Council was dissolved in 2010, a victim of Conservative spending cuts. Created in 2000 to distribute lottery funds more efficiently, its beneficiaries included *This Is England* (Meadows, 2007) and the Academy Award-winning *The King's Speech* (Hooper, 2010). Most of its functions were passed to the BFI. 'Abolishing the most successful film support organisation the UK has ever had is a bad decision, imposed without any consultation or evaluation,' said Working Title's Tim Bevan (Shoard 2010) at the time, while stars as diverse as Bill Nighy and Clint Eastwood petitioned the government to reconsider (BBC 2010).

Due to the growing multiplex mentality – with more screens showing fewer, bigger films – British cinema, indeed cinema in general, has been forced to streamline itself for the global market, or remain a niche concern. Producer Stephen Woolley explains:

> Now the world is smaller, we're all seeing the same reviews and numbers and awards ceremonies. Film fans are part of a global audience now, they're not part of individual nationalistic idea. There are freaks, of course, strange films that work only in Spain or Germany, but the only way you can go beyond a million pounds to make a film is if you get investment outside of the UK, so where does that come from?
>
> (2016)

In fact, British hits such as *Four Weddings* (Newell, 1994) and *The Full Monty* (Cattaneo, 1997) have always required American studio backing to penetrate the world market – and cycles of boom and bust are inherent in any industry. But the polarization of our national cinema into huge franchises such as *James Bond* and *Harry Potter*, and smaller, inward-looking offerings like *I, Daniel Blake* (Loach, 2016), has squeezed out the fertile middle ground where Britpop cinema once flourished. According to producer Jeremy Thomas:

> It started to change in 2000 because video killed the radio star. There was a time when I started in the film industry in the 1960s when cinema was a very important part of culture. But today you have to make movies that are instantly consumable and can be attractive to audiences to make them go out to the movie houses, and that's changed dramatically because of what's available. You've got brilliant TV, multiple channels, great shows of every type, unbelievable sport, to say nothing of what's available on your mobile device. You know what's happened to the video and the DVD markets, so then you're left with streaming or downloading – and look what happened to the record business. People are not wanting to pay a lot of money to download a movie. I used to be able to take one of my films and find people around the world who wanted to support it for more than it cost, so you'd get back more than it cost to make and distribute, you didn't have to go to multiple sources. The film itself had a value, and then that stopped.
>
> (2016)

Macdonald blames the dispiriting political climate among other things:

> Basically the Tories ran out of ideas, then along came Blair and then he ran out of ideas, and now we're probably in a bit of a stupor. I don't know what British films there are now that are exciting. *I, Daniel Blake* is obviously very good. *American Honey,* a lot of people like it, but it's

> not my cup of tea. The rest of them are small, very small. And the problem of why they're very small is because, in general, I think people aren't interested in cinema as much as they were. The 1990s generation went to the cinema, but if they were that age now they'd probably be more interested in what's on Netflix and all the rest of it. I mean *The Night Of* or *Game of Thrones* are more exciting.

It is hard to argue with the latter point. In recent years Britpop cinema directors such as Shane Meadows, Danny Boyle, Paul McGuigan and Peter Cattaneo have all dabbled – or disappeared – into TV, often with impressive results. Even Guy Ritchie's *Snatch* (2000) has been turned into a series by online content provider Crackle, though one sample review states, 'In no way, viewed from any conceivable angle, is *Snatch* a good television programme' (Heritage 2017). There is even talk of a *Four Weddings and a Funeral* TV show from American streaming service Hulu, presumably with a younger cast, or more funerals.

But before we sound the death knell for British film, it should be noted that, in many respects the industry is flourishing. UK cinema admissions have gone up, pretty much year on year, from 123.5 million in 1994 to 168.3 million in 2015 (BFI 2017a), with grosses swelling more dramatically due to increased ticket prices. And not just Hollywood blockbusters. The market share of studio-backed UK films such as *Slumdog Millionaire* (Boyle, 2008) went up from 21.8 per cent in 2006, to 28.5 per cent in 2016, with these releases spending longer in cinemas than their Tinseltown equivalents (BFI 2017b). Yet what has been lost is the individuality of that output; a sense of national identity; the idea that we can make original, entertaining films purely for ourselves and, if the rest of the world wants in, all the better.

Although it is reductive and overly romantic to place the films of the past on a pedestal, the Britpop cinema era can now be viewed as something of a golden age for UK films that stood apart from the traditional Merchant Ivory/Mike Leigh trappings. In 1994 the top release at the UK box office was *Four Weddings and A Funeral*. *Trainspotting* (Boyle, 1996) reached No.10 in 1996; *The Full Monty* was No.1 in 1997; *Lock, Stock and Two Smoking Barrels* (Ritchie, 1998) was No.8 in 1998; and *Billy Elliot* (Daldry, 2000) No.5 in 2000.[1] In 2016 the top five films at the UK box office that qualify, apparently, as British, were the mega-budget international sequels/ remakes *Rogue One* (Edwards), *Fantastic Beasts and Where to Find Them* (Yates), *Bridget Jones's Baby* (Maguire), *The Jungle Book* (Favreau) and *Jason Bourne* (Greengrass). These may have had British directors, stars or source novels, but it is hard to argue they represent vital, homegrown cinema, or have much to say about our country or culture. Says Macdonald of the Britpop cinema years:

> There was a boom, wasn't there? It was a great time, with an unbelievable amount of British films being made that had a chance. There are still a lot of films we make, but most of them, I don't think anybody ever sees. I think what is interesting was that there was time to do working-class stories, there was time to do regional stories, time to try and access [our own] entertainment. Everybody was rude about Richard Curtis films

> but it was what he knew and I can promise you that people – men, women, kids from all backgrounds and races – like those films, the same as they like *The Full Monty*: you don't have to be from Sheffield. But they were honest and true in the same way we were with Edinburgh. There was a thing there for a moment where the films weren't quite as worthy, I guess, not quite as film festival-friendly, but they were still accessible.

Producer Allan Niblo is more sceptical:

> You could define it as a boom as the kind of box office these films achieved hadn't been achieved before. It was a boom culturally, being at the forefront, with *Trainspotting* and *Lock, Stock*. But it's your definition of a boom – my definition of a boom would be that suddenly there's a sustainable industry on the rise. This was more like there were several films that really showed that, 'Hey, we can be commercial and British and unique.'
>
> (2016)

That uniqueness is, perhaps, the key. Britpop cinema efforts such as *Shallow Grave* (Boyle, 1995), *Sexy Beast* (Glazer, 2001) and *Billy Elliot* sought to celebrate our eccentricities, accents and all, rather than erase them – in sharp contrast to more obviously exportable titles such as *Bean* (Smith, 1997), *Shakespeare in Love* (Madden, 1998) and *Bridget Jones's Diary* (Maguire, 2001). Recalls director Edgar Wright:

> I felt that around that time, the late 1990s/early 2000s, there were a lot of British films that were trying to be transatlantic in an attempt to appeal overseas. And I always think people can smell a rat on both sides of the pond when that happens.
>
> (2017b)

By contrast, the best of Britpop cinema chose regional authenticity over international appeal, good actors instead of global stars, and the playful above the profound. According to director Paul McGuigan:

> I think that what's interesting about the 1990s films, a little bit like Britpop music itself, is it was populist culture, but not necessarily *Four Weddings*. It was *Trainspotting* and *Shallow Grave* – movies that another generation are going to go and see, not just your granny or your auntie. They were making money as well, people were going to the cinema to watch British movies.
>
> (2016)

If the quality varied wildly – step forward *Spice World* (Spiers, 1997) – the confidence was tangible. Says Eaton:

> I think it goes back to self-belief and thinking that you have enough interesting stories of your own to tell. It's strange, because you look at the French, the Germans or the

> Italians and they've been doing that for a long time. I think it's because we share the same language with America, which has such a massive cinema industry. But they've got a bigger military arsenal than us, too, it's not a reason to feel that you're a second-rate citizen.

Director Gillies MacKinnon cites the likes of *East Is East* (O'Donnell, 1999) as a valiant attempt to tell our own stories:

> It was exactly the right moment to see a film about an Asian family in the north of England. The same for *The Full Monty*, these films just sprang out of nowhere, and that doesn't really happen much now with British films. In the 1990s, there was a string of them and in a way I'm just not sure we're able to do that anymore. Maybe it's because everything gets so processed by so many people with notes and things that anything surprising doesn't seem to pop out of the woodwork anymore. But it can still happen, I'm just not sure it's happening here.
>
> (2016)

Of course, there is always a flipside to being unique – and successful – in the entertainment industry. Says Woolley:

> *Four Weddings* showed that the impossible was achievable, and the problem with that, if you look at the landmark films that go on beyond, is that there's always this point afterwards where there's a drought. You have these idealistic notions that anything we can do can achieve success; but the reality is these films are freaks. They come out of nowhere and you can't replicate them easily. You don't build an industry around it. OK, you might make another *Notting Hill* (Michell, 1999), but that won't be for another two or three years afterwards. You don't roll them off a conveyer belt.

Actor Nick Moran puts it more succinctly:

> The film industry at the moment is suffering because there's too much pressure on making it a business, whereas those great films [of the Britpop cinema era] were accidentally fucking massive. You can't stand around in the rain with a bottle to catch lightning, it will happen when it happens.
>
> (2016)

Meanwhile, Britpop has become big business once again. Blur, Suede, Sleeper and more have re-formed; memoirs from Jarvis Cocker and Brett Anderson caused bidding wars at the 2017 London Book Fair (Kean 2017); while documentaries such as *Oasis: Supersonic* (Whitecross, 2016) look back in fond befuddlement at the excesses of the era.

On 27 January 2017, a frustratingly inelegant 20 years, 11 months after the release of its crowning glory, came the Britpop cinema sequel we had all been waiting for: *T2*

Trainspotting (Boyle, 2017), featuring most of the original cast and based, very loosely, on Irvine Welsh's *Porno* (2002). Introducing the film at the UK press screening, Boyle admitted that, between takes, he could see the actors watching him, thinking, 'Don't fuck this up!' In fact, the film took $42 million worldwide on a budget of $18 million (Box Office Mojo 2018j) and was warmly reviewed, but even its many fans had to acknowledge there was something missing: the thrill of the new.

It begins, once more, on Renton's sprinting feet. But it is a running machine, now, and he is in Amsterdam failing to flee the past; rather than Edinburgh, failing to flee the police. He suffers a minor heart attack, is fitted with a stent (although, strangely, nobody calls him 'Stentboy'), and heads home to Edinburgh to face his demons. Here we catch up with the other characters: older, sadder, but largely unchanged. Sick Boy is still a scammer/pimp; Spud still a junkie; and Begbie is in jail, but not for long.

As the four reconnect, often violently, there are touching moments, broadly comic setpieces, and plenty of Boyle's cinematic dazzle. Edinburgh has never looked more beautiful, and the soundtrack, ranging from the classic (Underworld, Iggy Pop) to the cutting-edge (Young Fathers, Wolf Alice), is as strong as ever. But the film's iconography is, by necessity, borrowed. 'You're a tourist in your own youth,' Sick Boy tells Renton, once they have punched and made up. 'What other moments will you be revisiting?' True to form, most of the film's best scenes nod to that imperfect past – a blast of 'Lust for Life' here; a wry reunion with Diane (Kelly Macdonald) there; more time spent in terrible toilets. It even takes a turn into meta-fiction, inferring that Spud will write a memoir that is effectively Irvine Welsh's *Trainspotting*, thus becoming his own creator. It is a striking idea, but how do you come back down to earth afterwards? The original film delighted in breaking the fourth wall; this smashes it to pieces.

T2 Trainspotting is not a bad film by any stretch of the imagination, just one that suffers from its own inbuilt obsolescence. There is no reason for its existence, except nostalgia; nowhere for these characters to turn, but to the past. Where *Trainspotting* was a film about escape, *T2 Trainspotting* is a film about the impossibility of escape, but – irony of ironies – it never quite steps out of the shadow of the original. Perhaps this should serve as the last word on the Britpop cinema legacy: a series of unique films, made under unique conditions, reflecting unique times. There will be other booms, other golden ages, other glories. But you can never go back, only visit.

THE END

Note

1 These Top 10 figures were sent directly to the author by BFI research manager Ian Cade on 20 November 2011.

References

Adams, Tim (2009), 'A shiny, happy place, relaxed about the filthy rich, insatiable in its optimism, in love with happy endings, and very New Labour. Welcome to Curtisland…', *The Guardian*, 22 March, https://www.theguardian.com/film/2009/mar/22/richard-curtis-the-boat-that-rocked. Accessed 14 January 2018.

Albarn, Damon (1997), 'Making of', *Face*, DVD extras, UK: Paramount.

Allen, Kevin (1997), *Twin Town*, UK: Agenda, Aimimage Productions, Figment Films.

——— (2017), telephone interview, 9 January.

Amalou, J.K. (1996), *Hard Men*, UK: Dacia Films.

Anastasia, George and Macnow, Glen (2013), '100 greatest gangster films: *Sexy Beast* #24', *Calit Review*, 5 May, http://calitreview.com/32694/100-greatest-gangster-films-sexy-beast-24/. Accessed 22 January 2018.

Anciano, Dominic and Burdis, Ray (1998), *Final Cut*, UK: Fugitive Features.

——— (2000), *Love, Honour and Obey*, UK: British Broadcasting Corporation, Fugitive Features, L. H. and O. Limited.

Anderson, Paul W.S. (1994), *Shopping*, UK: Channel 4 Films, Impact Pictures, Kuzui Enterprises, PolyGram Filmed Entertainment, WMG Film.

——— (1995), *Mortal Kombat*, USA: Threshold Entertainment.

Armstrong, Gillian (2002), *Charlotte Gray*, UK: Film4, Senator Film, Ecosse Films.

Arnold, Andrea (2006), *Red Road*, UK: Advanced Party Scheme, BBC Films, Glasgow Film Office, Scottish Screen, Sigma Films, UK Film Council, Verve Pictures, Zentropa Entertainments.

Aukin, David (2016), in person interview, London, UK, 19 November.

Ayoade, Richard (2010), *Submarine*, UK: The Weinstein Company, Warp Films, Film4, UK Film Council.

Baird, Jon S. (2013), *Filth*, UK: Steel Mill Pictures, Logie Pictures, Altitude Film Entertainment, Egoli Tossell Film, Entre Chien et Loup, Film House Germany, Film i Väst, Filmgate Films, Maven Pictures.

Barker, Emily (2015), '30 minutes or less! 19 famous songs written at staggering speed', *NME*, 8 September, http://www.nme.com/photos/30-minutes-or-less-19-famous-songs-written-at-staggering-speed-1422651. Accessed 10 January 2018.

Barra, Allen (2015), 'The twin gangsters who ruled London', *Daily Beast*, 22 November, https://www.thedailybeast.com/the-twin-gangsters-who-ruled-london. Accessed 23 January 2018.

Barron, Steve (2001), *Mike Bassett: England Manager*, UK: Artists Independent Productions Film Council, Hallmark Entertainment.

BBC (1998a), 'The full monarchy', BBC online, 13 November, http://news.bbc.co.uk/1/hi/uk/213847.stm. Accessed 22 January 2018.

——— (1998b), 'Ginger Spice sells out', BBC online, 16 September, http://news.bbc.co.uk/1/hi/entertainment/172717.stm. Accessed 21 January 2018.

——— (1998c), 'Vinnie Jones guilty of assault', BBC online, 2 June, http://news.bbc.co.uk/1/hi/uk/105051.stm. Accessed 22 January 2018.

——— (1998d), 'Bowie returns to Stardust', BBC online, 23 July, http://news.bbc.co.uk/1/hi/entertainment/138290.stm. Accessed 23 January 2018.

——— (2002), 'FilmFour failure is sad day', BBC online, 9 July, http://news.bbc.co.uk/1/hi/entertainment/2118221.stm. Accessed 24 January 2018.

——— (2003), 'Simon Fuller: Guiding pop culture', BBC online, 18 June, http://news.bbc.co.uk/1/hi/entertainment/2999872.stm. Accessed 21 January 2018.

——— (2010), 'Clint Eastwood writes plea to save UK Film Council', BBC online, 9 August, http://www.bbc.co.uk/news/entertainment-arts-10911948. Accessed 21 January 2018.

Benedictus, Leo (2011), 'How the British fell out of love with drugs', *The Guardian*, 24 February, https://www.theguardian.com/society/2011/feb/24/british-drug-use-falling. Accessed 23 January 2018.

Bevan, Nathan (2013), '*Human Traffic* director Justin Kerrigan sets his sights on celebrity culture for latest film', Wales Online, 22 April, http://www.walesonline.co.uk/whats-on/film-tv/human-traffic-director-justin-kerrigan-2963448. Accessed 23 January 2018.

Bird, Antonia (1997), *Face*, UK: BBC Films.

Blackman, Shane J. (2004), *Chilling Out: The Cultural Politics of Substance Consumption, Youth and Drug Policy*, London: McGraw-Hill International.

Blur (1995), 'The Universal', CD, London: Food.

——— (1996), 'Beetlebum', CD, London: Food.

——— (1997), 'Song 2', CD, London: Food.

Box Office Mojo (2018a), '24 Hour Party People', http://www.boxofficemojo.com/movies/?id=24hourparty.htm. Accessed 26 January 2018.

——— (2018b), '28 Days Later', http://www.boxofficemojo.com/movies/?id=28dayslater.htm. Accessed 24 January 2018.

——— (2018c), 'Billy Elliot', http://www.boxofficemojo.com/movies/?id=billyelliot.htm. Accessed 14 January 2018.

——— (2018d), 'Brassed Off', http://www.boxofficemojo.com/movies/?id=brassedoff.htm. Accessed 14 January 2018.

——— (2018e), 'Four Weddings and a Funeral', http://www.boxofficemojo.com/movies/?id=fourweddingsandafuneral.htm. Accessed 14 January 2018.

——— (2018f), 'The Full Monty', http://www.boxofficemojo.com/movies/?id=fullmonty.htm. Accessed 14 January 2018.

——— (2018g), 'Resident Evil franchise', http://www.boxofficemojo.com/franchises/chart/?id=-residentevil.htm. Accessed 24 January 2018.

——— (2018h), 'Shaun of the Dead', http://www.boxofficemojo.com/movies/?id=shaunofthe-dead.htm. Accessed 29 January 2018.

——— (2018i), 'Trainspotting', http://www.boxofficemojo.com/movies/?id=trainspotting.htm. Accessed 14 January 2018.

——— (2018j), 'T2 Trainspotting', http://www.boxofficemojo.com/movies/?id=trainspotting2.htm. Accessed 28 January 2018.

Boyle, Danny (1995), *Shallow Grave*, UK: Film4.

——— (1996), *Trainspotting*, UK: Film4.

——— (1997), *A Life Less Ordinary*, USA: Figment Films, Film4.

——— (2000), *The Beach*, USA: Figment Films.

——— (2002a), *28 Days Later*, UK: DNA Films, British Film Council.

——— (2002b), '*28 Days Later* production notes', Cinema.com, http://cinema.com/articles/1465/28-days-later-production-notes.phtml. Accessed 24 January 2018.

——— (2004), *Millions*, UK: Pathé Pictures, UK Film Council, BBC Films, Mission Pictures, Inside Track 2, Ingenious Film Partners.

——— (2009a), 'Director's commentary', *Shallow Grave Special Edition*, DVD extras, UK: Film4.

——— (2009b), 'Deleted scenes', *Trainspotting*, Blu-ray extras, UK: Film4.

——— (2017), *T2 Trainspotting*, UK: Artbees, DNA Films, Decibel Films, Cloud Eight Films, TriStar Pictures, Film4, Creative Scotland.

Bradshaw, Peter (1999), 'Both feet in the rave', *The Guardian*, 4 June, https://www.theguardian.com/film/News_Story/Critic_Review/Guardian/0,,55313,00.html. Accessed 17 January 2018.

——— (2001), 'Dead Babies', *The Guardian*, 26 January, https://www.theguardian.com/books/2001/jan/26/martinamis.film. Accessed 22 January 2018.

——— (2009), 'The irony about Nick Love's *Outlaw* DVD commentary', *The Guardian*, 23 September, https://www.theguardian.com/film/filmblog/2009/sep/23/nick-love-outlaw-dvd-commentary. Accessed 17 January 2018.

Brass Eye (1997–2001, UK: TalkBack).

Bremner, Ewen (2017), interviewed by Graham Norton, *The Graham Norton Show*, BBC1, 27 January.

British Film Institute (BFI) (2016), *Top Films of All Time at the UK Box Office*, London: BFI, http://www.bfi.org.uk/sites/bfi.org.uk/files/downloads/bfi-top-films-of-all-time-2015-2016-04.pdf. Accessed 28 January 2018.

——— (2017a), 'New BFI statistics show robust year for film in the UK in 2016', London: BFI, 26 January, http://www.bfi.org.uk/news-opinion/news-bfi/announcements/highest-grossing-films-uk-box-office-2016. Accessed 28 January 2018.

——— (2017b), *BFI Statistical Yearbook 2017*, London: BFI, https://www.bfi.org.uk/sites/bfi.org.uk/files/downloads/bfi-statistical-yearbook-2017.pdf. Accessed 21 January 2018.

Brown, Geoff (2005), 'Something for everyone: British film culture in the 1990s', in R. Murphy (ed.), *British Cinema of the 90s*, London: BFI, pp. 27–36.

Brown, Kat (2014), 'Stanley Kubrick too "cheap" to pay for *Singin' in the Rain*', *The Telegraph*, 2 December, http://www.telegraph.co.uk/culture/film/film-news/11267306/stanley-kubrick-cheap-singin-in-the-rain.html. Accessed 10 January 2018.

Bye, Ed (2000), *Kevin & Perry Go Large*, UK: Tiger Aspect Pictures.

Caffrey, David (1998), *Divorcing Jack*, UK: Scala Productions.

Cannon, Danny (1993), *The Young Americans*, UK: PolyGram Filmed Entertainment, StudioCanal, Working Title.

Cattaneo, Peter (1995), *Loved Up*, UK: BBC.

——— (1997), *The Full Monty*, UK: Redwave Films, Film4.

——— (2017), telephone interview, 12 January.

Catterall, Ali and Wells, Simon (2002), *Your Face Here: British Cult Movies Since the Sixties*, London: Fourth Estate.

Chadha, Gurinder (2002), *Bend It Like Beckham,* UK: Kintop Pictures, The Film Council, Filmförderung Hamburg, BskyB, British Screen Productions, Bend It Films, Roc Media, Road Movies Filmproduktion, Future Films.

Channel 4 (2015), 'Interview with Shane Meadows for *This Is England '90'*, Channel4.com, 7 September, http://www.channel4.com/info/press/news/shane-meadows-interview. Accessed 25 January 2018.

Charity, Tom (1996), 'The other side of the tracks', *Time Out*, 31 January–7 February, pp. 16–19.

Chibnall, Steve (2005), 'Adventures in lad land', in R. Murphy (ed.), *The British Cinema Book Second Edition*, London: BFI, pp. 281–91.

'Cherubim & Seraphim' (1992), Danny Boyle (dir.), *Inspector Morse*, Series 6 Episode 5 (15 April, UK: Zenith Productions).

Church Gibson, Pamela (2005), 'Fewer weddings and more funerals: Changes in the heritage film in British cinema of the 90s', in R. Murphy (ed.), *British Cinema of the 90s*, London: BFI, pp. 115–24.

Clarke, Alan (1982), *Made in Britain*, UK: Central Independent Television.

——— (1989a), *The Firm*, UK: BBC.

——— (1989b), *Elephant*, Northern Ireland: BBC Northern Ireland.

The Clash (1985), 'This Is England', vinyl, London: CBS.

Coogan, Steve (2003), 'Audio commentary', *24 Hour Party People*, DVD extras, UK: Pathé.

Corbijn, Anton (2007), *Control*, UK: Becker Films, CINV, Claraflora, European Regional Development Fund, IFF, NorthSee, Three Dogs and a Pony, Warner Music.

Cottrell-Boyce, Frank (2017), e-mail to author, 14 February.

Criminal Justice and Public Order Act (1994), C.33.63.1a, https://www.legislation.gov.uk/ukpga/1994/33/part/V/crossheading/powers-in-relation-to-raves. Accessed 23 January 2018.

Crook, Simon (2017), e-mail to author, 12 March.

Curtis, Richard (2003), *Love Actually*, UK: Universal Pictures, StudioCanal, Working Title, DNA Films.

Daldry, Stephen (2000), *Billy Elliot*, UK: StudioCanal, Working Title Films, BBC Films, Arts Council of England, Tiger Aspect.

Davis, Phil (1995), *I.D.*, UK: BBC Films.

——— (2016), telephone interview, 14 December.

Dawson, James (2016), 'Remembering Ian Curtis on what would have been his 60th birthday', Lad Bible, 15 July, http://www.ladbible.com/now/music-remembering-ian-curtis-on-what-would-have-been-his-60th-birthday-20160715. Accessed 23 January 2018.

De Semelyn, Nick (2015), 'Edgar Wright's *A Fistful of Fingers*: Once upon a time in the west country', *Empire* online, 18 November, https://www.empireonline.com/movies/features/upon-time-west-country/. Accessed 24 January 2018.

Donen, Stanley and Kelly, Gene (1952), *Singin' in the Rain*, USA: MGM.

Dowse, Michael (2004), *It's All Gone Pete Tong*, UK and Canada: True West Films, Vertigo Films.

Duerden, Nick (2003), 'Brett Anderson: "I was a very strange human being indeed"', *The Independent*, 17 October, http://www.independent.co.uk/arts-entertainment/music/features/brett-anderson-i-was-a-very-strange-human-being-indeed-91337.html. Accessed 22 January 2018.

Duta, Soma (2015), '16 best-selling girl groups of all time', Insider Monkey, https://www.insidermonkey.com/blog/16-best-selling-girl-groups-of-all-time-377221/?singlepage=1. Accessed 21 January 2018.

Dyer, Danny (2011), *Danny Dyer: Straight Up*, London: Arrow Books.

Dyja, Eddie (2010), *Studying British Cinema: The 1990s*, London: Auteur.

Eaton, Andrew (2016), in person interview, London, UK, 15 November.

Ebert, Roger (2000), '*Human Traffic* review', Roger Ebert, 12 May, https://www.rogerebert.com/reviews/human-traffic-2000. Accessed 23 January 2018.

Elton, Ben (2000), *Maybe Baby*, UK: Pandora Cinema, BBC Films.

Evans, David (1997), *Fever Pitch*, UK: Film4.

Finn, Jon (2016), telephone interview, 16 November.

Fitzgerald, John (2010), *Studying British Cinema 1999–2008*, Leighton Buzzard: Auteur.

Follows, Stephen (2013), 'The numbers on 20 years of film rental', Stephen Follows homepage, 14 October, https://stephenfollows.com/the-numbers-on-20-years-of-film-rental/. Accessed 25 January 2018.

Fontaine, Rex (1998), 'People: Early to bed for Anne and Oscar', *The Independent*, 29 March, https://www.independent.co.uk/life-style/people-early-to-bed-for-anne-and-oscar-1153273.html. Accessed 21 January 2018.

Fowler, Christopher (2013), *Film Freak*, London: Doubleday.

Frost, Sadie (2016), telephone interview, 7 December.

Fulci, Lucio (1979), *Zombie Flesh Eaters*, Italy: Variety Film Production.

Fuller, Graham (2007), 'Boys to men', *Film Comment*, July/August, pp. 44.

Gibson, Mel (1995), *Braveheart*, USA: Icon Entertainment International, The Ladd Company, Icon Productions.

Giese, Maria (1996), *When Saturday Comes*, UK: Guild, Pint O'Bitter Productions.

Gilbert, Lewis (1966), *Alfie*, UK: Paramount Pictures.

Glazer, Jonathan (2000), *Sexy Beast*, UK: Film4, Kanzaman S.A., Recorded Picture Company, Jeremy Thomas Productions.

Glennie, Alasdair (2013), '"My character was in love... not even thinking about the fricking rain!" Andie MacDowell defends THAT *Four Weddings* line', *Daily Mail*, 29 March, http://www.dailymail.co.uk/tvshowbiz/article-2301060/Andie-MacDowell-defends-THAT-Four-Weddings-Funeral-line.html. Accessed 14 January 2018.

Godfrey, Alex (2000), '8 things you should know about *Sexy Beast*', Scotts, http://blog.scottsmenswear.com/8-things-you-should-know-about-sexy-beast/. Accessed 22 January 2018.

Goodall, Nigel (2011), *Ray Winstone: The Biography*, London: John Blake.

Graham, Jamie (2014), 'It shouldn't happen to a film journalist', *Total Film*, 222, pp. 25.

——— (2016), 'Ewan McGregor', *Total Film*, 245, pp. 121–25.

Gritten, David (2003), 'When the joking has to stop', *The Telegraph*, 11 November, http://www.telegraph.co.uk/culture/film/3606290/When-the-joking-has-to-stop.html. Accessed 14 January 2018.

The Guardian (2007), 'I was a skinhead myself in 1983', 1 April, https://www.theguardian.com/film/2007/apr/01/2. Accessed 25 January 2018.

Guillen, Michael (2008), 'Noir City 6 – James Ellroy intro to Dalton Trumbo doublebill', *The Evening Class*, 28 January, http://theeveningclass.blogspot.co.uk/2008/01/noir-city-6james-ellroy-intro-to-dalton.html. Accessed 15 January 2018.

Haines, Luke (2010), *Bad Vibes*, London: Windmill.

Harris, John (2003), *The Last Party: Britpop, Blair and the Demise of English Rock*, London: Harper Perennial.

Harvey, Chris (2015), '*This Is England*, Shane Meadows on his era-defining drama', *The Telegraph*, 13 September, http://www.telegraph.co.uk/culture/tvandradio/11859462/This-Is-England-Shane-Meadows-on-his-era-defining-drama.html. Accessed 25 January 2018.

Hassan, Tamer (2017), telephone interview, 26 April.

Hattenstone, Simon (2002), 'The film factory', *The Guardian*, 29 March, https://www.theguardian.com/film/2002/mar/29/artsfeatures1. Accessed 23 January 2018.

Haynes, Eric Ngowani (1998), 'The Making of *Human Traffic*', *Human Traffic: Remixed*, DVD extras, UK: Starlight Films.

Haynes, Todd (1988), *Superstar: The Karen Carpenter Story*, USA: Iced Tea.

——— (1998), *Velvet Goldmine*, USA and UK: Killer Films, Newmarket Capital Group, Film4.

Herbert, Mark (2016), telephone interview, 16 December.

Herman, Mark (1996), *Brassed Off*, UK: Film4, Miramax, Prominent Features.

——— (2017), e-mail to author, 6 February.

Heritage, Stuart (2017), '*Snatch* review', *The Guardian*, 16 March, https://www.theguardian.com/tv-and-radio/2017/mar/16/snatch-remake-review-rupert-grint-guy-ritchie-crackle. Accessed 28 January 2018.

Heydon, Robert (2011), *Irvine Welsh's Ecstasy*, Canada and UK: Ecstasy Film Production Services, Rob Heydon Productions.

Hills, Paul (1995), *Boston Kickout*, UK: Boston Films.

Hodge, John (1996), *Trainspotting & Shallow Grave*, London: Faber & Faber.

Holmwood, Leigh (2009), 'Channel 4's extra £20m for drama to fund Shane Meadows' TV debut', *The Guardian*, 26 August, https://www.theguardian.com/media/2009/aug/26/shane-meadows-channel-4. Accessed 26 January 2018.

Hook, Peter (2010), *The Haçienda: How Not to Run a Club*, London: Pocket Books.

Hoyes, Mel (2016), 'Infographic: The true picture for black actors in the UK film industry', BFI, 19 December, http://www.bfi.org.uk/news-opinion/news-bfi/features/black-actors-british-film-industry-statistics. Accessed 14 January 2018.

Hudson, Hugh (1981), *Chariots of Fire*, UK: Allied Stars, Goldcrest Films, Enigma Productions, The Ladd Company.

Hurst, Andy (1999), *You're Dead*, UK: Atlantic Streamline.

IMDB (2018a), 'Human Traffic', http://www.imdb.com/title/tt0188674/. Accessed 23 January 2018.

——— (2018b), 'Gangster No. 1', http://www.imdb.com/title/tt0210065/?ref_=nv_sr_1. Accessed 22 January 2018.

——— (2018c), 'Lock, Stock and Two Smoking Barrels', http://www.imdb.com/title/tt0120735/. Accessed 22 January 2018.

——— (2018d), 'Mike Newell biography', http://www.imdb.com/name/nm0001565/bio?ref_=nm_dyk_trv_sm#trivia. Accessed 29 January 2018.

——— (2018e), 'Sexy Beast', http://www.imdb.com/title/tt0203119/?ref_=nv_sr_1. Accessed 22 January 2018.

——— (2018f), 'Shallow Grave', http://www.imdb.com/title/tt0111149/. Accessed 15 January 2018.

——— (2018g), 'Shaun of the Dead', http://www.imdb.com/title/tt0365748/?ref_=fn_al_tt_1. Accessed 24 January 2018.

——— (2018h), 'The Football Factory', http://www.imdb.com/title/tt0385705/. Accessed 27 January.

The Independent (1997), 'Drugs are like a cup of tea, says Noel', 30 January, http://www.independent.co.uk/news/drugs-are-like-a-cup-of-tea-says-noel-1285833.html. Accessed 23 January 2018.

James, Nick (2007), 'Shane Meadows: At the edge of England', *Sight & Sound*, May, pp. 41.

Jenkins, Milly (1996), '*Trainspotting* made easy – for Americans', *The Independent*, 25 May, http://www.independent.co.uk/news/uk/home-news/trainspotting-made-easy-for-americans-1349197.html. Accessed 10 January 2018.

Jones, Vinnie (2013), *It's Been Emotional*, London: Simon & Schuster.

Jordan, Neil (1992), *The Crying Game*, UK: Palace Pictures, Film4.

Jovy, Alexander (2000), *Sorted*, UK: Excell Film Agentur, Jovy Junior Enterprises.

Kane, David (1999), *This Year's Love*, UK: Entertainment Film Distributors, Kismet Film Company.

Kapur, Shekhar (1998), *Elizabeth*, UK: PolyGram Filmed Entertainment, Working Title Films, Film4.

Kashner, Sam (2014), 'Making Beatlemania: *A Hard Day's Night* at 50', *Vanity Fair*, 2 July, https://www.vanityfair.com/hollywood/2014/07/a-hard-days-night-making-of. Accessed 10 January 2018.

Kean, Danuta (2017), 'London book fair: Not so common deal for Jarvis Cocker as publishers chase Britpop stars', *The Guardian*, 15 March, https://www.theguardian.com/books/booksblog/2017/mar/15/london-book-fair-deal-for-jarvis-cocker-publishers-chase-britpop-stars. Accessed 28 January 2018.

Keay, Douglas (1987), 'AIDS, education and the year 2000!', *Woman's Own*, 31 October, pp. 8–10.

Kelly, Ben (2009), '*Slumdog Millionaire* director Danny Boyle almost became a priest', *The Telegraph*, 14 January, http://www.telegraph.co.uk/culture/film/4238043/Slumdog-Millionaire-director-Danny-Boyle-almost-became-a-priest.html. Accessed 15 January 2018.

Kelly, Guy (2014), '20 amazing facts from 20 years of the National Lottery', *The Telegraph*, 14 November, http://www.telegraph.co.uk/finance/personalfinance/11228989/National-Lottery-20-amazing-facts-from-20-years-of-creating-millionaires.html. Accessed 14 January 2018.

Kenworthy, Duncan (2016), telephone interview, 11 November.
Kermode, Mark (2002), 'Bloomin' Nora this man's a star', *The Independent*, 7 April, http://www.independent.co.uk/arts-entertainment/films/features/ewan-mcgregor-bloomin-nora-this-mans-a-star-9241555.html. Accessed 15 January 2018.
Kerrigan, Justin (1999), *Human Traffic*, UK: Irish Screen, Fruit Salad Films.
——— (2008), *I Know You Know*, UK: The Film Agency.
——— (2016), telephone interview, 12 May.
King, John (1997), *The Football Factory*, London: Jonathan Cape.
——— (1998), *Headhunters*, London: Vintage.
——— (2017), e-mail to author, 31 January.
King, Paul (2017), *Paddington 2*, UK: StudioCanal, Heyday Films, Marmalade Films.
Kirwan, Sian (2014), '*Two Weeks Notice*', BBC online, 24 September, http://www.bbc.co.uk/films/2003/01/31/hugh_grant_two_weeks_notice_interview.shtml. Accessed 14 January 2018.
Klein, Joshua (1999), 'Guy Ritchie', AV Club, 10 March, https://www.avclub.com/guy-ritchie-1798207984. Accessed 22 January 2018.
Kray, Reggie (1991), *Born Fighter: An Autobiography of Vicious Crime and Lifelong Punishment*, London: Arrow.
Kubrick, Stanley (1972), *A Clockwork Orange*, UK: Polaris Productions, Hawk Films.
Kuhn, Michael (2003), *One Hundred Films and a Funeral*, London: Thorogood.
——— (2016), in person interview, London, UK, 15 December.
Lamont, Tom (2014), '*Four Weddings and a Funeral* 20 years on – in pictures', *The Guardian*, 27 April, https://www.theguardian.com/film/gallery/2014/apr/27/four-weddings-and-a-funeral-20-years-in-pictures. Accessed 18 January 2018.
Lawrenson, Edward (2004), 'Austen power', *Sight & Sound*, October, pp. 36–37.
Leigh, Mike (1993), *Naked*, UK: Film4, British Screen Productions, Thin Man Films.
——— (1996), *Secrets & Lies*, UK: Film4, CiBy 2000, Thin Man Films.
Lester, Richard (1964), *A Hard Day's Night*, UK: United Artists.
Leyfield, James (2015), 'Ronnie and Reggie Kray HATED Martin and Gary Kemp's *The Krays* biopic film', *The Mirror*, 1 July, http://www.mirror.co.uk/tv/tv-news/ronnie-reggie-kray-hated-martin-5980535. Accessed 22 January 2018.
Leyland, Richard (1998), 'Making of *Lock, Stock and Two Smoking Barrels*', *Lock, Stock and Two Smoking Barrels*, DVD extras, UK: Universal.
Lock, Stock (2000), UK: Ginger Productions.
Lodge, Guy (2016), '*Superstar*: Todd Haynes's banned Karen Carpenter movie is visionary', *The Guardian*, 11 August, https://www.theguardian.com/film/2016/aug/11/superstar-todd-haynes-banned-karen-carpenter-movie. Accessed 23 January 2018.
Love, Nick (2001), *Goodbye Charlie Bright*, UK: Bonaparte Films.
——— (2004), *The Football Factory*, UK: Vertigo Films, Rockstar Games.
——— (2005), *The Business*, UK: Vertigo Films.
——— (2016), in person interview, London, UK, 14 December.
Lynskey, Dorien (2011), 'Castlemorton triggers the rave crackdown', *The Guardian*, 15 June, https://www.theguardian.com/music/2011/jun/15/castlemorton-triggers-rave-crackdown. Accessed 23 January 2108.

Macdonald, Andrew (2016), in person interview, London, UK, 9 December.
MacKinnon, Gillies (2003), *Pure*, UK: A Bad Way Ltd, Kudos Productions Ltd, Little Wing Films.
——— (2016), telephone interview, 4 May.
Macnab, Geoffrey (1997), 'Made in Wales', *The Independent*, 3 April, https://www.independent.co.uk/arts-entertainment/made-in-wales-1264852.html. Accessed 18 January 2018.
Major, John (1993), '1993 – Mr Major's Speech to the Conservative Group for Europe', John Major Official Website, n.d., http://www.johnmajor.co.uk/page1086.htm. Accessed 14 January 2018.
Marsh, William (2000), *Dead Babies*, UK: Civilian Content, Gruber Films, Outer Edge.
Mather, Nigel (2006), *Tears of Laughter: Comedy–Drama in 1990s British Cinema*, Manchester and New York: Manchester University Press.
Maylam, Tony (1992), *Split Second*: UK: Muse Productions, Challenge Films.
McDowell, Malcolm (2008), 'Interview', *Gangster No.1*, DVD extras, UK: Film4.
McGuigan, Paul (1998), *The Acid House*, UK: Channel 4 Films.
——— (2000), *Gangster No. 1*, UK: Film4, Pagoda Film.
——— (2016), telephone interview, 11 November.
Meadows, Shane (1996), *Where's the Money, Ronnie?*, UK: Big Arty Productions.
——— (1998), *Twenty Four Seven*, UK: BBC Films.
——— (1999), *A Room for Romeo Brass*, UK: BBC Films, October Films, Company Pictures.
——— (2004), *Dead Man's Shoes*, UK: Warp Films, Big Arty Productions, EM Media, Film4.
——— (2007), *This Is England*, UK: Warp Films, Film4.
——— (2008), 'Audio commentary', *This Is England*, DVD extras, UK: Optimum.
Medak, Peter (1990), *The Krays*, UK: Fugitive TV Productions, Fugitive Features, Parkfield Entertainment.
Mersey Beat (2008), 'Beatles Browser Four', n.d., http://triumphpc.com/mersey-beat/beatles/beatlesbrowser-four3.shtml. Accessed 14 January 2018.
Michell, Roger (1999), *Notting Hill*, UK: PolyGram Filmed Entertainment, Working Title Films, Bookshop Productions, Notting Hill Pictures.
Miller, Toby (2005), 'The film industry and the government: "endless Mr Beans and Mr Bonds?"', in R. Murphy (ed.), *British Cinema of the 90s*, London: BFI, pp. 37–47.
Monk, Claire (2005), 'Men in the 90s', in R. Murphy (ed.), *British Cinema of the 1990s*, London: BFI, pp. 156–66.
Montgomery, Hugh (2015), 'Director Shane Meadows and others pay tribute to the late great singer-songwriter Gavin Clark', *The Independent*, 29 November, http://www.independent.co.uk/arts-entertainment/music/features/director-shane-meadows-and-others-pay-tribute-to-the-late-great-singer-songwriter-gavin-clark-a6751726.html. Accessed 25 January 2018.
Moran, Nick (2016), in person interview, London, UK, 14 November.
Morris, Chris (2010), *Four Lions*, UK: Film4, Warp Films, Wild Bunch, Optimum Releasing.
Morrison, Alan (2003), 'The Making of *Trainspotting*', *Empire*, 169, July, pp. 115–21.
Mullinger, James and Sothcott, Jonathan (2013), *The Films of Danny Dyer*, London: Caffeine Nights.
Munro, John Neal (2013), *Lust for Life: Irvine Welsh and the Trainspotting Phenomenon*, London: Polygon Books.

Murray, Jonathan (1993), *The New Scottish Cinema*, London: IB Tauris.
Newell, Mike (1994), *Four Weddings and a Funeral*, UK: PolyGram Filmed Entertainment, Film4, Working Title.
Niblo, Allan (2016), in person interview, London, UK, 18 May.
Nighy, Bill (2017), in person interview, London, UK, 13 October.
Oasis (1994), 'Supersonic', CD, London: Creation.
Odell, Michael (2011), 'Noel Gallagher: 'I'm a frontman who takes out the bins. It's OK', *The Times*, 15 October, https://www.thetimes.co.uk/article/noel-gallagher-im-a-frontman-who-takes-out-the-bins-its-ok-wd7mbs0c5b6. Accessed 10 January 2018.
Ogborn, Kate (2005), 'Pathways into the industry', in R. Murphy (ed.), *British Cinema of the 90s*, London: BFI, pp. 60–67.
Parker, Alan (1982), *Pink Floyd – The Wall*, UK: MGM.
Parry, Nick (2007), 'Festival reunites cult film cast', BBC online, 31 March, http://news.bbc.co.uk/1/hi/wales/south_west/6510027.stm. Accessed 22 January 2018.
Pasolini, Uberto (2016), telephone interview, 12 December.
Patterson, Sylvia (2016), 'The 1990s were the best of times … until the Spice Girls ruined everything', *The Guardian*, 4 July, https://www.theguardian.com/commentisfree/2016/jul/04/1990s-spice-girls-celebrity-culture. Accessed 20 January 2018.
Pegg, Simon (2018), telephone interview, 5 July.
Pendreigh, Brian (2000), 'Sights unseen', *The Guardian*, 7 January, https://www.theguardian.com/film/2000/jan/07/2. Accessed 22 January 2018.
Pennington, Adrian (1996), 'Such a perfect day', *Premiere UK*, March, pp. 59–61.
Peretti, Jacques (2000), 'Shame of a nation', *The Guardian*, 26 May, https://www.theguardian.com/film/2000/may/26/1. Accessed 10 January 2018.
Pertwee, Sean (2016), telephone interview, 13 December.
Pickadolla (2010), 'Stylorouge – *Trainspotting*', 7 May, https://pickadolla. wordpress.com/tag/claire-allfree/. Accessed 15 January 2018.
Pop, Iggy (1977), 'Lust for Life', vinyl, New York: RCA.
Postlethwaite, Pete (2012), *A Spectacle of Dust*, London: Phoenix.
Prechezer, Carl (1995), *Blue Juice*, UK: Skreba Films.
Prior, Neil (2017), '*Twin Town* 20 years on: "It belched in people's faces"', BBC online, 3 August, http://www.bbc.co.uk/news/uk-wales-40800777. Accessed 22 January 2018.
Pulp (1995), 'Common People', CD, London: Island.
Raphael, Amy (2013), *Danny Boyle: Creating Wonder*, London: Faber & Faber.
Reade, Lindsay (2009), *Torn Apart: The Life of Ian Curtis*, London: Omnibus Press.
Reed, Lou (1972), 'Perfect Day', *Transformer*, London: RCA.
Reuters (2007), '*Purple Rain* greatest film soundtrack: *Vanity Fair*', 25 October, https://www.reuters.com/article/us-soundtracks/purple-rain-greatest-film-soundtrack-vanity-fair-idUSN2335552920071025. Accessed 23 January 2018.
Ritchie, Guy (1998), *Lock, Stock and Two Smoking Barrels*, UK: HandMade Films, SKA Films, The Steve Tisch Company, Summit Entertainment.
——— (2000), *Snatch*, UK: Columbia Pictures, SKA Films.
Robertson, Fran (1997), 'Shoot out in Swansea: The making of *Twin Town*', *Twin Town*, DVD extras, UK: BBC.

Roddam, Franc (1979), *Quadrophenia*, UK: The Who Films, Polytel.

Romero, George A. (1968), *Night of the Living Dead*, USA: Image Ten, Laurel Group, Market Square Productions, Off Color Films.

——— (1978), *Dawn of the Dead*, USA: Laurel Group, Dawn Associates.

——— (1985), *Day of the Dead*, USA: Dead Films Inc. Laurel Group.

——— (2005), *Land of the Dead*, USA: Universal Pictures.

Ross, Andrew (1996), 'The fall and fall of Bob Dole', *Salon*, 19 September, https://www.salon.com/1996/09/19/news_544/. Accessed 15 January 2018.

Rumley, Simon (2002), *Club Le Monde*, UK: 2M Films, Screen Production Associates.

Russell, Ken (1975), *Tommy*, UK: RSO Records.

Savage, Jon (2007), '*This Is England* review', *Sight & Sound*, May, pp. 38–42.

Sawyer, Miranda, (2017), 'Ewan McGregor: "What if I'm not Scottish enough any more?"', *The Guardian*, 14 January, https://www.theguardian.com/film/2017/jan/14/ewan-mcgregor-t2-trainspotting-scottish-enough. Accessed 21 January 2018.

Schwartz, Stefan (1997), *Shooting Fish*, UK: Gruber Bros, Tomboy Films, Winchester Multimedia PLC, Arts Council of England.

Shim, Andrew (2016), telephone interview, 21 December.

Shoard, Catherine (2010), 'Government to axe UK Film Council', *The Guardian*, 26 July, https://www.theguardian.com/film/2010/jul/26/uk-film-council. Accessed 28 January 2018.

Shyer, Charles (2004), *Alfie*, USA and UK: Paramount Pictures.

Skolnick, Barry (2001), *Mean Machine*, UK: Paramount Pictures, Ska Films.

Smith, Cathy (2016), in person interview, London, UK, 12 April.

Smith, Murray (2002), *Trainspotting*, London: BFI.

Softley, Ian (1993), *Backbeat*, UK: Channel 4 Films, Fortbeam, PolyGram Filmed Entertainment, Royal, Scala Productions, Wildgaze Films.

——— (1997), *The Wings of the Dove*, UK: Renaissance Dove.

Solomons, Jason (2007), 'Shane Meadows', *The Guardian*, 25 April, https://www.theguardian.com/film/2007/apr/25/guardianinterviewsatbfisouthbank. Accessed 25 January 2018.

Solomons, Jason and Hoggard, Liz (2006), 'Ready for our close-up', *The Guardian*, 12 February, https://www.theguardian.com/film/2006/feb/12/features.review. Accessed 24 January 2018.

Spiers, Bob (1997), *Spice World*, UK: PolyGram Filmed Entertainment, Fragile Films, Icon Entertainment International, Spice Productions.

Stewart, Dave A. (2000), *Honest*, UK: Honest Productions, Pathé Entertainment, Seven Dials Films.

Stewart, Olivia (2016), telephone interview, 14 December.

Suede (1993), 'So Young', CD, London: Nude.

——— (1994), 'The Living Dead', CD, London: Nude.

Tarantino, Quentin (1992), *Reservoir Dogs*, USA: Live America Inc, Dog Eat Dog Productions.

——— (1994), *Pulp Fiction*, USA: A Band Apart, Jersey Films.

Temple, Julien (1986), *Absolute Beginners*, UK: Goldcrest Films, Palace Pictures, Virgin Films.

——— (2000), *The Filth and the Fury*, UK: Film4, Jersey Shore, Nitrate Film, Panacea Entertainment, The Sex Pistols Residuals.

The 90s, 10 Years that Changed the World, Nico Wasserman (dir.) (13 June 2015, UK: Nerd TV).

Thomas, Ed (2000), *Rancid Aluminium*, UK: Ballpark Productions Partnership, Entertainment Film Distributors, Fiction Factory.
Thomas, Jeremy (2016), in person interview, London, UK, 19 December.
Thompson, Annie, (1994), '*Four Weddings and a Funeral* a surprise hit', *Entertainment Weekly*, 6 May, http://ew.com/article/1994/05/06/four-weddings-and-funeral-surprise-hit/. Accessed 14 January 2018.
Thorpe, Vanessa and Barnett, Antony (2000), 'Lottery movies: 9 hits 121 misses', *The Guardian*, 12 March, https://www.theguardian.com/film/2000/mar/12/news.focus. Accessed 21 January 2018.
Tickell, Paul (2000), *Christie Malry's Own Double-Entry*, UK: Delux Productions, Kasander Film Company, Movie Masters, Woodline Films.
Todd, Peter (2005), 'The British film industry in the 1990s', in R. Murphy (ed.), *British Cinema of the 90s*, London: BFI, pp. 17–26.
Travis, Alan (2012), 'Illicit drugs going out of fashion', *The Guardian*, 28 September, https://www.theguardian.com/society/2012/sep/27/illicit-drugs-out-of-fashion. Accessed 23 January 2018.
Tufano, Brian (2016), telephone interview, 12 December.
Turner, Alwyne (2013), *A Classless Society: Britain in the 1990s*, London: Aurum Press.
UK Film Council (2006), 'UK Film Council Statistical Yearbook 2006/07', London, UK Film Council, http://www.bfi.org.uk/sites/bfi.org.uk/files/downloads/uk-film-council-statistical-yearbook-2006-2007.pdf. Accessed 26 January 2018.
Underworld (1996), 'Born Slippy', CD, London: Junior Boy's Own.
Vaughn, Matthew (2004), *Layer Cake*, UK: Sony Pictures Classics, Marv Films.
Venville, Malcolm (2009), *44 Inch Chest*, UK: Anonymous Content.
Walker, Alexander (2005), *Icons in the Fire: The Rise and Fall of Practically Everyone in the British Film Industry 1984-2000*, London: Orion Books.
Walker, Rob (2000), *Circus*, UK: Circus Pictures, Film Development Corporation.
Walters, Mark (2004), 'Talking *Shaun of the Dead* with Edgar Wright, Simon Pegg, and Nick Frost', Big Fan Boy, 4 September, http://www.bigfanboy.com/pages/interviews/shaunofthedead/shaunofthedeadinterviews.html. Accessed 24 January 2018.
Watson, Neil (2005), 'Hollywood UK', in R. Murphy (ed.), *British Cinema of the 90s*, London: BFI, pp. 80–87.
Weintraub, Steve (2010), 'Producer Nira Park on set interview: *Paul*', Collider, 15 July, http://collider.com/paul-producer-nira-park-interview-on-set/. Accessed 24 January 2018.
Weitz, Chris and Weitz, Paul (2002), *About a Boy*, UK: Universal Pictures, StudioCanal, Tribeca Productions, Working Title Films.
Welsh, Irvine (1995), *The Acid House*, London: Vintage.
——— (2013), *Trainspotting*, London: Vintage.
——— (2016), telephone interview, 15 December.
Williams, Paul Andrew (2006), *London to Brighton,* UK: Steel Mill Pictures, Wellington Films, LTB Films Limited, UK Film Council.
Williams, Richard (2004), '*The Football Factory*: irresponsible, ill-timed and risible', *The Guardian*, 12 May, https://www.theguardian.com/football/2004/may/12/sport.comment. Accessed 18 January.

Wilson, Tony (2002), *24 Hour Party People: What the Sleeve Notes Never Tell You*, London: Channel 4 Books.

Winterbottom, Michael (1996), *Jude*, UK: BBC Films, PolyGram Filmed Entertainment, Revolution Films.

——— (1999), *Wonderland*, UK: BBC Films, Kismet Film Company, PolyGram Filmed Entertainment, Revolution Films, Universal Pictures.

——— (2000), *The Claim*, UK, France and Canada: Alliance Atlantis, Arts Council of England, BBC Films, Canal+, Grosvenor Park Productions, Revolution Films.

——— (2002), *24 Hour Party People*, UK: Film4, Revolution Films.

——— (2004), *9 Songs*, UK: Revolution Films.

——— (2005), *A Cock and Bull Story*, UK: BBC Films, Baby Cow Productions, EM Media, East Midlands Media Initiative, Revolution Films, Scion Films.

——— (2016), in person interview, London, UK, 14 November.

Wheatley, Ben (2011), *Kill List*, UK: Warp X, Rook Films.

——— (2012), *Sightseers*, UK: StudioCanal, Film4, BFI, Big Talk Productions, Rook Films.

White, Allen (1998), 'Interview: director Guy Ritchie', Unclean Arts, https://uncleanarts.com/interview-guy-ritchie/. Accessed 22 January 2018.

Wikipedia (2018), 'Perfect Day – Lou Reed Song', https://en.wikipedia.org/wiki/Perfect_Day_(Lou_Reed_song). Accessed 23 January 2018.

Woolley, Stephen (2016), telephone interview, 15 November.

Wright, Edgar (1995), *A Fistful of Fingers*, UK: Edgar Wright.

——— (2004), *Shaun of the Dead*, UK: StudioCanal, Working Title, Big Talk Productions, Film4.

——— (2007), *Hot Fuzz*, UK: Universal Pictures, StudioCanal, Working Title, Big Talk Productions.

——— (2013), *The World's End*, UK: Universal Pictures, Relativity Media, Working Title, Big Talk Productions.

——— (2017a), *Baby Driver*, USA: Big Talk Productions, Working Title.

——— (2017b), telephone interview, 1 May.

Wright, Joe (2007), *Atonement*, UK: Universal Pictures, StudioCanal, Relativity Media, Working Title.

Wynn Davies, Patricia (1997), 'East 17 singer sacked for making ecstasy remarks', *The Independent*, 18 January, http://www.independent.co.uk/news/east-17-singer-sacked-for-making-ecstasy-remarks-1283668.html. Accessed 17 January 2018.

Index

www.ingramcontent.com/pod-product-compliance
Lightning Source LLC
LaVergne TN
LVHW080831240826
846232LV00015B/55
9781783209873